The Neo-Latin Verse of
Urban VIII, Alexander VII
and Leo XIII

BLOOMSBURY NEO-LATIN SERIES

Series editors: William M. Barton, Stephen Harrison,
Gesine Manuwald and Bobby Xinyue

Early Modern Texts and Anthologies
Edited by Stephen Harrison and Gesine Manuwald

Volume 10

The 'Early Modern Texts and Anthologies' strand of the *Bloomsbury Neo-Latin Series* presents editions of texts with English translations, introductions and notes. Volumes include complete editions of longer single texts and themed anthologies bringing together texts from particular genres, periods or countries and the like.

These editions are primarily aimed at students and scholars and intended to be suitable for use in university teaching, with introductions that give authoritative but not exhaustive accounts of the relevant texts and authors, and commentaries that provide sufficient help for the modern reader in noting links with classical Latin texts and bringing out the cultural context of writing.

Alongside the series' 'Studies in Early Modern Latin' strand, it is hoped that these editions will help to bring important and interesting Neo-Latin texts of the period from 1350 to 1800 to greater prominence in study and scholarship, and make them available for a wider range of academic disciplines as well as for the rapidly growing study of Neo-Latin itself.

Also available in this series
An Anthology of British Neo-Latin Literature edited by Gesine Manuwald, L. B. T. Houghton and Lucy R. Nicholas
An Anthology of European Neo-Latin Literature edited by Gesine Manuwald, Daniel Hadas and Lucy R. Nicholas
An Anthology of Neo-Latin Poetry by Classical Scholars edited by Gesine Manuwald, Stephen Harrison, Bobby Xinyue and William M. Barton
An Anthology of Neo-Latin Literature in British Universities edited by Gesine Manuwald and Lucy R. Nicholas
De persecutione Anglicana by Robert Persons S.J.: A Critical Edition of the Latin Text with English Translation, Commentary and Introduction edited by Victor Houliston and Marianne Dircksen (with the assistance of Koos Kritzinger)
Ermolao Barbaro's On Celibacy 1 and 2 edited by Gareth Williams
Ermolao Barbaro's On Celibacy 3 and 4 and On the Duty of the Ambassador edited by Gareth Williams
Japan on the Jesuit Stage by Akihiko Watanabe
Roger Ascham's Themata Theologica by Lucy R. Nicholas

The Neo-Latin Verse of Urban VIII, Alexander VII and Leo XIII

Three Papal Poets from Baroque to Risorgimento

Stephen Harrison

BLOOMSBURY ACADEMIC
LONDON • NEW YORK • OXFORD • NEW DELHI • SYDNEY

BLOOMSBURY ACADEMIC
Bloomsbury Publishing Plc, 50 Bedford Square, London, WC1B 3DP, UK
Bloomsbury Publishing Inc, 1359 Broadway, 12th Floor, New York, NY 10018, USA
Bloomsbury Publishing Ireland, 29 Earlsfort Terrace, Dublin 2, D02 AY28, Ireland

BLOOMSBURY, BLOOMSBURY ACADEMIC and the Diana logo are trademarks of Bloomsbury Publishing Plc

First published in Great Britain 2024
This paperback edition published 2026

Copyright © Stephen Harrison, 2024

Stephen Harrison has asserted his right under the Copyright, Designs and Patents Act, 1988, to be identified as Author of this work.

For legal purposes the acknowledgements in the Preface on pp. vii–viii constitute an extension of this copyright page.

Cover image: St Peter's Basilica, The Vatican, Rome, Italy © joe daniel price/Getty

All rights reserved. No part of this publication may be: i) reproduced or transmitted in any form, electronic or mechanical, including photocopying, recording or by means of any information storage or retrieval system without prior permission in writing from the publishers; or ii) used or reproduced in any way for the training, development or operation of artificial intelligence (AI) technologies, including generative AI technologies. The rights holders expressly reserve this publication from the text and data mining exception as per Article 4(3) of the Digital Single Market Directive (EU) 2019/790.

Bloomsbury Publishing Inc does not have any control over, or responsibility for, any third-party websites referred to or in this book. All internet addresses given in this book were correct at the time of going to press. The author and publisher regret any inconvenience caused if addresses have changed or sites have ceased to exist, but can accept no responsibility for any such changes.

A catalogue record for this book is available from the British Library.
Library of Congress Cataloging-in-Publication Data
Names: Harrison, Stephen, 1948– author.
Title: The Neo-Latin verse of Urban VIII, Alexander VII and Leo XIII : three papal poets from baroque to resorgimento / Stephen Harrison. Other titles: Bloomsbury Neo-Latin series. Early modern texts and anthologies ; v. 10. Description: New York : Bloomsbury Publishing Plc, 2024. | Series: Bloomsbury neo-latin series: early modern texts and anthologies; vol 10 | Includes bibliographical references and index. | Latin texts and English translations; commentary in English. Identifiers:
LCCN 2023039114 (print) | LCCN 2023039115 (ebook) |
ISBN 9781350292383 (hardback) | ISBN 9781350292376 (paperback) |
ISBN 9781350292390 (pdf) | ISBN 9781350292406 (ebook)
Subjects: LCSH: Urban VIII, Pope, 1568–1644–Criticism and interpretation. Alexander VII,Pope, 1599–1667–Criticism and interpretation. | Leo XIII, Pope, 1810–1903–Criticism and interpretation. | Latin poetry, Medieval and modern–History and criticism.
Classification: LCC PA8050 .H37 2024 (print) | LCC PA8050 (ebook) |
DDC 871/.0409—dc23/eng/20231201
LC record available at https://lccn.loc.gov/2023039114
LC ebook record available at https://lccn.loc.gov/2023039115

ISBN: HB: 978-1-3502-9238-3
PB: 978-1-3502-9237-6
ePDF: 978-1-3502-9239-0
eBook: 978-1-3502-9240-6

Bloomsbury Neo-Latin Series: Early Modern Texts and Anthologies

Typeset by RefineCatch Limited, Bungay, Suffolk

For product safety related questions contact productsafety@bloomsbury.com.

To find out more about our authors and books visit www.bloomsbury.com and sign up for our newsletters.

Contents

List of Figures	vi
Preface	vii
Introduction	1
1 Maffeo Barberini (1568–1644; Pope as Urban VIII 1623–44)	9
2 Fabio Chigi (1599–1667; Pope as Alexander VII 1655–67)	93
3 Vincenzo Pecci (1810–1903; Pope as Leo XIII 1878–1903)	181
Appendix: Table of Latin Metres	251
Notes	255
Bibliography	267
Index of Names and Places	275

Figures

1. Pope Urban VIII, bust by studio of Gianlorenzo Bernini, photo by Sailko — 8
2. Pope Alexander VII, bust by Melchiore Cafà, photo by Giovanni Piscina — 92
3. Pope Leo XIII, photo by Francesco De Federicis, 1898 — 180

Preface

This book considers the Latin poetry of Popes Urban VIII, Alexander VII and Leo XIII, in each case by treating in some detail a select group of substantial poems of particular interest in literary and cultural terms. It presents the first modern commentary on this body of work in English, and in many cases the first translation of a particular poem into English. It aims to present these poems in a form that can be used by non-specialist modern Anglophone readers.

The Introduction to the whole volume gives a brief biography of each of the volume's three popes as a background to their poetry, while the introductions to the sections on each poet set out to provide a similarly concise context for his work. I have selected poems which engage with particular flair in the creative appropriation of classical Latin poetry (especially of Horace); the volume thus hopes to make a contribution to classical reception studies as well as to the study of neo-Latin poetry and cultural history. In this sense this volume is parallel to my 2017 Bloomsbury volume *Victorian Horace: Classics and Class*, which sought to analyse and contextualize some of the many British Horatian receptions of the nineteenth century.

The Latin texts used in this volume are based on the major printed editions or occasionally on manuscripts, of which details are given for each poet; I have felt free to alter punctuation and orthography to those conventional in modern classical Latin texts for the ease of the modern reader. In the commentary 'cf.' points to a likely source for a phrase or idea, while an asterisk (*) indicates that a word or phrase occurs in the same metrical position in another text, again indicating a probable model; the works of Vergil (the most frequent parallels) are cited in full title without the name of the author (so simply *Aeneid*, *Georgics* or *Eclogues*). References to other classical works generally follow the conventions of the *Oxford Latin Dictionary*. The *Oxford Latin Dictionary* itself is referred to as *OLD*, the *Thesaurus Linguae Latinae* as *TLL*, and the excellent online Italian Poetry in Latin database *Musique Deoque* (http://mizar.unive.it/poetiditalia/public/index), covering 1200–1600, as *MQDQ*. Quotations from the Bible in Latin are from the Vulgate, in English from the Authorised Version of 1611. A table of the Latin metres used is given in an Appendix. All www. locators were functional at the date of going to press.

I have a number of debts to record. I owe many thanks to my fellow-editors of the Bloomsbury Neo-Latin series, Gesine Manuwald, William Barton and Bobby Xinyue, for taking on this volume, to the editorial staff at Bloomsbury, especially Alice Wright, Lily Mac Mahon and Zoe Osman, for all their help and support, to Merv Honeywood at RefineCatch for his production management, to Sarah Webb for her copy-editing, to the anonymous referee for Bloomsbury for their suggestions, and (especially) to John Trappes-Lomax for reading the whole text, saving me from many errors and making two excellent conjectures in Chigi poems 2 and 21. Further, I am most grateful to Andrea Cucchiarelli and La Sapienza, Università di Roma for a period as visiting professor in Rome in 2020, to Luca Graverini and the Università degli Studi di Siena for a period as visiting professor in Siena in 2022, to Hélène Casanova-Robin and Sorbonne Université for a period as visiting professor in Paris in 2023, and to Federica Bessone and the Università degli Studi di Torino for a period as visiting professor in 2023; all enjoyable visits during which I was able to work on the project. Finally, I would like to thank Corpus Christi College, Oxford, my main academic home for more than thirty-five years, most warmly for all its various kinds of support, and especially for electing me in 2020 to a Senior Research Fellowship which has allowed me the ideal conditions in which to work on this book.

Stephen Harrison
Oxford, August 2023

Introduction

1. Papal poets

Not many popes have been substantially productive poets. The first known is Damasus (pope 366–384), whose relatively brief Latin verse inscriptions (largely in hexameters) in honour of saints and martyrs can still be found in many of the churches and tombs around Rome which he constructed or embellished.[1] In the late antique period, we find several celebrated episcopal Latin poets, such as Ambrose of Milan (fourth century), Paulinus of Nola (fourth to fifth century) and Venantius Fortunatus of Poitiers (sixth century),[2] but no major poetic popes. The next substantial poet to be elected to the papacy was Enea Silvio Piccolomini (pope as Pius II, 1458–64) who wrote a range of elegant neo-Latin poems in his younger days as a humanist courtier.[3] The baroque period, one of the high points of neo-Latin poetry in Italy and elsewhere,[4] saw two distinguished papal Latin poets, Maffeo Barberini (Urban VIII, 1623–44) and Fabio Chigi (Alexander VII, 1655–67); there then follows a gap of more than two centuries until Leo XIII (1878–1903), the last pope to write extensive Latin verse; the most recent pontifical poet, John Paul II (1978–2005), preferred his mother tongue of Polish.[5] This volume treats Urban VIII, Alexander VII and Leo XIII.

2. Maffeo Barberini (1568–1644; pope as Urban VIII 1623–44)[6]

Maffeo Barberini was born in 1568 into the minor noble family of Barberini in their Tuscan home town of Barberino Val d'Elsa between

Florence and Siena. His father died when Maffeo was young and he moved to Rome under the tutelage of his uncle Francesco Barberini, a protonotary apostolic (high clerical official) in the papal administration; he received an excellent Jesuit education at the Collegio Romano. In his youth he cultivated the friendship and literary advice of Aurelio Orsi (*c.* 1550–*c.* 1591), secretary and court poet of the senior church leader and major artistic patron Cardinal Alessandro Farnese (1520–89), and followed Orsi's example in writing Latin poems in praise of the cardinal and (especially) the cardinal's nephew, his homonym the celebrated general Alessandro Farnese (1545–92), Duke of Parma and Governor of the Spanish Netherlands for his uncle Philip II (1578–92). Items 1 and 2 in the material on Barberini below are drawn from these works linked with the Farnese.[7]

After studying for the degree of Doctor of Laws from the University of Pisa (1586–9), he began a career in the papal service, following his uncle. His career moved forward rapidly under Clement VIII (1592–1605), who made him Governor of Fano, protonotary apostolic like his uncle, and (1601) papal legate to France; in 1604 he was appointed titular Archbishop of Nazareth and papal nuncio in Paris. Paul V (1605–21) created him a cardinal (1606), Bishop of Spoleto (1608), legate of Bologna (1611) and prefect of the Signatura (1617); he was elected to the papacy in 1623. Items 3, 4 and 5 come from this period, marking his rise in the papal service (3), his patronage of younger men (4) and his combination of diplomacy with poetic ambition (5); in these years he also featured anagrammatically as the character Ibburanes in his friend John Barclay's Latin novel *Argenis* (1621).[8]

He was the longest-serving pope since Alexander III (1159–81). In foreign policy, he generally allied with France via Cardinal Richelieu and was mistrustful of the power of the Habsburgs; in the Thirty Years' War (1618–48) he provided only very limited support to German Catholic forces and was an advocate of peace. Within Italy, he strengthened the defences of the papal territories, reinforcing the Castel Sant'Angelo in Rome, establishing a major naval base at Civitavecchia and expanding the papal arsenal at Tivoli. In 1626 he extended his domains by annexing the Duchy of Urbino, gifted to him by the della Rovere family; his final War of Castro (1642-4) against the Farnese family of Parma was less successful, ending in defeat at the hands of an international coalition. He condemned the operation of the slave trade in Catholic countries overseas (Brazil and the West Indies).

In Rome he founded (1627) the Collegium Urbanum, now transformed into the Pontifical Urban University, for the training of missionaries, and embellished the existing Sapienza university, approving the appointment of Borromini as architect of its splendid church, S. Ivo alla Sapienza. Painted as a young man by Caravaggio (1598), as Pope he employed Bernini for key commissions at St Peter's, including the famous Baldacchino and his own tomb (finished in 1647). He was a collector of sculpture and antiquities, making or facilitating for his family famous acquisitions such as the Barberini Faun, the Barberini Apollo and the Barberini Vase (now the Portland Vase in the British Museum).

He also had some importance as a literary patron. The Polish Jesuit Maciej Kazimierz Sarbiewski (1595-1640), perhaps the finest Latin poet of the period, addressed several poems to him and made him the dedicatee of his Horatianizing collection of four books of *Odes* with one of *Epodes* (1632);[9] Urban presented Sarbiewski with a gold medal for his verse and employed him during his residence in Rome (1623-6) as part of a team revising the Latin hymns of the Breviary.[10] At the time of his election to the papacy, Urban's status as a Latin poet was already well known internationally; this is evidenced for example by his exchange of Latin epigrams with the major English poet George Herbert, then Public Orator of the University of Cambridge.[11]

He has been criticized for his extravagant expenditure (which put the papacy in deep debt) and for nepotism:[12] he made his nephews Francesco and Antonio Barberini cardinals in their twenties, and their brother Taddeo Prince of Palestrina and Prefect of Rome at a similarly early age, while his brother Carlo became head of the papal armies and Duke of Monterotondo. Francesco and then Taddeo rebuilt a former Sforza residence on the Quirinal as the splendid Palazzo Barberini (now the home of the Galleria Nazionale d'Arte Antica) with the help of Maderno, Borromini and Bernini (John Milton and John Evelyn were welcomed there in 1639 and 1644). He has also been criticized for his treatment of Galileo: earlier a friend of the great scientist, Urban called him to Rome in 1633 and forced him to recant his heliocentric theory of the universe, keeping him in effect under house arrest in Tuscany thereafter.

3. Fabio Chigi (1599–1667; pope as Alexander VII 1655–67)[13]

Fabio Chigi was born in 1599 in Siena into privilege as a member of the famous Sienese banking family, and as the great-nephew of Paul V, pope during his youth (1605–21). After an initial education in Siena, he came to Rome and rose in the service of Urban VIII, becoming vice-papal legate at Ferrara (1627), Inquisitor of Malta (1634) and Bishop of Nardò in southern Italy (1635). In 1639–51 he was papal nuncio in Germany, taking a key part in the complex negotiations (1643–8), leading to the Treaty of Westphalia and the end of the Thirty Years War (1648). In 1651 he was recalled to Rome by Innocent X and appointed Secretary of State; in 1652 he was created a cardinal and Bishop of Imola, and in the conclave of 1655 he was elected pope as Innocent's successor.

As pope, he was the host in Rome of the mercurial Christina, the Catholic convert daughter and successor of the great Protestant warrior-king Gustavus Adolphus of Sweden, who had abdicated her throne at the age of twenty-seven in 1654, and was a keen patron of European intellectual activity.[14] Alexander welcomed her to Rome at the start of his reign, and she lived there for much of the time until her death in 1689; there were tensions in their relationship, not least when Christina intrigued with Cardinal Mazarin over the political control of Naples.

Alexander's antagonistic relationship with Mazarin, the chief minister of Louis XIII and Louis XIV, went back to his earlier diplomatic days, and his relations with France, often tense and complex, were the major foreign policy issue of his reign. In 1662 there was a quarrel with Louis XIV over a supposed violation of the diplomatic immunity of the French embassy in Rome, as a result of which the papal territory of Avignon was briefly annexed by France; the dispute was resolved by the Treaty of Pisa in 1664. Alexander and Louis were subsequently (1665) able to agree on the condemnation of Jansenism, the views associated with the Dutch theologian and Bishop of Utrecht Cornelis Jansen (d. 1638) on predestination and other topics.

In Rome, Alexander was, like Urban VIII, a major patron of Bernini, whose work for him included the Scala Regia between the Vatican and St Peter's Basilica, the Chair of St. Peter in the basilica itself and the famous colonnade in the piazza in front of it. He made many further contributions to the urban landscape of Rome, promoting grand and theatrical spaces and vistas such as the Piazza del Popolo.[15] As a published poet himself, he was the dedicatee of a significant anthology of neo-Latin poetry by an international group of poets, the *Septem illustrium virorum poemata* of 1662,[16] and of the massive theological elegiac cycle *Urania Victrix* (1663) by the major German neo-Latin poet Jakob Balde (1604–68).[17] He initially rejected nepotism, but then made his nephew Flavio Chigi (who had served with him in Germany) a cardinal at the age of twenty-six (1657); he also created his nephew Agostino Chigi Duke of Ariccia and enabled him to buy and embellish the Palazzo Chigi, now the official home of the Italian Prime Minister.

4. Vincenzo Pecci (1810–1903; pope as Leo XIII, 1878–1903)[18]

Vincenzo Pecci was born in Carpineto Romano near Rome in 1810 to a family of minor nobility, and studied initially in the Jesuit college in Viterbo; from 1824 he attended the Jesuit Collegio Romano in Rome, followed by the Pontifical Ecclesiastical Academy, and was ordained priest in 1837. Promoted by Gregory XVI (1831–46), after spells as papal legate in Benevento and Perugia, in 1843 he was appointed papal nuncio to Belgium, and in 1846 returned to Perugia as bishop, where he stayed for many years, being made cardinal in 1853. Pius IX (1846–78), with whom he had a complex relationship, eventually made him papal chamberlain in 1877, and he was elected as Pius' successor in 1878. He retained the episcopate of Perugia until 1880.

He was the fourth longest-serving pope of all time, and the first for a millennium not to rule the papal states, which had become part of the Kingdom of Italy in 1871; a key feature of his reign was the tension with the recently established Italian state and its lay character. He was concerned to defend the position of the Church in a modern and laicized Europe, both in Italy and in a rapidly secularizing France; he was able to defuse a crisis between Germany and Spain in 1885 about the Pacific Caroline Islands, and to mitigate the considerable hostility to the Church in Germany which had developed under Pius IX in the 1870s. He encouraged missionary activity in the European colonies in Asia and Africa.

But the focus of his papacy was generally on social, moral and theological issues rather than international affairs. In the encyclical *Rerum novarum* of 1891 he set out workers' entitlement to fair pay and conditions and to trade union membership, but also supported property rights and rejected socialism as perilous and anarchic. He was especially interested in Marian devotion, issuing eleven encyclicals on the rosary, and in promoting the cult of the Holy Family. In 1879 he elevated both John Henry Newman and his own distinguished Jesuit brother Giuseppe Pecci simultaneously to the cardinalate; like his brother, he was an advocate of the revival of Thomism, the philosophy of Thomas Aquinas, a stance which many saw as unprogressive.

5. Common elements and divergences

These three papal poets have a number of features in common in addition to their pontifical status. Barberini and Chigi belonged to the same Roman classicizing movement in the baroque period, which promoted a more strictly antique Latin poetic style, especially imitating Horace and Vergil, in contrast with contemporary mannerist tendencies.[19] All three were highly educated in classical Latin poetry, both in extensive reading of it and in its composition; in the cases of Barberini and Pecci this was a consequence of the top-class Jesuit instruction of the Collegio Romano.[20] All three are part of the long story of the European reception of the most important classical Latin poets, especially Horace, and all produce work which uses classical models in a creative and sophisticated way: studying them is an informative and entertaining exercise in classical reception.

All of them are interested in the mixing of the traditional genres of classical Latin to achieve novel effects, something which is a constant feature of neo-Latin verse. Barberini is particularly adept at this, combining Vergilian pastoral and Claudianic encomium (item 2), Catullan hendecasyllable and Horatian epistle (item 4), and Pindaric triads, Horatian lyric and Prudentian martyr-poetry (item 5), while Chigi combines Horatian epistle, Lucanian civil war epic and Ovidian exile poetry (item 8). Pecci is straighter in some of his classical imitation (Propertian elegy in item 2 and Horatian satire in item 4), but like Barberini is interested in combining or at least juxtaposing Christian and pagan forms (item 1) and drawing on Christian Latin prose texts of hagiography (item 1) and historiography (item 3). The two seventeenth-century poet-popes show themselves as thoroughly at home in original Latin composition, and largely echo and rework classical models with an impressive freedom and sophistication; Pecci in the nineteenth century sticks more closely to the imitation of his Roman originals, with more direct repetition of classical phrasing.[21]

But all of them show a fascinating deployment of classical poetic resources for high political or diplomatic purposes as cardinal or pope, whether honouring a martyr in order to please Spain (Barberini, item 4), exposing the problems of the negotiations around the Peace of Westphalia (Chigi, item 8) or seeking to reinforce Catholicism in a rapidly laicizing France (Pecci, item 3). There has been little analysis of their verse in modern Anglophone scholarship; this selective anthology aims to show that its close study is fully worthwhile, and to provide the first close translation and commentary in English for a modern readership.[22]

Figure 1 Pope Urban VIII, bust by studio of Gianlorenzo Bernini, photo by Sailko. *Source*: Wikimedia Commons https://commons.wikimedia.org/wiki/File:Gianlorenzo_bernini,_busto_di_urbano_VIII_02.JPG.

1

Maffeo Barberini (1568–1644; Pope as Urban VIII 1623–44)

Barberini wrote poetry in Latin over more than half a century,[1] and his highly accomplished verse was widely read in his lifetime, especially during his papacy, when a number of editions of his collected Latin poems appeared.[2] This selection of his poems comprises work written over more than three decades, and seeks to show the diversity and skill of his reception and reworking of the major classical Latin poets, especially Horace and Vergil.

It begins with a pair of his highly accomplished youthful compositions, one of the several Horatian odes he wrote to celebrate the leading general the Duke of Parma (item 1 below), and the Vergilianizing eclogue praising the same great man (item 2 below). These come from the 1580s, when the teenage Barberini was under the mentorship of Aurelio Orsi, the house poet of Parma's Roman family the Farnese (see Introduction).[3] They cover several different genres, rising from short epigrams through Horatian lyrics of moderate length to an encomiastic Vergilian-style pastoral in almost a hundred hexameters, and show the young author's desire to please both his subject and Orsi as well as to demonstrate his emerging poetic talent and first-class classical education.

Over the next two decades as a rising cleric Barberini wrote a number of moralizing and didactic poems on the virtuous life, often addressed to members of his own family, which showed limited engagement with classical models and literary dynamism.[4] But in mid-career as cardinal and senior papal official, he composed a number of attractive secular poems to friends of similar high education and literary interests deploying a wide range of classical allusion. Included in this selection are two fine verse letters of the period 1609–15, one in Horatian hexameters to his friend and brother-in-law Lorenzo Magalotti, another learned cleric (item 3), and one in Catullan hendecasyllables to the young aristocratic intellectual Virginio Cesarini (item 4). Both show an interesting combination of ancient poetic sources from different generic traditions.

These secular poems form a smaller proportion of Barberini's overall Latin output than his sacred poems. The sacred poems are usually placed at the start of the printed collections[5] and ultimately take up more than half their space, fully understandable for such an author publishing as cardinal and supreme pontiff. Many of these are biblical paraphrases, and most often use Horatian metres. They include the songs of Moses (Exodus 15, in eighteen Sapphic stanzas, and Deuteronomy 32, in hexameters), the song of Hannah (I Samuel 2, in fifteen Second Asclepiad stanzas), the songs of Isaiah and Hezekiah (Isaiah 12 and 38, the former in alternating iambic trimeters and dimeters, the latter in alternating hexameters and iambic dimeters, both metres from Horace's *Epodes*) and the song of Habbakuk (Habbakuk 3, in hexameters). Versions of canticles and psalms are also prominent: the Benedicite (Daniel 3, in the stichic asclepiads of Horace *Odes* 1.1), the Magnificat (Luke 1, in Ambrose-style iambic dimeter stanzas), the Benedictus (Luke 1, in hexameters), the Nunc Dimittis (Luke 2, in two Sapphic stanzas), the Te Deum (in alternating hexameters and iambic dimeters) and Psalms 1 (in six Alcaic stanzas), 116 (praise of God, fittingly in the four-line stanzas of Catullus' hymn to Diana, three glyconics followed by a final pherecratean) and 136 (the lament for Jerusalem, appropriately in sorrowing elegiacs).

There are also more original and interesting religious poems, for example a lyric dialogue in seven Alcaic stanzas between Christ on the cross and his sorrowing mother. The most ambitious of these are the long 'Pindaric' lyric odes in strophic triads using combinations of Horatian metrical lines celebrating particular saints, written when he was a cardinal (1606–23): these take as their topics St John the Baptist, St Mary Magdalen, St Louis of France and St Laurence; the last, also looking back to the late antique Christian martyr poetry of Prudentius, is included in full here (item 6 below).[6]

The earliest collections of his Latin poems, put together when he was still a cardinal, contained some thirty items, but by the time of the final edition published in his lifetime this had grown to more than 150.[7] After his death only one complete edition appeared, in Protestant Oxford (Barberini 1726).[8] Further poems have been published since from manuscript and other sources (see Sacré 2007 and especially Wiendlocha 2005).

He was at the centre of a group of poets in Rome for whom a relatively restrained classical form and imitation was fundamental in both Latin and Italian, and whose output presented a clear contrast with the other contemporary strand in Italian baroque poetry, the colourful and dramatic mannerism of Gianbattista Marino (1569–1625);[9] this circle was a key influence for Fabio Chigi (Alexander VII), our next papal poet. His work is consistently elegant in its diction and creative in its adaptation of classical models for the context of Baroque Rome, and thoroughly deserves revival in the modern study of Neo-Latin.

1. Encomiastic lyric: ode to Alessandro Farnese (*c.* 1585)

This ode in Horatian Alcaic stanzas[10] celebrates the campaigns in the Netherlands in the 1580s of Alessandro Farnese, Duke of Parma, to whose family the teenage Barberini was attached (see above). Farnese served his uncle, Philip II of Spain, as captain-general and governor-general of the Netherlands in the years 1578–89, a relatively successful period for Spanish arms in Flanders.

The close of this poem seems to place it at a moment of major victory in the Duke's Flemish campaigns, perhaps his capture of Antwerp in 1585.[11]

Here Barberini's main classical antecedents are the pair of Alcaic odes addressed by Horace to the two stepsons of Augustus, Drusus and the future emperor Tiberius, *Odes* 4.4 and 4.14, celebrating their victorious campaigns of 15 BCE in central Europe. Similar Horatianizing lyric poems celebrating military victories were common in sixteenth-century neo-Latin, for example the Alcaic odes written by George Buchanan on Henri II's capture of Calais (1558) and relief of Metz (1553)[12] or (especially) those composed to celebrate the very Battle of Lepanto in which Farnese had featured some years before; the lyrics by Aurelio Orsi himself on that occasion will have been a particular stimulus.[13]

This ode was not published until 2005; the printed editions of Barberini's poems include only a ten-line epigram congratulating Parma on his victory in Flanders in general terms. It is included here as an example of Barberini's apprentice work and of his detailed reception of Horace's political odes, a road that would also be followed by Fabio Chigi/Alexander VII (see further below).

This poem was first published from the Vatican Codex Barberini Latinus 1919 (probably the author's autograph; now online at https://digi.vatlib.it/view/MSS_Barb.lat.1919) by Wiendlocha 2005 as Ode II, from which my text is taken with some minor adjustments of punctuation.

Text and translation

Dum Belga uires spernit Iberiae
Ducisque uanos Austriaci impetus,
  Hispaniae rex ius in omnes
    Farnesio tribuit phalanges.
Rex quippe norat, per maris aequora 5
Cum uectus orae Thrax ferus Italae
  Magnam minaretur ruinam
    Ut ruerit medios in hostes,
Et quot minantum corpora miserit
Thracum sub Orcum factaque nomine 10
  Maiora prudentemque mentem,
    Norat et inscia corda uinci.
Ergo ille Belgis obuius aduolat
Irasque dictis suscitat agmini
  Hostes in aduersos et ipse 15
    Fulmineam quatit acer hastam,
Iamque in feroces irruit hostium
Turmas et amplas ense sibi uias
  Substernit et Belgarum aceruat
    Corpora corporibus cadentum, 20
Qualis rubenti fulmina Iuppiter
Dextra e superno cum iacit aethere,
  Miscentur horrendo fragore
    Aequora et igne polus coruscat.
Disiecta quercus fulmine concidit 25
Aut pinus alta, et comminus omnia
  Diffringit ac nix magna dirae
    Grandinis insequiturque nimbus,
Iamque ecce ab altis montibus irruit
Torrens et alnos saxaque et obuia 30
  Quaecumque fert secum per arua et
    In mare praecipitat profundum.
Talis timendus consilio, horrida

Maffeo Barberini (1568–1644; Pope as Urban VIII 1623–44)

While the Fleming rebuffed the might of Iberia
And the vain attacks of the Austrian general,
The king of Spain consigned to Farnese
Command over all his regiments.
   For the king knew how, when the fierce Turk   5
Was borne through the ocean's waters,
And threatened mighty ruin to Italy's shore,
He rushed against the thick of the enemy,
   And knew how many bodies he dispatched
Of threatening Turks to Hades, and of his deeds   10
Accomplished even beyond his name and wise mind,
And of his heart that knows not defeat.
   And so he flew to confront the Flemings
And roused passions in the army by his words
Against their opposing foes, and himself fiercely   15
Wielded his lightning spear,
   And now charged the fierce enemy squadrons
And razed ample paths for himself
With his sword, and heaped up bodies
On bodies of the falling Flemings,   20
   Just as, when Jupiter hurls his thunderbolts
With ruddy hand from the heaven above,
The seas are stirred with a terrible crash
And the sky flashes with fire,
   An oak-tree falls shattered by the bolt   25
Or a lofty pine, and smashes everything nearby,
And a mighty blizzard of terrible hail follows,
And a storm-cloud, and look,
   A stream rushes from the mountain heights
And carries with it through the fields alder-trees,   30
And rocks and whatever is in its path and
Sends it crashing into the depths of the sea.
   Such is Farnese, formidable for his forethought,

Timendus hasta, nominis Itali
   Spes una Mauortisque fulmen,   35
      Farnesius tonat inter hostes.
Contortus igni moenia ferreus
Infringit orbis, terraque murmure
   Dissultat, obducitque fumus
      Aethereum nebulis Olympum,   40
Passimque grando plumbea depluit,
Et Belga passim perfidus occidit,
   Ac trunca diffuse tumescens
      Membra vehit fluuius cruoris.
I, disce foedus, perfide, rumpere!   45
I, disce, ferrum, Belga, resumere!
   Non te amplius tolles, superbe,
      Fabula ni renovatur Hydrae.

Formidable for his fearsome spear, the one hope
Of Italy's fame and the bolt of Mars   35
As he thunders amidst the enemy.
   The iron ball hurled by fire smashes through
The wall, and the earth splits with the roar,
And the smoke covers heavenly Olympus
With mists, and on every side a hail of lead   40
   Pours down, on every side the faithless Fleming falls
And a river of blood, swelling and spreading,
Carries along severed limbs.
   Go on, learn what it is to break a treaty, traitor!
Go on, learn what it is to take up the sword again, Fleming!   45
You will not rise up again, proud one,
Unless the myth of the Hydra is renewed.

Commentary

1–12 The poem's opening stanzas look back to Parma's succession to Don John of Austria as Spanish governor in the Netherlands (1578) and to his role as Don John's lieutenant at the crucial naval Battle of Lepanto against the Ottomans (1571). Horatian colour is clear here. The idea that the Ottoman Turks threatened *ruina* to Italy at Lepanto recalls Horace's account in the same metre in *Odes* 1.37 of the battle of Actium, commonly compared to Lepanto in the poems celebrating that similarly naval victory of West over East in much the same location,[14] in which Cleopatra is said to menace the same for the Capitol at Rome (1.37.6–8 *dum Capitolio / regina dementis ruinas / funus et imperio parabat*), as well as using Horatian poetic topographical language in *orae . . . Italae* (6–7; cf. *Odes* 3.8.21 *Hispanae . . . orae*) and *maris aequora* (5, repeated from *Odes* 4.5.10). In line 10 'Thracians' = 'Turks' as often in neo-Latin, reflecting the Ottoman occupation of northern Greece and utilizing the local classical name (though *Turcus* is also frequent). The praise of Farnese's *prudentem . . . mentem* (11) recalls Horace's commendation of another general and politician, the Lollius of *Odes* 4.9, for his *animus . . . / rerum. . . prudens* (4.9.34–5). The idea that Parma has surpassed his name (11) points encomiastically to his homonym the classical conqueror Alexander the Great.

13–20 Parma's role in the Netherlands is celebrated in terms of Homeric and Vergilian epic heroism as well as Horatian lyric military encomium. He is both a speaker of words and doer of deeds (cf. *Iliad* 9.443), his spear flies like a thunderbolt (cf. *Aeneid* 12.919–25), and he creates heaps of dead enemies in battle (cf. *Aeneid* 10.509); his vigorous personal engagement with enemy forces recalls that of Horace's Drusus at *Odes* 4.14.22–3 *impiger <u>hostium</u> / vexare <u>turmas</u>*, while his opening up of a wide path in battle with his own sword echoes Aeneas at *Aeneid* 10.513–4 *latumque per agmen / ardens limitem agit ferro* (for the image see also *Iliad* 11.68). *hastam* (16) recalls the fearsome Roman warrior of *Odes* 3.2.4 *eques metuendus hasta* in both stanza-final position and sense; note the splendidly forceful triple alliteration of 20 *corpora corporibus cadentum*.

21–32 This disproportionately long simile recalls the two similar images of unusual length to be found in Horace's ode to Drusus, 4.4.1–16 (Drusus is compared to an eagle attacking sheep or snakes, or a lion attacking goats) and 4.4.57–68 (the Romans are like an oak-tree that gains strength from attempts to cut it down); Barberini's falling *quercus* (deciduous oak, 25) perhaps recalls and inverts Horace's non-falling *ilex* (evergreen oak, 57), though his falling pine (25–6 *concidit* ... / ... *pinus*) looks to Vergil (*Aeneid* 5.448–9, the fall of Entellus: <u>*concidit*</u>, *ut quondam caua* <u>*concidit*</u> *aut Erymantho / aut Ida in magna radicibus eruta* <u>*pinus*</u>). Likewise, Jupiter's hurling of his thunderbolts (21–4) echoes the stormy weather-scene at the opening of Horace *Odes* 1.2 where Jupiter similarly hurls thunderbolts *rubente / dextra* (2–3); *grandinis ... nimbus* (28) points to the similar extended simile comparing battle and its hail of weapons (for the image see further on line 41 below) to hostile weather at *Aeneid* 10.803–10 (esp. 803 *grandine nimbi*), while the image of the violent stream carrying rocks and trees before it (29–32) picks up another simile from the war-narrative of the *Aeneid* describing Turnus on the charge (12.684–90, esp. 889 *inuoluens secum*).

33–48 The description of Parma as *horrida / timendus hasta* (33–4) recalls *Odes* 3.2.4, describing the Roman cavalryman with similar encomiastic colour as *eques metuendus hasta* (a line already echoed at 16 above); *fulmen* (35) is picked up by *tonat* (36), suggesting Parma is like Jupiter the thunderer in war, recalling Vergil's compliment to the young Caesar at the end of the *Georgics* (4.561 *fulminat ... bello*). The final section of the poem (37–48) confronts a common issue for neo-Latin: how to Latinize post-classical technological developments, in this case the artillery which was central to late sixteenth-century sieges.[15] Here Barberini draws on a classical account of an erupting volcano; the description of cannon-fire in lines 37–44 recalls the account of Etna at *Aeneid* 3.572–4, which like artillery expels igneous balls into the air and creates obscuring smoke (*interdumque atram prorumpit* <u>*ad aethera nubem*</u> */ turbine* <u>*fumantem*</u> *piceo et candente fauilla, / attollitque globos* *flammarum et sidera lambit*); likewise, the 'hail of lead' here (41 *grando plumbea*) adds a contemporary colour to the traditional classical metaphor of a 'hail of weapons', foreshadowed in 28 *grandinis*; for example Ennius' *ferreus imber* or 'iron rain' (*Ann*.266 Sk.; cf. also Vergil *Aeneid* 9.666-71). The other imagery in 37-48 is also strongly classical: the picture of the river of blood (44) goes back to Lucan's melodramatic battlefields (4.785, 7.292, both similarly *fluuios . . . cruoris*); the idea that such a gory river carries limbs is a variation of the classical battle-epic trope of a normal river bearing the bodies of the dead (Homer *Iliad* 21.218-20, 300-2, 324-5, Catullus 64.359-60, Vergil *Aeneid* 8.538-40, Lucan 2.209-20). The pairing of hail and river in lines 40-44 thus repeats the weather imagery of lines 25-32 in shorter and more condensed form.

The taunting and admonition of defeated miscreants in lines 45-6 picks up *Aeneid* 9.634 *i, uerbis uirtutem inlude superbis* and *Aeneid* 6.620 *discite iustitiam moniti et non temnere diuos*.

The concluding image of the Hydra (48) recalls the imagined words of Hasdrubal about the Romans at *Odes* 4.4.61-2: *non Hydra secto corpore firmior /vinci dolentem crevit in Herculem*. If Flanders rises again (Hydra-like), like the Romans against Carthage, the mighty Parma will be ready with the punishing might of a Hercules to suppress its repeated resurgence. This final and flattering classical allusion fittingly reminds us of one of the poem's key metrical and thematic models.

2. Pastoral encomium of Alessandro Farnese – *Alexander: Ecloga* (1586-8)

This poem of 93 hexameters,[16] classified by its author as an 'eclogue', is an encomium of Parma: it looks to be written after the involvement of the English under the Earl of Leicester in the Dutch conflict in late 1585, probably soon after the capture of Antwerp in 1585 (see 1 above) and very likely before Parma's key role in the Spanish Armada of 1588.[17] The harnessing of the originally pastoral eclogue form to the praise of the great was familiar from the fourth *Eclogue* of Vergil, which celebrated the peace pact of Brundisium between the future Augustus and Antony in 40 BCE and was much imitated in the Renaissance period;[18] such encomiastic eclogues were common in neo-Latin pastoral from the middle Quattrocento.[19]

In this poem a Vergilian bucolic framework is present only in the imitation of *Eclogue* 6 with which the poem opens, and its modest length;[20] most of its material is the kind of classical Latin hexameter military panegyric to be found in the Augustan *Panegyricus Messallae* preserved in the poems of Tibullus (3.7/4.1), and in the poems written by Claudian in late antiquity celebrating the deeds of generals such as Stilicho.[21] The Poem's opening also marks a transition rooted in the poet's own literary career: the pastoral mode he seeks to move on from is that of his earlier three *Eclogues* (I–III Wiendlocha), which are more conventionally bucolic with herdsmen, love and singing-contests.[22]

The text followed here is that of Barberini 1642, the author's final version; the earlier manuscript text printed as Eclogue IV in Wiendlocha 2005 was much altered in the later rewriting.

Text and translation

Quae solita es pecudes inter frondentis in umbra
Ilicis agrestes calamos inflare, Thalia:
Linque casas nemorum cultuque ornata decenti
Desuper excelsas turres pete: digna sonorae
Voce tubae heroum molimur maxima facta.   5
Non facit atrocem ad Martem rude carmen auenae.
  Ecquis Alexandri possit tam grande sonanti
Carmine complecti laudes, ut facta canendo
Aequarit? Nec enim tantum ducis incluta uirtus
Caesaris ingentes animos imitatur, et ausus   10
Scipiadum Fabiive moras: quot protulit umquam
Roma ducum claras uirtutes excitat uno
In Duce ALEXANDRO.
                        Mauors Thrax efferus ensis
Fulmineos ictus sensit, cum caerula passim
Aequora Turcarum fuso rubuere cruore,   15
Qua mare Naupacti fluctu caua litora plangit.
Hic iterum fractae uires Orientis ab armis
Hesperiae, hic sacram captae uidere triremes
Per sua transtra Crucem victricia pandere signa.
Acer in aduersos illum rapit impetus hostes,   20
Nulla uiro uirtus obstat, uis nulla resistit
Herois gladio: nigras mors explicat alas
Lunigeras puppes super, ac truncata cadentum
Membra cruentati fluitant per marmora ponti.
Hellespontiaca Byzantii in sede tyrannum   25
Fama uolans tantae turbatum nuntia cladis
Perculit: huc illuc trepide per compita fertur
Correptum pauidis uulgus praecordia curis.
Quisque fugam meditans, incertis anxius haeret
Consiliis. Facile poterat perterritus hostis   30
Ad priscas Tanais cogi remeare latebras

Maffeo Barberini (1568–1644; Pope as Urban VIII 1623–44)

Thalia, you who have been used to play the rustic pipes
Amongst flocks in the shade of a flourishing holm-oak:
Leave your cottages in the woods and, decked in fair array,
Come down and seek lofty towers: I am labouring at
Mighty deeds of heroes worthy of the voice of the
   loud-sounding trumpet: 5
The crude song of the straw-pipe does not suit fierce Mars.
   Could anyone encompass the praise of Alexander
In so lofty-sounding a song as to equal his deeds
By singing? His famed courage does not only imitate
The mighty spirit of Caesar the general,   10
Or the daring of the Scipios or the delays of Fabius:
As many noble qualities as Rome ever produced in its generals
It now arouses in one single leader ALEXANDER.
Fierce Thracian Mars has felt the thunderous blows of his sword,
When the blue surface of the sea turned red with the blood
   of the Turks,   15
Where the sea strikes the concave shore of Naupactus with its waves,
Here once again the might of the Orient was broken by the arms
Of the West, here captured triremes saw the sacred Cross
Spread its victorious standards over their benches.
A fierce spirit drove him against the enemies opposite,   20
No power could withstand the warrior, no force resist
The hero's sword: death spread its dark wings
Over the ships that bore the crescent, and the severed limbs
Of the fallen floated through the bloodied marble surface of the sea.
In his seat on the Hellespont flying rumour struck   25
And shook the despot of Byzantium as messenger
Of such a disaster: the people rushed here and there
Through the crossroads, their hearts seized with panic and anxiety.
Each of them envisaging flight stopped still with worry
Their plans all uncertain. The terrified enemy could easily   30
Have been driven to return to their ancient lair on the Don,

Ni fera Christicolis uario discordia motu
Distractis, meritae rapuisset praemia palmae.
Sic placitum superis nostrae ob contagia culpae
Gaudentis patrio perfundere sanguine campos. 35
   Nec tua, ALEXANDER, tantum decora incluta nouit
Qui colit Eoas oras, et clara tropaea
Miratur, captasue dolet praedasque uirosque
Armatamque timet funesta in proelia dextram:
Nouere Ausonii, Bataui sensere subacti. 40
Hi magnos ausus animi metuendaque fortis
Damna manus; illi meritos ex hoste triumphos
Et summos immortalis uirtutis honores.
Hique tuam noscent uentura in saecula famam
Quos et uterque polus, quos Taurus claudit et Atlas, 45
Quique sua inuertunt nostris uestigia plantis.
   Nulla tuas poterit laudes abolere uetustas
Dum Scaldis tumidum rapidis irrumpet in aequor
Fluctibus, et stabit celsis Antuerpia muris
Bellica dum Belgae suboles nomenque manebit. 50
Nam quid ego hostiles summa uirtute fugatas
Commemorem turmas debellatasque phalanges?
Quid fluuii clausum per aquas iter obice pontis,
Quem ratis incassum tentauit perdere nitri
Freta dolis, iussasque ferens in tempore flammas? 55
Seu quid consilio pernicique oppida capta
Aduentu? uel aquis cinctas et moenibus arces
Assiduis uictas studiis urbesque subactas?
Nec tibi res fuerat tantum contra horrida Belgae
Arma, nec aduersus munitas aggere fossas: 60

Had not fierce discord stolen the reward of their merited victory
From the Christians when they were riven by varied dissension.
Thus did it please the gods through the contagion of our fault
To soak the rejoicing plains with the blood of their own country.   35
   Nor is it only the inhabitant of the Eastern shores
Who knows your distinguished glories and wonders at
Your famed trophies, or grieves over the capture of men and plunder,
Or fears your right hand armed for deadly battle:
The Italians know you, the conquered Dutch have felt your might,   40
The latter the great daring of your spirit and the fearsome losses
Inflicted by your arm, the former your deserved triumph over the enemy
And the highest honours paid to your immortal courage,
Those too will also come to know your fame in centuries to come
Who are bounded by the two poles, by Taurus and Atlas,   45
And who place their footsteps opposite to the soles of our feet.
   No age will be able to wipe away your achievements
For as long as the Scheldt spills into the swelling ocean
With its swift streams, and Antwerp stands with its lofty walls,
As long as the warlike race of Flanders and its name shall live.   50
For why should I mention the squadrons of the enemy
Routed by your high courage and the formations you defeated?
Why mention the route down the river's waters closed by the barrier of the bridge,
Which a ship tried in vain to destroy relying on the trick
Of gunpowder and carrying the ordered flames at the right moment?   55
Or the towns captured by your planning and rapid arrival?
Or the citadels surrounded by waters and fortifications
Overcome by your continuous efforts, and the cities you subdued?
Nor did you just have to do with opposing the dreadful
Arms of Flanders, or ditches protected with a mound: 60

Saepe Britannorum saeua undique circumuentum
Gallorumque acie regio te Belgica uidit
Ac tria deuicto referentem ex hoste tropaea.
Non tibi tormentis saeuos imitantibus ictus 65
Fulminis aut lymphis circumstagnantibus altae
Vrbis agrum, est aditus clausus: non fluminis undis
Qua celeres furtim lintres alimenta ferebant
Hostibus obsessis: uictor tanta urbe potiris.
   Qualis in Alpino nodosa cacumine quercus 70
Saepius incursus Boreae frustrata frementis
Et quamquam insolito miscetur turbine caelum
Stat tamen immota, et uenti uix frondis honorem
Decutiunt: tenues fulmen si forte per auras
Iuppiter in quercum contorserit, illa repente 75
Concidit et campis infert segetique ruinam:
Palantes fugiunt pecudes pecudumque magistri;
At sibi tota timet subsultans murmure silua.
Talis, ut herois generosae robora dextrae
Sensit, Iberorum consueta euadere nisus 80
Cedit et admittit victorem Antuerpia portis.
   Iam pauor excurrit mortis, iam terror oberrat
Exitii. Quid agat? tantis circumdatus armis
Quid tentet? Veniam supplex sibi Belga precatur.
Et licet incensum ualido cor ferueat aestu, 85
Tu tamen, antiquae FARNESI gloria gentis,
Supplicibus ueniam defers, et bile tumentis
Vltores animi sedas in pectore motus.
Hoc uirtutis opus. Nunc o quantum libet illa
Nunc tui Alexandri facta incluta Graecia iacta. 90
Est et ALEXANDER Romae, aeque fortis in armis,
Maior in hoc: nec enim tantum deuicerit hostes,
Hostibus at uictis sese quoque uincit et iram.

Often the region of Flanders saw you surrounded
By a battle-line of Britons or Gauls
And winning three trophies from a conquered enemy.
Your way was not closed off by the machines
Imitating the fierce blows of the thunderbolt					65
Or by the waters pooling around the territory of the lofty city,
Nor by the streams of the river by which swift boats
Secretly carried provisions to your enemies under siege:
As victor you mastered such a mighty city.
   As a knotty oak-tree on an Alpine peak					70
Repeatedly resists the incursions of the roaring North Wind
And, though the heaven is confounded by an unprecedented storm,
It stands unmoved, and the winds barely knock down
The ornament of its branches; if it happens
That Jupiter hurls a bolt against that oak-tree					75
Through the thin air, the tree falls rapidly
And brings destruction to both plains and crop:
The flocks and the flocks' herdsmen scatter and flee,
But the whole wood fears for itself leaping at the din.
Just so, when it felt the strength of the hero's noble right hand
Antwerp, accustomed to escape the efforts of the Spanish,		80
Yielded and admitted the victor by its gates.
   Now a fear of death ran wild, now a terror of extinction
Ranged about. What was she to do? What could she attempt,
Surrounded as she was by such great forces?
Flanders in supplication begged pardon for herself.
And though your heart burned with a mighty heat,				85
Yet you, Farnese, the glory of your ancient house,
Grant pardon to the suppliants, and quiet the motions
Swelling with bile of your avenging spirit in your heart.
That is the task of virtue. Now, Greece, go ahead and boast
Of the glorious deeds of your own Alexander:					90
Rome too has an Alexander, equally brave in war,
But greater in this: he does not just defeat his enemies,
But when he has done so conquers himself and his anger.

Commentary

1–6 This preface reworks the similarly programmatic opening of Vergil's sixth *Eclogue* with clear lexical echoes (6.1–9, 2 *Thalia*, 8 *agrestem*). In Vergil the poet is diverted from his intended theme of epic battle by the intervention of Apollo who turns him towards pastoral; here the pastoral Muse Thalia is invoked to adapt epic battle to the bucolic form by the poet himself, a neat variation. There are other clear traces of the *Eclogues* here: *umbra*, shade, *pecudes*, flocks, the *ilex* or holm-oak, and the pipe (*calami*, *avena*) are all characterizing elements in Vergil's pastoral collection.[23] Barberini's opening also echoes another preface, the lines prefixed to the beginning of the *Aeneid* by an early reader[24] and commonly believed at his time to be authentically Vergilian:

> *Ille ego, qui quondam gracili modulatus auena*
> *carmen, et egressus siluis uicina coegi*
> *ut quamvis auido parerent arua colono*
> *gratum opus agricolis, at nunc horrentia Martis*
> *arma uirumque cano . . .*

Using the same symbolic keywords *auena* and *Mars*, these lines represent the passage of the poet from pastoral to epic which Barberini adopts in his preface, jumping the intermediate didactic stage of the *Georgics* in his career ascent within hexameter genres.

7–13a These lines introduce the object of the poet's praise. The opening rhetorical question (7–9), asking whether there could be a poet adequate to the epic task in hand, fittingly echoes the words of Statius' introduction to his catalogue of the Seven against Thebes (*Thebaid* 4.145–6) *quis numerum ferri gentesque et robora dicto / aequarit mortale sonans?*, an enquiry with a prominent literary history;[25] the passage also appropriately picks up the description of the great epic poet Homer in the Underworld in Silius Italicus (13.787–9) *et fuit in tanto non paruum pectore numen: / carmine complexus terram, mare, sidera, manes / et cantu Musas et Phoebum aequauit honore*. The comparison of Parma with the great commanders of Roman antiquity, common in neo-Latin encomium, is expressed in classical phrases: *incluta virtus* is once again from Statius (*Theb*.11.412), *ingentes animos* from Vergil (*Georgics* 3.27), while the references to the Scipios and Fabius look back to their appearance together in Vergil's Show of Heroes (*Aeneid* 6.843 *Scipiadas*, 6.845 *Fabii*) as well as to Propertius (3.3.9 *uictricesque moras Fabii*). The passage climaxes mid-line with the proper name which Parma shares with the greatest conqueror of the Greek world, capitalized as in the original edition.

13b–35 This section looks back to the younger Farnese's service at the crucial naval battle of Lepanto (1571) as lieutenant of Don John of Austria. The description of Lepanto here incorporates a topos of its contemporary celebration, its approximate co-location with and symbolic repetition of (17 *iterum*) the Roman naval battle of Actium (31 BCE).[26] Actium had been fought in the Gulf of Ambracia some 100 kilometres north of the site of Lepanto in the Gulf of Patras; both were historically decisive conflicts in which a 'Western' force defeated an 'Eastern' one (the future Augustus/Antony and Cleopatra, the Holy League/the Ottoman Empire) on the same central-western coast of Greece.[27] In line 13 'Thracian' = 'Ottoman', reflecting the location of Constantinople in Eastern Thrace (cf. *Ode* II.10 above), but also recalling Mars' traditional association with the area in classical poetry (e.g. Ovid *Ars* 2.588, *Fasti* 5.257–8, Manilius 4.691). For the classicizing comparison of weapons and thunderbolts (14) see on *Ode* 2.16 (above) *fulmineam quatit acer hastam*; the detail of the sea turning red with blood (15) recalls Vergil's description of Actium (*Aeneid* 8.695 *arua noua Neptunia caede rubescunt*), as does the phrase *uires Orientis* (17) to describe the Eastern enemy (8.687 *uirisque Orientis*); for *fractae uires* (17) cf. *Odes* 2.7.11 *cum fracta uirtus* (of the battle of Philippi), for *uictricia signa* (19) see Lucan 1.347, for the dark wings of death (22) cf. Seneca *Oedipus* 164–5 *Mors atra* ... / ... *omnis explicat alas*, for *marmora ponti* (24) cf. Catullus 63.88 *marmora pelagi* and for *per compita* of rumour (27) cf. *Satires* 2.6.50. Line 31 refers to the Ottoman expedition to the river Don (north-east of the Caucasus) in 1569,[28] but also invokes the river's classical role as a distant border of the Roman empire (cf. *Odes* 3.10.1, 3.29.8, 4.15.24, Propertius 2.30.2). The final moralizing remark (34–5) on the tensions in the Holy League after Lepanto which prevented an effective follow-up to the victory also echoes the Roman poetry of civil war: the plains soaked with blood[29] present a hyperbolic echo of those at the end of *Georgics* 1 linked with the battles of Pharsalus and Philippi (cf. *G.*1.491–2 *nec fuit indignum superis bis sanguine nostro / Emathiam et latos Haemi pinguescere campos*). As at the end of the poem (92–3), a moral forms a conclusion (here to the account of Lepanto).

36–46 This section provides a transition to the Duke's command in the Netherlands from 1578. For 36–7 cf. Seneca *Medea* 130 *inclitum ... decus*, Cicero *Inv.*1.67 *claro ... tropaeo*, Valerius Flaccus 1.43–4 *Scythiam Phasinque rigentem / qui colit*; note how a noun/adjective pair encloses line 39 (cf. similarly Ovid *Met.*8.421 *uictricemque ... dextram*), and lines 43 and 44 both end with similarly shaped nouns referring to military glory (*triumphos, honores*). Lines 40–6 echo Roman poetic encomia: the idea that defeated foreign peoples have witnessed the might of a great commander picks up the praise of Drusus in *Odes* 4.4.17–18 *uidere Raeti bella sub Alpibus / Drusum gerentem Vindelici*,[30] while the notion of the merited triumph and the idea that the fame of the great man will extend across all of space and time derive similarly from the poetic praise of great Romans: 42 *meritos ex hoste triumphos* recalls Manilius on Pompey's military career (4.52) *et tris emenso meritos ex orbe triumphos*, while *uentura in saecula* (44) looks to Silius' praise of Cicero (8.406-7) *quantumque ... Ausoniae populis uentura in saecula ciuem*, and the mention of Atlas as the distant limit of fame (45) echoes Anchises' encomium of Augustus which identifies Atlas as the far-off limit of his rule (Vergil *Aeneid* 6.796). Line 46 in effect translates the Greek *Antipodes*, 'opposing our feet'; for both phrasing and idea see Cicero *Lucullus* 123 *e contraria parte terrae qui aduersis uestigiis stent contra nostra uestigia, quos ἀντίποδας uocatis*.

47–69 Here we reach the chief subject of the poem, the capture of Antwerp. The statement that Parma's fame will last as long as Antwerp, the Scheldt and Flanders themselves (47–50) is a version of Vergil's famous prophecy that the glory of Nisus and Euryalus will endure as long as the Julian dynasty will rule Rome and its empire (*Aeneid* 9.447–9): <u>nulla</u> *dies umquam memori uos eximet aeuo,/ <u>dum</u> domus Aeneae Capitoli immobile saxum / accolet imperiumque pater Romanus <u>habebit</u>,* and also echoes[31] the assertion of the lasting fame of Daphnis (Vergil *Eclogues* 5.76–8): <u>*Dum*</u> *iuga montis aper, fluuios <u>dum</u> piscis amabit, / <u>dum</u>que thymo pascentur apes, <u>dum</u> rore cicadae, / semper honos <u>nomen</u>que tuum laudesque <u>manebunt</u>,* as well as Ovid's promise of eternal life for his *Metamorphoses* at the end of the poem (15.871–2): *Iamque opus exegi, quod nec Iouis ira nec ignis / nec <u>poterit</u> ferrum nec edax <u>abolere uetustas</u>.* The encomiastic series of four rhetorical questions in lines 52–8 recalls a similar sequence in the praise of Italy at *Georgics* 2.158–64, a passage which refers similarly to the mastering and constraining of great waters by human ingenuity in a military context. In Vergil this happens in the context of the Portus Iulius naval base project of Agrippa near Naples, in Barberini in Parma's blockade of the Scheldt and construction of a spectacular pontoon bridge:[32]

> *an mare quod supra <u>memorem</u>, quodque adluit infra?*
> *anne lacus tantos? te, Lari maxime, teque,*
> *fluctibus et fremitu adsurgens Benace marino?*   160
> *an <u>memorem</u> portus Lucrinoque addita claustra*
> *atque indignatum magnis stridoribus aequor,*
> *Iulia qua ponto longe sonat unda refuso*
> *Tyrrhenusque fretis immittitur aestus Auernis?*

Other linguistic details in this section look back to Roman triumphal poetry: the *oppida capta* of line 56 occur in Propertius' prospective Eastern triumph of Augustus (3.4.16) and in Ovid's imagined triumph of Tiberius (*Tristia* 4.2.20), both similarly at line-end, while the *tria ... tropaea* of line 64 (defeating Dutch, French and English)[33] recall both Manilius' description of the three triumphs of Pompey already echoed in line 42 (4.52 *tris . . . triumphos*) and the two trophies of the victorious Augustus at *Georgics* 3.32 (*duo rapta manu diuerso ex hoste tropaea*).

70–81 The city of Antwerp is compared in an elaborate simile to an oak-tree which resists storms but then suddenly collapses, echoing the famous image at Vergil *Aeneid* 4.441–9:

> ac uelut annoso ualidam cum robore <u>quercum</u>
> Alpini Boreae nunc hinc nunc flatibus illinc
> eruere inter se certant; it stridor, et altae
> consternunt terram concusso stipite <u>frondes</u>;
> ipsa haeret scopulis et quantum uertice ad <u>auras</u>   445
> aetherias, tantum radice in Tartara tendit:
> haud secus adsiduis hinc atque hinc uocibus <u>heros</u>
> tunditur, et magno persentit pectore curas;
> mens <u>immota</u> manet, lacrimae uoluuntur inanes.

Here Aeneas' unresponsiveness to Anna's pleas for Dido is represented like a great unmoveable tree, whose leaves may be stripped off by the wind but which remains firmly rooted and upright.

This Vergilian immobility is modified by Barberini into a great tree which repeatedly resists but then actually falls, suitable for the long but ultimately successful siege of Antwerp which lasted more than a year. In this there are also lexical echoes of the tree-like tower cut down by the Trojans in the sack of Troy in *Aeneid* 2 (465–6 *ea lapsa <u>repente ruinam</u> / cum sonitu trahit*) which can be seen as a symbol for the fall of Troy itself; this would be a neatly appropriate echo for Barberini's context of the fall of the Troy-like Antwerp. The same verb *concidit* (76) is also used (twice) in a tree simile for the fall of the wrestler Entellus at *Aeneid* 5.448–9 *concidit, ut quondam caua concidit aut Erymantho/ aut Ida in magna radicibus eruta pinus*, a passage also echoed in *Odes* II above, while *murmure* (78) and *misceturque turbine caelum* (72)[34] both look back to the storm during the hunt at *Aeneid* 4.160 *magno miscetur murmure caelum*. Not unexpectedly, this long simile looks back firmly to Vergilian epic in both its style and subject matter.

82-93 The poem's final section focusses on Parma's magnanimity in victory. This kind of mercy is a conventional classical virtue, going back to the traditional *clementia* of Roman emperors; the language of line 88 also suggests Cicero's definition of temperance (*frugalitas* = Greek *sophrosyne*) at *Tusculans* 3.17 as <u>motus animi</u> appetentis regere et <u>sedare</u>, while *hoc uirtutis opus* echoes Jupiter's firmly Roman definition of virtue at *Aeneid* 10.468–9 as seeking fame by deeds (*famam extendere factis, / hoc <u>uirtutis opus</u>*); its reapplication to mercy might represent a Christian correction of pagan ethics. Like the heroes of old, Parma brings glory to his family, *gloria gentis* (86); this matches one of Aeneas' royal ancestors seen in the Show of Heroes at *Aeneid* 6.767 *Troianae gloria gentis*.[35] Parma might well have acted differently on the surrender of Antwerp: its inhabitants, and contemporaries elsewhere such as Barberini, would only too easily recall the infamous 'Spanish Fury' of November 1576, when mutinous Spanish troops had brutally sacked the same city, inflicting thousands of casualties.[36] Barberini's concluding commendation of Parma's contrasting self-restraint at the moment of military triumph, and the idea of the simultaneous conquest of one's enemies and one's own lower nature, irresistibly recall Cicero's praise of Julius Caesar for not taking vengeance against his adversaries at the end of the civil war against the Pompeians (*Pro Marcello* 8): *animum vincere, iracundiam cohibere, uictoriam temperare ... haec qui fecit, non ego eum cum summis uiris comparo, sed simillimum deo iudico*. Like Caesar, Parma has overcome both his opponents and his own basic instinct for revenge, thus attaining a glory which fits the highest standards of both Roman imperial and Christian values (*clementia* and mercy). The comparison with Alexander the Great triggered by Parma's name (1–2) is also a standard way of praising Roman heroes,[37] and here the modern hero outdoes his ancient counterpart, given Alexander's notoriously unrestrained personal passions for which he was sometimes criticized by Christian writers.[38] The moralizing close is typical of Barberini; cf. 34–5 above and the close of the epistle to Magalotti (see 5 below).

3. Hexameter epistle – letter to Lorenzo Magalotti (1609–11)[39]

This 149-hexameter[40] epistle belongs to the period 1609–11 (when Barberini was already a cardinal and bishop but more than a decade before his papacy) and is addressed to his friend and relative by marriage Lorenzo Magalotti (1584–1637), whose older sister Costanza had married Barberini's brother Carlo in 1594. Magalotti was then serving in the papal Curia as referendary of the Tribunals of the Apostolic Signatura (i.e. as a canon lawyer concerned with responding to petitions to the Pope)[41] and was later appointed by Urban as Secretary of State (1623–8) and created a cardinal (1624), but after differences with his master ended his career in exile from Rome as bishop of Ferrara (1628–37).[42]

The poem is framed as an invitation by Barberini to his friend to leave behind the business of the Curia in Rome and come for relaxation to the papal estate at Castel Gandolfo in the Alban Hills 20 kilometres south-east of the city. It was the supposed site of the ancient city of Alba Longa, traditionally founded by Aeneas' son Ascanius/Iulus and the original home of Romulus and Remus;[43] its early history and that of the neighbouring Nemi is alluded to at length in lines 107–40. This estate had been acquired by Clement VIII in 1596; Urban himself as Pope was later to convert the castle there into the extant papal palace, until recently a papal summer retreat and now a papal museum, with magnificent gardens and spectacular views over Lazio.[44] Barberini's poem presents a rich description of the country pleasures of the estate, and evokes its supposed view of the city of Rome, emphasizing the current major building programme there of the then Pope Paul V Borghese.

Almost every line of the poem contains phrases taken or adapted from the classical Latin poets, of which the more significant are noted in the commentary below; it also incorporates a number of larger literary themes and frameworks from the same sources. As a hexameter poem of more than 100 lines addressed to a friend in epistolary form, it is closest in format to the *Silvae* of Statius amongst classical Latin texts. Rediscovered in 1417–18 by Poggio Bracciolini, these occasional poems from the Flavian period (late first century CE) were prominently imitated by Poliziano at the end of the fifteenth century and enjoyed much popularity as models for neo-Latin poets until the eighteenth century.[45] One partial model for Barberini's poem is the 105-line *Silvae* 4.4, a verse letter written in 94–96 CE to M.Vitorius Marcellus, a key statesman under Domitian and Nerva;[46] at the time he was supervisor of Domitian's road project constructing the *uia Latina* (4.4.60), so a busy official working for the emperor, parallel to Magalotti's role in the Curia serving the Pope, and Statius' poem hopes that he has escaped the summer heat of Rome to a cool hill-resort like Castel Gandolfo (4.4.12–19).

Further connections with the *Silvae* and Domitian emerge in Barberini's poem. Lines 136–8 note that Statius' imperial master Domitian once built a palace at Castel Gandolfo which is now an overgrown ruin.[47] This looks like an inversion of the encomia in the *Silvae* of Domitian and his grandiose building projects (1.1 on his colossal equestrian statue of himself, 4.3 on more road construction, the *Via Domitiana*), just as lines 138 criticize Domitian's luxurious and debauched character. These ideas link with the poem's climax in reflecting on the impermanence of human pretensions and achievements (141–7): the sad fate of the palace of Domitian, the benighted and decadent pagan ruler of Rome, is presented as a striking contrast with the magnificent new monuments built by Paul V, Rome's pious Christian sovereign (see below).

Horace is also a prominent model. *Odes* 3.29 begins by addressing the Augustan poet's great patron Maecenas with an initial invitation to lay aside his urban cares in Rome and come to a symposium in the country at Horace's Sabine estate (1–28). This evidently matches Barberini's opening call to Magalotti to leave Rome for Castel Gandolfo, which like Horace's country home is in pleasant hill country not too far from the city; like Barberini's poem, *Odes* 3.29 also turns to philosophical reflection in its latter part (3.29.29–64). There are a number of verbal allusions to this ode in Barberini's poem (see commentary on lines 52 and 145–6). Another element from Horace's *Odes* in Barberini's poem is the *fons Bandusiae*, a cool, clear spring probably on Horace's Sabine estate and famously described in *Odes* 3.13 as well as several other poems; prominent allusions to it appear in lines 27–8, 107–8 and 134. This evocation of a familiar Horatian landmark is matched in the view of Mt Soracte in lines 76–8, recalling the famous opening of *Odes* 1.9.

A further Horatian framework here is that of the first book of hexameter *Epistles*, in which the poet regularly presents the advantages of the country or similar tranquil locations to Rome-based friends (1.2, 1.7, 1.10, 1.14). The way in which Barberini's essentially descriptive poetic letter of invitation turns at its end to sententious moralizing (noted above) also recalls a feature of that Horatian collection (1.4.12–14, 1.7.96–8, 1.11.22–30, 1.14.43–4). Perhaps the closest of these epistles to Barberini's letter in content is *Epistles* 1.16, where Horace describes the healthy summer delights of his Sabine estate to his friend Quinctius, apparently in Rome, where the poet promises to return in autumn when the heat is over (echoed at lines 27–8 and 38).

A more recent Horatianizing analogue in hexameters is the 90-line epistle of Girolamo Fracastoro, written before 1534 and published in 1550, to his friend Francesco della Torre, inviting him to his country villa in the hills near Verona.[48] This similarly urges in detail the pleasures of a rustic existence in a restful location with views of a city and water and includes a section of compliment to their mutual friend the bishop of Verona Gian Matteo Giberti, a match for Pope Paul V in Barberini's poem (see below).

Another relevant classical author here is Martial, who addresses an epigram (5.71) to his literary friend Faustinus, representing Faustinus' own country house in the Sabine hills (not far from Horace's estate) as itself inviting him to visit and cool down in the summer. This poem seems to be specifically recalled in the opening of Barberini's epistle (see on lines 1–3). Prominent too are the echoes of passages from Vergil's *Aeneid* which describe the same region of Latium in its catalogue of Italian warriors ranged against Aeneas (7.696–7, 762–80; see commentary on lines 111–16).

A more contemporary element is the description in lines 79–90 of the city of Rome with its emphasis on the recent and current urban building projects of Pope Paul V Borghese (1550–1621, pope 1605–21);[49] there is some suggestion that he here follows and outdoes pagan Roman imperial buildings in the city as a latter-day Christian monarch, just as the papal palace at Castel Gandolfo outdoes and outlasts the nearby ruins of Domitian's residence (see above).

This is a work of rich poetic texture, achieved by combining components from a number of diverse classical generic traditions into an attractive new form which gives a vivid impression of the papal estate at Castel Gandolfo. Its ancient literary ancestry also leads subtly to the positive comparison of the modern pope as ruler with Roman emperors, suggesting the superiority of Christian and papal Rome to its pagan and classical counterpart. The text followed here is that of Barberini 1642.

Text and translation

Laurentium Magalottum utriusque signaturae Referendarium rusticatum invitat.

Arua madent pluuiis, et amabilis aura calores
Iam fregit, celerique fuga se proripit aestas:
Rura uocant, laetisque patens in collibus aer.
Hic recreor spatiorque libens, ubi libera longos
Lumina metiri gaudent obtutibus agros.   5
Hic reficit corpus uires seniumque moratur:
Hic bona sollicitam tranquillant otia mentem.
Si, Magalotte, placet tristes deponere curas,
Qua lacus Albanus uitreis diffunditur undis.
Gandulphi pagus, ueteris pars altior Albae,   10
Excipiet lare nos modico, qui sufficit usus,
Quos parvo contenta petit natura. Superbae
Non sedes, animi requies facit una beatos.
Hanc tibi, quae cordi, solum parat ardua uirtus.
  Huc igitur secede: bonis, quae detulit anni   15
Hora, parensque sua tellus dat sponte, frueris:
Nec uitulus lactens et odoro gramine ueruex
Pastus abeat: dant oua cibum piscesque recentes.
Aucupium iuuat? Hic stipulis ager abdit alaudas,
Hic nutu signata canis capienda coturnix   20
Obtentu retis; lini seu fallere nexu
Seu uisco turdos libeat, uenantis in usum
Est nemus aptatum: perdix et Phasidis ales

Maffeo Barberini (1568–1644; Pope as Urban VIII 1623–44)

He invites Lorenzo Magalotti, Referendary of both Signaturas, to spend time in the country.

The fields are soaked with rain, and the lovely breeze
Has already broken the spells of heat, and the summer rushes
    away in swift flight:
The country calls and the open air on the joyful hills.
Here I enjoy rest, and walk gladly, where my eyes are free
To enjoy traversing the distant fields with their gazing.   5
Here the body recovers its strength, and arrests its ageing:
Here kindly leisure calms the troubled mind.
If, Magalotti, you please to lay down your stressful cares
Where the Alban Lake spreads wide with its glassy waters,
The village of Gandolfo, the higher part of Alba of old,   10
Will receive us with modest hospitality, which provides such
    entertainment
As a nature content with a little seeks. It is not lofty houses
But mental rest alone which makes men happy;
This is the relaxation, one dear to your heart, which only high
    virtue readies for you.
So retreat here: you will enjoy the benefits brought by the
    season of the year,   15
Which mother earth gives of her own accord;
The calf full of milk is there and the sheep
Fed on fragrant grass: eggs and fresh fish provide food.
Do you like hunting birds? Here the field conceals larks in
    its straw,
Here the quail, marked out by the hound's pointing, is to be
    captured   20
By extending a net: and whether you please to deceive thrushes
    by a bond of thread,
Or by bird-lime, the forest is suited to the use of the hunter:
The partridge and pheasant are to be found, and you will catch

> Non desunt, capies lepores capreasque fugaces,
> Qua prope frugiferis tellus fert pabula campis. 25
> Cetera formosus quae praestat commoda collis,
> Accipe. Fons gelidum deductus munere Pauli
> Fundit aquae riuum, cordique salubrior aether
> Influit: huc siquidem spirans non amplius Auster
> Aduehit umentes uicina e ualle uapores, 30
> Uberibus segetem glaebis herbasque virentes
> Nutrit humus, nuper caeno lymphaque palustri
> Obruta.
>   Cum terras oriens lux aurea Solis
> Exhilarat, summo ducet te semita cliuo,
> Unde lacum spectare licet, quem scaena coronat 35
> Frondea: nam gemini coeuntes more theatri
> Undique protenso tollunt se margine ripae;
> Quas illinc auium sedes et quercus et ilex,
> Populus hinc ambit sociataque uitibus ornus.
> Non procul obliquo curuat litus orbita flexu, 40
> Adsurgensque nouae templum superimminet Albae,
> Francisci cui sacra cohors famulatur: ad aram
> Hic tibi fas superos in uota uocare sacerdos
> Dum sancte peragit passi mysteria Christi.
> Mox gradiens uario qua tramite diuidit hortus 45
> Areolas, mixtoque olerum florumque colore
> Pingit humus, nemoris gratas ascende per umbras,
> Est montis apex: capiet te mira voluptas.
> Si circumspicias, aspectu uideris uno
> Oppida, camporum tractus siluasque comantes, 50
> Pascua, clementes colles, uineta lacumque,
> Et maria et montes augustaque moenia Romae.

Hares and fleeing deer, where the earth brings forth fodder
Close by on the plains which bear the crops. 25
Hear the other benefits which the fair hill offers:
A cool fountain, directed by the gift of Paul, pours a stream of water,
And a healthier air floods into the heart:
Here, even if it blows, the South Wind no longer brings
Damp exhalations from the neighbouring valley: 30
The earth feeds the crop with its rich clods, and the green grasses,
The earth recently drowned under mud and marshy water.
   When the rising golden light of the sun gladdens the lands,
A path will lead you to the top of the slope,
From where you can gaze at the lake, crowned by a leafy stage: 35
For, converging like a double theatre, the banks
Raise their heads all around with extensive edge:
These are surrounded on one side by the homes of birds, oak and holm-oak,
On the other by the poplar, and the ash linked with vines.
Close by the track curves round the side with crooked bend, 40
And the rising sanctuary of the new Alba hangs over it,
Served by the sacred team of Francis: at its altar
It is right for you to call on the gods for your prayers, while the priest
Performs with reverence the mysteries of Christ's passion.
Next, stepping where the garden divides with various paths its small sections, 45
And the earth paints them with mixed colours of vegetables and flowers,
Climb up through the welcome shadows of the wood,
Where the hill's top is – wondrous pleasure will overcome you:
If you look around, you will see at a single glance
Towns, expanses of plain, leafy-haired woods, 50
Pastures, gentle hills, vineyards, the lake,
And the seas and the mountains and the august walls of Rome.

  Nunc age sollertes protende per omnia uisus.
En prope subiectis uites in collibus uuam
Obiiciunt oculis ostro quae certat et auro,   55
Et latices fundit, referunt qui uina Falerni.
Ostentat Pomona suos ex arbore fetus,
Quoque fluant multo promit sua prela Lyaeus.
Aspice planitiem, gregibus quae gramina passim
Exhibet et late campos quos praebet arandos,   60
Ut larga Tiberis ditescant horrea messe,
Quae populum reserata beant sub principe Paulo.
Hinc etiam diffusa procul maris aequora cernas,
Quaeque ferunt celeres albentia carbasa puppes
Cum uitreum radiis dorsum Sol desuper ambit   65
Mobile lucis iter format miroque nitori
Non impar, quem sideribus compacta minutis
Aeris in sudo noctu uia lactea pandit.
Longius exsurgunt altae fastigia rupis,
Quam Circe tenuit: pelagi se prodit ab undis   70
Pontia, nunc dumis horrens et inhospita, quondam
Christiadum exiliis celebris, cum dira premebat
Saeuities Christi cultum. Vicinus in auras
Prominet Albanus uertex, ubi caeca Quiritum
Est aetas operata Ioui Latiaris ad aram.   75
Ardua Soractis ceruix ut in aera fertur!
Apparent Cimini montes collesque Sabini,
Et iuga Samnitum, summas aequantia nubes.
  Quam iuuat intuitu magnas discernere moles
Urbis! Ab Esquiliis celsa testudine culmen   80
Porrigit eximii species miranda sacelli,
Quod tibi, Christiparens, almi lux prima pudoris,

Come now, extend your acute gaze over it all:
See nearby the vines on the hills underneath
Present their grapes, which contend with purple and gold, to
   the eye, 55
And they pour out their juices, which recall the wines of Falerii.
Pomona shows off her offspring from the tree:
And Lyaeus presents his wine-presses to flow with rich must.
Look at the plain, which yields grass everywhere for flocks,
And the fields which it presents far and wide for ploughing, 60
So that the granaries of Tiber may be rich with a bounteous crop,
Which when opened up gladden the people under Paul's
   princedom.
From here too you may see the waters of the sea spread afar off,
And the white sails which carry swift ships:
When the Sun from above covers the glassy surface with its rays, 65
It shapes a moving road of light, not unlike the wondrous sheen
Which the Milky Way, compressed of tiny stars,
Spreads out at night in the clear part of the air.
Further away arise the peaks of the lofty rock,
Which Circe once held; Ponza projects from the sea's waves in
   the ocean, 70
Now bristling with bushes and inhospitable, once
Famed for the exile of Christ's followers, when terrible cruelty
Pressed hard on the worship of Christ. Nearby the peak of Alba
Projects, where the benighted age of the Romans
Performed sacrifice at the altar of Jupiter Latiaris. 75
How the high neck of Soracte pushes itself into the air!
The mountains of Cimino stand out clear and the Sabine hills
And the ridges of the Samnites, equalling the clouds on high.
What a pleasure it is to make out with one's gaze the great masses
Of the city! From the Esquiline the wondrous appearance of the
   outstanding shrine 80
Stretches out its tower with its interlocking roof,
Which was established for you, mother of Christ, first luminary
   of motherly chastity,

Addictum posuit studium pietasque dicauit,
Qua coluit puroque colit te pectore Paulus:
Cuius opus pulchro surgens in colle Quirini   85
Se domus extollit, regali condita sumptu.
Excelsi tholus en templi se proximus infert
Sideribus, pia quod uasto molimine cura
Pontificum struxit Petro. Te, Paule, loquetur
Posteritas, laudemque tuis hanc laudibus addet: 90
Nam tibi debetur tantae pars maxima molis.
  Sed tua dum uario Laurenti lumina pascis
Prospectu, rapidos caeli per inane iugales
Phoebus agens minuit iucundas altior umbras.
Qua tamen hac Albam prono petit obuia ductu,   95
Hinc iter inflectens reduces in limine sistet
Nos uia, nec uenti flabris nec peruia Soli:
Arboreis etenim ramis utrimque uirescens
Explicat umbriferum gratissima tegmen eunti.
Post epulas dulci dederis cum membra quieti,   100
Et medium Phoebus caelum transmiserit axe,
Non procul in siluam sonipes te deferet: illam
Huc illuc gressu placido peragrasse iuuabit:
Hic tibi castaneae frondentia bracchia pandunt
Quercubus admixtae, fessoque umbracula texunt: 105
Siue per annosos raeda uectabere saltus,
Qua late montana patent aequata uiarum
Strata rotae, nemus hac petitur speculumque Dianae:

By faithful devotion, and dedicated by piety, with which Paul
Has worshipped you and worships you now in his pure heart;
Whose own work, his House, projects itself high, rising 85
On the fair Quirinal hill, founded with funding on a royal scale.
Behold, the dome of the lofty Church enters the view, so close
  to the stars,
Which the pious care of the popes has built with vast effort for
  Peter.
Posterity will speak of you, Paul, and will add this praise to
  your praises: 90
For the largest part of this great mass is owed to you.
  But while you, Lorenzo, feed your gaze with this varied
    prospect,
Phoebus, driving his swift team through the heaven's void,
Has risen higher and reduced the pleasant areas of shade.
But the road on this side that makes for Alba with its sloping
  course, 95
Bending its path from here will set us as we double back on
  the threshold,
Is not exposed to the blasts of the wind or to the Sun;
Indeed, green on both sides with tree branches, most pleasingly
It unfolds a shady covering for the traveller.
When after dinner you consign your limbs to sweet sleep, 100
And when Phoebus has crossed the middle of heaven with his
  chariot,
A horse will bear you to the wood close by; it will give you
  pleasure
To traverse it in this direction and that at a peaceful pace.
Here chestnuts spread out their leafy branches for you,
Mixed with oaks, and weave shade for you when tired; 105
Or if you will ride through the aged groves in a carriage:
Where the flattened mountain offers wide passage to the wheel,
That is the way to head for the Grove (Nemus) and the mirror of
  Diana;

Hoc lacui nomen fecit, quae pura liquentis
Lympha uitri speciem referens, sinuatur in orbem. 110
   Abditus hic inter siluas est creditus aeuum
Hippolytus duxisse, nouo de nomine dictus
Virbius, auxilio Triuiae reuocatus ad auras
Aethereas: arcebat equos hinc uana uetustas,
Quod pauidis abreptus equis per deuia leto 115
Sit datus Hippolytus. Valeant insomnia Pindi!
Vt ueterum, quae uera, uirum iucunda recursant
Mentibus, apta facem rebus praeferre gerendis!
   Hinc oriens primum Romana potentia fluxit,
Post uarios casus dubiique pericula Martis: 120
His pater Aeneas profugus consedit in oris,
Quem tandem rapiens absorbuit unda Numici.
Filius Ascanius constructis moenibus Albae
Dat regum seriem, quorum de sanguine felix
Romulus auspiciis aeternam condidit urbem. 125
Linquimus Egeriae lucum, quo prouida uirtus
Aucta Numae, populumque rudem belloque ferocem
Formauit studio pacis. Non funere fratrum
Territus, hic ternos prostrauit Horatius hostes.
Immodicis Albanus aquas lacus auctibus olim 130
Extulerat, nullis manantibus aethere nimbis.
'Si ripis emissa, maris non influet aequor
Vnda lacus', Delphis inquit consultus Apollo,
'Romani capient obsessos milite Veios':
Permeat hinc subiens caesi per uiscera montis 135
iugis aquae riuus.
              Species ambesa theatri
Stirpibus innatis squalet: quater hostibus Alba

This made the name for the lake, the clear pure water
Which, recalling the sheen of clear glass, is bent into a circle. 110
   Here it is believed Hippolytus spent his life hidden
Amongst the woods, called Virbius with a new name,
Recalled by Trivia's aid to the upper air:
An empty ancient belief barred horses from here, since
Hippolytus had been consigned to death torn away by
   his horses 115
Through the wilds: farewell to those vain visions of Pindus!
May the true pleasant thoughts of men of old return
To our minds, apt to light the way for the doing of great deeds!
   Arising from here first the power of Rome flowed forth,
After various vicissitudes and the perils of doubtful battle: 120
On these shores father Aeneas the refugee settled,
He whom in time the waters of Numicius snatched and swallowed.
His son Ascanius built the walls of Alba and gave issue
To a series of kings, from whose bloodline Romulus the fortunate
Established the Eternal City under his auspices. 125
We leave behind the grove of Egeria, in which the foreseeing virtue
Of Numa was increased, and shaped a people which was crude
   and fierce in war
By his passion for peace. Here Horatius, undaunted
By the death of his brothers, laid low his set of three foes.
Once the Alban lake had raised its waters with mighty increase 130
When there were no clouds dripping in the sky:
'If the water of the lake overflows the banks but does not
Flow into the plain of the sea', said Apollo consulted at Delphi,
'The Romans will capture Veii which has been besieged by their
   armies':
A continuous stream of water flowed from here passing
   underneath 135
Through the innards of an excavated mountain. The shape
   of a theatre is eaten out,
And is rough with tree-stocks growing there: four times Alba

Ludibrium iacuit. densis en obsita dumis
Regia, quam posuit Romani Flauius heres
Tertius imperii, fastu qui turgidus egit 140
Hic annos epulas inter mimosque loquaces,
Deliciis fractus: iactet nunc stemmata gentis!
Ignotos extrema dies insignibus aequat.
Ingentem subitus siluam cum corripit ignis,
Confundunt cineres quercus humilesque myricas. 145
Mitte superuacuum cultum, curisque solutus
Eripe te rerum strepitu. Sibi uiuere dulce est.
Viue Deo, tibi sic uiues. Te sola sequentur
Post cinerem bene facta: rapit reliqua omnia letum.

Lay low, a plaything to its enemies. See, it is covered with
The thick bushes of the palace, built by the third Flavian inheritor
Of the Roman empire, who, swollen with arrogance, lived here   140
For years amongst feasts and talkative mime-actors,
Broken by indulgence. Let him now parade the pedigree of his
   family!
The extremities of time make the unknown equal to the famous:
When a sudden fire takes hold of a mighty forest,
The oak and lowly tamarisks mix their ash together.   145
Leave aside your superfluous polish, and, freed from cares,
Tear yourself away from the hubbub of affairs. It is sweet to live
   for oneself.
Live for God, for so you will live for yourself. Only your good deeds
Will follow you after you are ash: death snatches all the rest away.

Commentary

1–14 This opening section establishes Barberini's presence in the country and his invitation to Magalotti to join him from the city. Its initial marking of the changed season and weather recalls the openings of some famous Horatian odes (1.4.1 *Soluitur acris hiems grata uice veris et Favoni*, 1.9.1–2 *Vides ut alta stet niue candidum / Soracte* (also referring to hills near Rome), 4.7.1 *Diffugere niues, redeunt iam gramina campis* (in the same hexameter metre), 4.12.1–2 *Iam ueris comites, quae mare temperant, / impellunt animae lintea Thraciae*; the idea that the country is more healthy than the city is prominent in Horace's *Epistles*, e.g. 1.7.1–13. Lines 1–3 also contain specific allusions to Martial 5.71, imagining the poet's addressee Faustinus' own country residence in the Sabine Hills as summoning its owner for the summer (see introduction above); Martial's poem supplies Barberini with the phrase and personification of *rura uocant* (line 3, cf. 5.71.3–5 *rura .../... /... vocant*) and the idea of the attractions of cool/damp fields in the heat (1 *arva madent*, cf. 5.71.2 *alget ager*), as well as the topic of spending a summer vacation period in hill-country near Rome. Note the triple alliteration in line 4 *libens ... libera longos* and the elegant ABCAB word order of line 7. It is only in line 9 (*lacus Albanus*) that the poet's location is specified as Castel Gandolfo, above the volcanic Lago Albano; the town's personification as host and the detail of modest hospitality in lines 10–11 *Gandulphi pagus ... / excipiet lare nos modico* recall the opening of *Satires* 1.5 (1–2) *Egressum magna me accepit Aricia Roma / hospitio modico*, fittingly as Aricia is close by, only 4 kilometres from Castel Gandolfo.

15–33a Here Barberini catalogues some key pleasures of country residence which might induce Magalotti to visit: the ready supply of fresh foods, rural recreations such as hunting, and the scenic and salubrious environment. Such attractions are often emphasised by Horace in his invitations of urban friends to the country (see introduction above). The list is enlivened with verbal ornament: note the triple assonance in line 19 *ager abdit alaudas*, the matching triple alliteration in line 20 *canis capienda coturnix* and the elegant enclosing of line 21 with the parallel instrumental ablatives *obtentu . . . nexu*. The use of bird-lime in fowling (22-3 *fallere . . . . / . . . visco*) recalls Georgics 1.139 *fallere uisco*, while the alternative possibilities of hunting animals (22-3 *seu . . . seu*) echo Silius Italicus 14.262-3 *seu siluis sectere feras seu retibus aequor/ uerrere seu caelo libeat traxisse uolucrem*. In lines 28-9 the words *fons, gelidus* and *riuus* all come from Horace's poem addressed to his beloved spring on his Sabine estate (see introduction above), the *fons Bandusiae* (3.13.1, 3.13.6, 3.13.7), while the combination *aquae riuum* recalls Horace's account of the same spring in a nearby ode (3.16.29 *purae riuus aquae*) and the pair of *fons* and *riuus* recall yet another description of it at Epistles 1.16.12-13 *Fons etiam riuo dare nomen idoneus, ut nec / frigidior Thracam nec purior ambiat Hebrus*. These classical allusions are appropriately used here to describe Paul V's recent restoration of the ancient Malafitto acqueduct serving Castel Gandolfo, in a compliment to the Pope which anticipates the praise of his larger-scale building programme in Rome at lines 79-91.

33b-52 These lines describe the attractive walking route up to the hill-town of Castel Gandolfo (426 metres above sea level) from the east, starting at Lago Albano (292 metres); the naming of the town as the 'new Alba' reflects its past as the ancient Alba Longa (see introduction). The idea that a wood can be a *scaena* (theatrical-style backdrop, 35) is derived from Vergil (*Aeneid* 1.164, 4.506-7); the steep and heavily wooded shores of the Lago Albano do indeed form a kind of green amphitheatre auditorium with the lake as the central arena. The two types of oak in line 38 (*et quercus et ilex*) exactly repeat words from Horace Epistles 1.16.9, another account of rural attractions (see introduction above). In line 40 *nouae . . . Albae* points to the transformation of pagan Alba into Christian Castel Gandolfo; the church mentioned in lines 40-3 belonged to a Franciscan monastery, later (after 1619) to be developed by Paul V into the church of Santa Maria Assunta. Lines 45-51 give a good impression of the grand terraced garden of the hilltop papal estate with its spectacular views of Rome and the rolling hills and plains down to the sea. This section of the poem ends in line 51 with the phrase *moenia Romae*, the final and climactic words of the preface of the *Aeneid* (1.7), introducing the idea of the view of the buildings of Rome which returns in lines 79–90; *Romae* at the end of a poetic line and sentence also recalls *Odes* 3.29.12 *fumum et opes strepitumque Romae*, where the sight of the city of Rome is again the object of an elevated view from a rural retreat (see introduction above).

53–78 Using the line-initial formula *Nunc age* typical of Lucretian didactic (15× in the *De Rerum Natura*), Magalotti is urged to enjoy the details of the spectacular views. Sights specified include the nearby vineyards of the Colli Albani (53–8), still noted for their white wines such as Frascati and here compared to the ancient Falernian vintages (56), consistently mentioned in Horace's *Odes* as some of the best in Italy (1.20.10. 1.27.10, 2.3.8, 2.6.9, 2.11.19, 3.1.43). Similarly, the mention of Pomona, Roman goddess of fruit trees (57), stresses the rich local orchards and olive groves, and stress is laid on the fertile cornfields of the Tiber valley to the north (59–61); line 62 compliments Paul V on his feeding of the population of Rome from the papal granaries, then situated in the former Baths of Diocletian and expanded by him in 1609–12, another subtle allusion to his city building programme as well as to his benevolence (cf. 79–91 below); note the emphatic triple alliteration in 62 *populum ... principe Paulo*. The popes followed the emperors in providing grain for the city (Augustus *Res Gestae* 5), and here *principe* (standard for Roman emperors and used of Popes since the fourteenth century – see Canning 1987: 72) encourages the analogy implicit throughout the poem between modern Pope and ancient emperor as ruler of Rome.

The sea is some 20 kilometres east of the papal gardens and larger vessels on it are clearly visible as described in lines 63–4; less visible is the island of Ponza, some 80 kilometres to the south, sometimes thought as here (70) to have been the home of the Odyssean Circe (cf. Vergil *Aeneid* 3.386). Lines 71–3 report the tradition that Ponza was the place of exile of another prominent female, the early Christian Flavia

Domitilla persecuted by Domitian (Jerome *Ep*.108.7), a neat link with the former palace complex of that same emperor from which the island is here being viewed, presumably the point of introducing this distant island. The prospect ends with the various hills and mountains supposedly to be seen from Castel Gandolfo (73–8). The Mons Albanus indeed looms just across the lake to the east, modern Monte Cavo (950 metres), noted here (75) as the site of the Roman cult of Jupiter Latiaris celebrated in the ancient annual festival *feriae Latinae*; such a benighted pagan ritual (74 *caeca*) is a neat contrast with the true Christian religion of Flavia Domitilla in the previous line. The Colli Sabini (77) might conceivably be visible beyond Rome some 40 kilometres to the north-west; but the claims (76–7) to see the long ridge of Monte Soratte (291 metres), some 70 kilometres north, and the volcanic cone of Monte Cimino (1,053 metres), some 100 kilometres in the same direction, seem improbable, as is any kind of view of the hills of Samnium which lie some 100 kilometres to the south-west (78). These last three landmarks are likely to appear because of their prominence in Roman poetry and history: line 76 *ardua Soractis ceruix ut in aera fertur!* is a reminiscence of *Odes* 1.9.1 *Vides ut alta stet niue candidum / Soracte* ...?, while Soratte/Soracte and Cimino/Ciminus appear together in Vergil's Latin Catalogue at *Aeneid* 7.696–7, an episode further used by Barberini in lines 111–16 below. The far-off *iuga Samnitium* (78) seem to recall the famous humiliation of a Roman army by the Samnites by being made to surrender and pass under a yoke after defeat at the battle of the Caudine Forks in 321 BCE (Livy 9.1–6, Tacitus *Ann*.11.24 *Samnitum iugum*); *iuga* ('ridges') here appears to play on the main sense of *iugum* ('yoke') with this in mind. The line initial and sentence-starting verb *apparent* in line 77 is a Vergilian stileme (5 × in *Aeneid*).

79–91 Magalotti's attention is called to the impressive prospect of the city of Rome, not actually visible from Castel Gandolfo but inserted here to praise the contemporary building programme of Paul V. The stress on Paul's worship at the great papal basilica of Santa Maria Maggiore on the Esquiline (80–4) alludes to the ongoing construction there (1606–12) by Flaminio Porzio of Paul's Borghese Chapel (Cappella Paolina),[50] while the reference to the house on the Quirinal (85–6) points to the papal Palazzo Qurinale, begun by Gregory XIII in 1583 and being extended by Porzio for Paul at the time of writing,[51] and the description of St Peter's with its mighty dome (87–90) marks Paul's extensive works there, including Carlo Maderno's massive main façade with Paul's huge and still prominent building inscription of 1612.[52] All this stresses the Pope's piety and beneficent power, and the promise of immortality as a result of the works at St Peter's (89–91) reaches a climax in line 91 *nam tibi debetur tantae pars maxima molis*, which matches Paul's achievement verbally with that of the Roman Empire itself in the famous climax of the preface of the *Aeneid* (1.33 *tantae molis erat Romanam condere gentem*), repeating the technique of line 52 above. Note here the alliterating and metrically matched initial nouns in 89 and 90 (*pontificum/posteritas*), and the emphatic final alliterative pair *maxima molis* (91).

92–110 Magalotti is imagined as the day goes on proceeding on the sheltered path through the woods fringing Lago Albano, and then travelling on to Nemi (modern Ariccia), its ancient shrine of Diana, and its further lake (Lago di Nemi) in the next valley, a prelude to the narrative of the story of Virbius/Hippolytus in the next section. This section has two indications of the passing of time, the ascent of the sun (93–4) and a mid-day meal with a subsequent siesta and an afternoon ride (100–2); the inclusion of a meal-break in a hexameter journey-narrative recalls Horace's journey to Brindisi in *Satires* 1.5 (1.5.25, 38, 70–4). The emphasis on the shade provided by trees (98–9, 104–5) both reflects the real topography of the area and recalls the idealised landscape of Vergil's *Eclogues* (105 *umbracula texunt* echoes *Eclogues* 9.42 *lentae texunt umbracula uites*). Arrival at Nemi forms the climax here: the conceit that the round, reflective lake next to the goddess's temple was the 'mirror of Diana' (108) is derived from Servius' commentary on Vergil (on *Aeneid* 7.515), while its description (109–10) as *pura liquentis / Lympha uitri speciem referens* echoes Horace's *fons Bandusiae* (see introduction above and which is *splendidior uitro* (*Odes* 3.13.1, 'more gleaming than glass') and has a *purae riuus aquae* (*Odes* 3.16.29, 'a stream of clear water').

111-18 The mention of Nemi here stimulates a retelling of Vergil's narrative in his Latin Catalogue at *Aeneid* 7.762-80, according to which the Athenian king Theseus' son Hippolytus was raised from the dead after his fatal chariot crash (famously narrated in Euripides' *Hippolytus* and Seneca's *Phaedra*) by the god Asclepius and given sanctuary at Nemi by his divine patron Diana under the appropriate new name Virbius ('second man'). These lines have many verbal echoes of the Vergilian original: stress on the wooded location (111 *inter siluas* ~ 7.776 *in siluis*), similarly phrased descriptions of the hero's renaming and resurrection (112-13 *nouo de nomine dictus / Virbius* ~ 7.777 *uersoque... nomine Virbius*, 113-14 *auxilio Triuiae reuocatus ad auras / aethereas* ~ 7.677-9 *ad sidera rursus / aetheria et superas caeli uenisse sub auras, / Paeoniis reuocatum herbis et amore Dianae*), of the local ban on horses as the his previous nemesis (114 *arcebat equos* ~ 779 *arcentur equi*), and an analogous witty unpacking in Latin of the Greek name Hippolytus, 'horse-torn' (115 *pauidis abreptus equis* ~ 7.767 *turbatis distractus equis*). The section ends with an expression of disbelief in this pagan myth, preferring to follow true examples from past history; this suggests that for Barberini the true resurrection narrative of Christ in the Gospels should give inspiration to his Christian times, not the false classical story of the revived Hippolytus in Vergil. At 116 the Macedonian mountain Pindus symbolizes the Muses of pagan poetry, with whom it is often associated (cf. e.g. *Eclogues* 10.11, *Odes* 1.12.6).

119-36a Here the poem returns to the history of Castel Gandolfo in its guise as ancient Alba Longa, drawing on the early books of Livy's history of Rome. Alba is described as the origin of Roman history (119) as the city built by Ascanius, son of Aeneas (123, Livy 1.3), after the latter had led his Trojan refugees to Italy (Livy 1.2, the plot of the *Aeneid*, the opening of which is echoed in 121 *profugus... in oris* ~ *Aeneid*

1.1–2 *ab oris* / ... *profugus*) and then vanished at the river Numicus (Livy 1.2; 122 *unda Numici* points to Tibullus' account of the episode, 2.5.43–4 *cum te ueneranda Numici / unda deum caelo miserit indigetem*); Tibullus like many Romans interprets this disappearance as an apotheosis, but this pagan aspect of deification is understandably not vouched for by the Christian Barberini. Line 125 on the foundation of Rome itself (by Romulus, born in Alba; for his ktistic *auspicia* see Livy 1.7) draws again on the proem of the *Aeneid* (*condidit urbem* ~ 1.10 *conderet urbem*) and Tibullus 2.5 (*aeternam* ... *urbem* ~ 2.5.23 *aeternae* ... *urbis*). Lines 126–8 refer to Numa, Romulus' successor, and his supposed consultations of his wife the nymph/prophetess Egeria, whom he visited in the nearby grove of Diana at Nemi (Livy 1.23, *Aeneid* 7.775); for the common idea that Numa civilized a warlike Rome with peace see Livy 1.19 (including the phrase *ferocem populum*, cf. 127). 128–9 refer to the famous battle in the reign of Tullus Hostilius (seventh century BCE) between the three Alban brothers the Curatii and the three Roman brothers the Horatii, won by the latter (Livy 1.23–6); note the matching final alliterative pairs 128 *Horatius hostes*, 129 *funere fratrum*. Barberini's mini-history of Alba then passes in lines 130–6 to a much later episode in Livy (5.15–19, during the war against Veii in 393 BCE), when there was a dramatic rise in the water level of Lago Albano and a Delphic prophecy foretold that Veii would not fall as long as the waters of the lake remained high or overflowed their usual route to the sea; following the instructions of an Etruscan prophet, the Romans were able to draw the water off onto the nearby fields by a newly excavated route, the water level fell, and Veii fell too. 136 *iugis aquae riuus* once again echoes a description of Horace's *fons Bandusiae*, *Satires* 2.6.2 *iugis aquae fons* (see introduction).

136b–49 The poem concludes with a Christian moralizing meditation on the vanity of earthly achievements, stimulated by a consideration of the ruins of Domitian's palace complex which included a theatre, the remains of which were (and are) still visible in the papal gardens. The statement that Alba was defeated four times (137–8), an example of human instability, seems to mean that after the city's initial conquest and absorption by Rome (Livy 1.29–30), it then shared Rome's three ancient captures (by the Gauls in 390 BCE, Alaric in 410 CE, and Totila in 546 CE). In lines 138–42 we find a moral condemnation of Domitian which echoes those by the Latin writers who survived his reign of terror: Suetonius refers (*Domitian* 5) to his dining with (low-status) mime-actors (cf. 141 *mimos*), while Juvenal describes a decadent dinner of the emperor's in *Satire* 4 (with 141 *epulas* compare the same word form at 4.28, and with 142 *deliciis* compare 4.4 *deliciae*). The idea that ancestry is nothing to boast about for the unvirtuous (140) is also a theme of Juvenal (*Satire* 8), and its framing rhetorical exclamation is a Juvenalian technique (cf. e.g. *Satires* 1.91,140, 5.24, 134). Barberini's phrase describing Domitian as the third Flavian emperor (139–40 *Romani Flauius heres / Tertius imperii* evidently) picks up the first line of an epigram which was at his time believed to be by another poet commenting adversely on his contemporary Donitian, Martial, a poem sometimes attached to the latter's *De Spectaculis* but unlikely to be genuine:[53] *Flavia gens, quantum tibi tertius abstulit heres*, 'Flavian family, how much your third inheritor has taken from you'.

In the final lines, 143–9, we find several closing allusions to Horace *Odes* 3.29, one of the poem's key models (see introduction above). Horace's famous Epicurean statement that the happy man is he who can say 'I have lived my life' (*uixi*, 3.29.43) is picked up and suitably Christianized in a triple repetition of the same verb in Barberini's lapidary *sibi uiuere dulce est. / uiue Deo, tibi sic uiues*, 'It is sweet to live for oneself. Live for God, for so you will live for yourself' (148–9).[54] Further, Barberini's *eripe te rerum strepitu*, 'Tear yourself away from the hubbub of affairs' (147) plainly picks up from Horace's poem both the injunction to Maecenas *eripe te morae*, 'tear yourself away from delay' (3.39.5) and the urban din disliked by the poet (3.29.12 *fumum et opes strepitumque Romae*). Line 143 likewise echoes the prominent Horatian idea that death does not discriminate between the great and the unknown (*Odes* 1.4.13–14, 1.28.15–16 and especially 3.1.13–14 <u>*aequa lege Necessitas / sortitur insignis et imos*</u>; the personification of *extrema dies* in the context of the destructive effect of time recalls *damnosa quid non imminuit dies?* at *Odes* 3.6.45), while the simile of 144-5 combines a similar comparison from the *Aeneid* (fire in a wood, 12.521-2 *immissi diuersis partibus ignes / arentem in siluam*) with prominent line-endings from Manilius (1.821 *corripit ignis*) and the *Eclogues* (4.2 *humilesque myricae*); note the fire-like sibilation of 143-5 and the triple assonance *ignotos . . . insignibus . . . ingentem*, the first and third terms balancing each other in length and line-initial position. The last line has an Ovidian opening (*post cinerem* = *Met.*8.459) and a nicely alliterative final phrase (*rapit reliqua omnia letum*) which appropriates the line ending of Catullus 64.187 *omnia letum*, echoes and reverses Propertius 4.7.1 *letum non omnia finit* and presents the finality of death as the last word, a brilliant element of poetic closure (cf. Roberts et al. 1997: 304). A similar technique is found in the last line of *Epistles* 1.16 (79), a poem imitated elsewhere in this one (see introduction above): *mors ultima linea rerum est* (1.16.79).

4. Hendecasyllabis letter to Virginio Cesarini (*c.* 1615)

Virginio Cesarini (1595-1624) was the son of Giuliano Cesarini, Duke of Civitanova, and his wife Livia Orsini.[55] As a boy he was sent to study at Parma, where he was hosted by Duke Ranuccio I Farnese; he suffered from poor health from early youth. He returned to Rome in 1610, and there pursued as a cleric a range of intellectual interests, writing poetry in both Latin and Italian; in 1618 he became a member of the recently established Accademia dei Lincei. It was here that he encountered both Galileo (whom he supported against his opponents) and the poet Giovanni Battista Ciampoli, another friend of Barberini mentioned in this poem; he was painted by Van Dyck (now in the Hermitage, St Petersburg) some time in the period 1621-4, possibly when he was appointed chamberlain to Urban (1623) before his early death the next year.[56] This poem dates to *c.* 1615; the text followed here is that of Barberini 1642.

A generation older than Cesarini, Barberini writes to him like Horace to younger literary friends in the *Epistles*, but uses the hendecasyllabic metre[57] and style of Catullus and a topic from the epigrams of Martial in a neat generic mix which his learned addressee would recognize as such. The opening greeting and question echo Catullus' hendecasyllabic letter to his friends on the staff of a Roman governor abroad (Catullus 28.1-4):

> *Pisonis comites, cohors inanis,*
> *aptis sarcinulis et expediti,*
> *Verani optime tuque mi Fabulle,*
> <u>*quid rerum geritis*</u>?

> Companions of Piso, starving staff,
> With packs prepared and lightly equipped,
> Excellent Veranius and you, my dear Fabullus
> How are you getting on?

But the multiple questions of the opening, several introduced by *ut*, also recall Horace's epistle to Florus, another hexameter letter to literary friends separated by provincial service (*Epistles* 1.3.6-15):

> *quid studiosa cohors operum struit? hoc quoque curo.*
> *quis sibi res gestas Augusti scribere sumit?*
> *bella quis et paces longum diffundit in aeuum?*
> *quid Titius, Romana breui uenturus in ora,*
> *Pindarici fontis qui non expalluit haustus,*
> *fastidire lacus et rivos ausus apertos?*
> <u>*ut*</u> *ualet?* <u>*ut*</u> *meminit nostri? fidibusne Latinis*
> *Thebanos aptare modos studet auspice Musa,*
> *an tragica desaeuit et ampullatur in arte?*

> What works are you, that literary entourage, creating? That too is my
>   concern.
> Who is taking upon himself the writing of the deeds of Augustus?
> Who is broadcasting war and peace to time everlasting?
> What is Titius up to, soon to come to the lips of Romans,
> Who has not paled before drinking from the spring of Pindar,

Daring to disdain the lakes and streams open to all?
How is he getting on? How does he remember me? Is he keen to fit
The measures of Thebes to the Latin lyre under the Muse's auspices,
Or does he rave and bluster in the art of tragedy?

Other poems in Horace's first book of *Epistles* are recalled here, both in terms of type of addressee (1.4: letter to a poetic friend, Tibullus) and in terms of topic (1.15: letter to a friend on a health cure by the sea).

A third classical author of close relevance to this poem is Martial. In 10.30 Martial (again in hendecasyllables) sketches the similarly salubrious pleasures of sailing and fishing at the seaside town of Formiae (Formia), close to Cesarini's Antium/Anzio on the same coast of Lazio south of Rome, a subject typically subverted by the poem's close which suggests that Apollinaris, the poem's addressee, is always too busy to travel from Rome to his villa which is enjoyed only by its staff. This poem is specifically echoed in lines 15 and 20 (see commentary below).

Text and translation

VIRGINI, decus eruditiorum,
Amor Castalidum, iubar Quiritum,
Quos uerae bona gloriae cupido
Pennis euehit aureis ad astra
Quid rerum geris? ut uales? ut oris   5
Antii recrearis? an tepore
Istic aeris, ut ferunt, iniquum
Bruma frigoris impetum remittit?
Floridi tibi ueris adflet aura,
Quae caelum sine nubibus recludat,   10
Ut dulces nemorum queas per umbras
Securus pede libero uagari,
Dum cantu querulo strepunt uolucres,
Seu malis placidum maris per aequor
Huc illuc agili uehi phaselo,   15
Quem litus prope remus hinc et inde
Impellat facili leuique motu.
Squamosum licet hic genus tueri
Lusus nectere lusibus, uel hamo
Piscem ducere, quam iuuat liquentis   20
Regni caeruleos obire tractus
Vago lumine, nigra dum per undas
Alis carbaseis uolat carina!
Nec gratum minus exhibet theatrum
Tellus gramine laeta, quam petulci   25
Huc haedi, pecudumque grex, et illuc
Immixti peragrant equis iuuenci.
Inter herbida prata se uirentes
Diffundunt segetes satis in agris.
Addunt se super eminentque dorso   30

Virginio, glory of the more learned,
Beloved of the Muses, bright light of those Romans
Whom a virtuous desire for true glory
Lifts on golden wings to the stars,
How do you fare? How is your health?   5
How are you recovering on the shores of Antium?
And has winter, as they report,
Softened the attack of its cold
Through the warmth of the air there?
May the breeze of flowery spring breathe on you,
And open up a cloudless sky   10
So that you can wander under the sweet shade
Of the woods, released from care and with free foot,
While the birds sound with their singing complaint.
Or, if you should prefer to be carried
Over the calm surface of the sea
Here and there in a nimble yacht,
Propelled near the shore in one direction or another   15
By an oar with easy and smooth motion:
Here you can see the scaly race
Join game to game, or draw up
Fish with a hook: what a pleasure it is
To cover the blue tracts of the clear sea   20
With wandering eye, while the dark keel
Flies through the waves on its wings of canvas!
Nor does the land present a less pleasant show,
Lush with grass, traversed here
By butting goats and a herd of sheep,   25
And there by steers mixed with horses.
The verdant crops spread themselves
In the sown fields between the grassy meadows:
Vine-bearing hills add themselves above
And project from the ridge, and you can see   30

Colles uitiferi, niuesue in altis
Procul montibus albicare cernis.
An non haec facies soli decora,
Prospectusque maris patens, et aer
Spiritus reficit, fugatque tristem 35
Languorem capitisque fluxionem
Qua fauces nimium soles peruri?
Mitte cum medicis graues medelas:
Curas excute noxias, cupitae
Valetudinis intimum uenenum, 40
Et caros iubeas abire libros:
Sat te Ciampolus allocutione
Librorum uice detinet. Valentem
(Haec si feceris, ut reor) reuisam
Te breui. Deus annuat benignum: 45
Sic vouet tua Roma, sic amici.

Snows gleaming white in the high mountains at distance.
Does not this fair appearance of the ground,
And the open prospect of the sea, and the breeze
Refresh the spirits and drive away
Your sad lassitude and the flux from your head,   35
With which your throat is wont to be so sore?
Shake off your unhealthy anxieties, the surest
Poison to the health you long for:
Leave aside the grievous cures along with doctors,
And bid farewell to your beloved books: 40
Ciampoli occupies you sufficiently with his talk
Instead of books. I will see you
In good health (if you do this, as I think you will)
Shortly. May God give you a kindly nod:
Such is the prayer of your devoted Rome and your friends.

Commentary

1–22 Opening address to Cesarini, and aquestions about his health and activities. As noted above, the initial questions recall the openings of Catullus 28 (5 *quid rerum geris* echoes 28.4 *quid rerum geritis?*) and Epistles 1.3 (5–6 *ut uales? Ut oris / Antii recrearis?* recalls 1.3.12 *ut valet? ut meminit nostri?*). The Catullan tone is emphasized by the affective comparative *eruditiorum* in line 1 (cf. Catullus 3.2 *uenustiorum*, 9.9 *beatiorum*), while the image of being carried to heaven by poetic ambition looks back to *Odes* 1.1.6 *euehit ad deos* and 2.20.1–2 *ferar / pinna . . . per liquidum aethera*. An of the whereabouts of the addressee (6) and the vision of healthy woodland walks (11–12) recall Horace's letter to the poet Tibullus (*Epistles* 1.4.4 *an tacitum siluas inter reptare salubris?*), while the location of Antium (6) picks up its mention in a list of salubrious resorts in Martial 10.30.7, a poem (see above) also echoed in the evocation of boating and fishing here (14 *phaselo* ~ 10.30.13 *phaselon*, 19 *piscem ducere* ~ 10.30.18 *trahit piscis*).

23–36 Further recommendations to Cesarini of Antium/Anzio as a health resort, this time for its pastoral landscape, with greenery descending to the sea as in the modern Riserva Naturale Regionale di Tor Caldara there. This aspect is underlined by echoes of Vergil's *Eclogues* and *Georgics* (24 *gramine laeta* ~ *Georgics* 2.525 *gramine laeto*, 24–5 *petulci / . . . haedi* ~ *Georgics* 4.10 *haedique petulci*, 25 *pecudumque grex* ~ *Eclogues* 2.30 *haedorumque gregem*). Note how line 26 is enclosed by the correlatives *huc . . . illuc*, line 27 by a participle and its noun *immixti . . . iuuenci*. Lines 28 and 31 echo phrases from Pliny's Natural History – cf. 33.89 *segetis laete uirentes* and 3.60 *uitiferi colles*. Line 32: the peaks of the Colli Albani such as Monte Cavo (925 metres) are indeed visible from the coast at Anzio some 25 kilometres south. Lines 35–6 point to Cesarini's medical condition, analysed according to the Hippocratic theory as a noxious flux (*fluxio* = Greek ῥόος) from the head to the throat (Hippocrates *Places in Man* 10.294).

37–45 The poet recommends a better cure than the painful ones of the doctors: Cesarini should free himself from stress and leave his beloved books aside, for his friend Giovanni Battista Ciampolli's conversation will be sufficiently stimulating in their place. As at Catullus 38.5 (in the same metrical position), *allocutione* (41) suggests comforting conversation in adversity from a literary friend (there the poet Q. Cornificius); as in the case of Catullus, Barberini's and Cesarini's circle of friends are often also poets. Ciampolli (1590–1643) was a poet of some reputation who like Cesarini was a cleric and friend of Barberini,[58] an associate of Galileo and (from 1618) a member of the Accademia dei Lincei; he was the close companion of the invalid Cesarini. Succeeding the latter as Urban's chamberlain, he was later (1632) prevented by Urban from becoming a Cardinal for his support of Galileo and exiled from Rome to a series of provincial governorships.[59] The concluding idea that Cesarini will return to Rome in better health in due course recalls Horace's promise to Maecenas at *Epistles* 1.7.11–12 *te, dulcis amice, reuiset / cum Zephyris, si concedes, et hirundine prima.*

5. Strophic lyric ode to St Laurence (1619)

Barberini's most ambitious Latin poems in formal terms are the four long strophic lyric odes celebrating particular saints, written when he was a cardinal (1606–23):[60] these take as their topics St John the Baptist (126 lines), St Mary Magdalen (144 lines), St Laurence (132 lines) and St Louis of France (165 lines). All use the triadic form of metrically identical strophe and antistrophe followed by a metrically different epode, a three-part unit which can then be repeated. This ambitious structure is derived from the epicinian odes of Pindar (*c.* 518–438 BCE), traditionally considered the greatest of the Greek lyric poets.[61]

Such triadic Pindarizing odes first emerged prominently in neo-Latin lyric in the poems of Benedetto Lampridio (Lampridio 1550), who like Barberini here used combinations of single lyric lines from Horace and Catullus in building up his stanzas (perhaps following Seneca's practice in constructing the lyric choruses of his tragedies, which are simpler, being largely non-stanzaic and without symmetrical architecture).⁶² The formal structure of Lampridio's 'Ad Cremonam patriam' is closely similar to that of this ode of Barberini to St Laurence, with a triad of strophe (10 lines), antistrophe (10 lines) and epode (12 lines) adding up to a total of 32 lines, which is then repeated twice with the same metrical forms (96 lines); Barberini uses a schema of strophe (12 lines), antistrophe (12 lines) and epode (9 lines), which is then exactly repeated three times (132 lines; for further details see the metrical analysis below).

Like Lampridio, Barberini does not attempt the virtuoso feat of the French Greek scholar Jean Dorat, who had exactly imitated the metre of Pindar's *Olympian* 4 in a 1550 ode of six triads (252 lines) in memory of the wife of the poet Jean Salmon Macrin;⁶³ but he is more ambitious than Milton in his 1646 strophic Latin ode to John Rouse, librarian of the Bodleian Library at Oxford, which has three strophes each followed by an antistrophe, with one epode rounding off the whole, all using Latin lyric metrical units (like Barberini) but without metrical or other responsion between stanzas, even in terms of length.⁶⁴

The ode to St Laurence, the Spanish-born Christian deacon traditionally roasted to death on a gridiron in the third century by the pagan authorities of Rome, is the most interesting of Barberini's strophic lyrics from a literary perspective and in terms of classical reception. Pindar's epinician odes of praise for victorious athletes, which often include mythological narratives with imagined speeches, provide a thematic as well as formal framework (see above) for this poem praising the 'athlete of Christ' and 'victor' Laurence (lines 80 and 130) which contains much direct speech. A more particular model is Horace *Odes* 3.5, which celebrates the heroic choice of the Roman general Regulus to undergo a parallel cruel martyrdom by torture (see note on line 16).⁶⁵ The late antique Spanish Christian poet Prudentius (348–after 404/5) had also written a long lyric hymn in iambic dimeter stanzas on his compatriot Laurence in his *Peristephanon* (2), a collection of martyr narratives.

Barberini follows Prudentius in dating Laurence's martyrdom to the reign of the emperor Valerian (253–60 CE) but varies his account by placing the emperor himself in charge of the execution (25–33). This detail might owe something to the most widely diffused medieval life of Laurence in the thirteenth-century *Golden Legend* of Jacobus de Voragine,⁶⁶ which records that Laurence died in the persecutions of the emperor Decius (249–251 CE), and presents Decius himself and the future emperor Valerian (as city prefect) as both present at his martyrdom (Jacobus' brief account of Laurence's end seems otherwise to be based on Prudentius' much longer narrative). Reputed relics of Laurence are still preserved in the Roman papal basilica of San Lorenzo fuori le mura, the successor of a Constantan oratory marking the traditional site of the saint's tomb.

Prudentius' poem presents a similarly dramatic account of the saint's end in its second half (2.313–584), which clearly influences some details as well as the general character of Barberini's poem: it supplies the comparison with the protomartyr Stephen (2.369–372, cf. 21–4), the idea of Laurence's defiant and black comic address to his tormentor from his gridiron (2.406–8, cf. 124–8) and the condemnation of the earlier tyrant Nero (2.469–71, cf. 58–66). In general, Prudentius' poem has much more direct speech with long discourses from both executioner and victim, each given only a few lines by Barberini.

The narrative of the analogy of the three faithful Jews consigned by Nebuchadnezzar to the burning fiery furnace in lines 79–109 is drawn from a biblical text, the Book of Daniel, the context for the canticle *Benedicite* familiar in regular Christian liturgy which Barberini himself paraphrased in Latin verse elsewhere.⁶⁷ Here the biblical episode is used merely for its parallel situation of the faithful witness victimized by a king, the key parallel with the story of Laurence (see commentary on 77–90 and 91–9 below).

The Spanish identity of Laurence also has contemporary political relevance. The initial honorific address to Spain and the mentions in the first strophe of Spain/Portugal's imperial dominions,⁶⁸ the past military glories of Charles V and the more restrained virtues of the contemporary Philip III are clearly a complimentary gesture to a key Catholic country from a major figure at the Vatican who had had significant diplomatic experience. The poem has a counterpart in Barberini's similarly elaborate strophic lyric hymn in praise of St Louis, which seems to have written at much the same time as a balancing gesture towards France, Spain's political rival and Europe's other great Catholic power.[69]

The stress on the physical burning of Laurence with its gory details (112–24) also reflects the context of contemporary Rome. The philosopher Giordano Bruno had been publicly burnt in the Campo dei Fiori by the Roman Inquisition in 1600 and Barberini's then master Pope Paul V had overseen the similar burning of the radical friar Fulgenzio Manfredi in the same location less than a decade before (1610).

This poem draws throughout on language and ideas from classical Latin literature, but is less dense and close in its allusions than poems written in more strictly Vergilian or Horatian form, thus showing a freer approach to imitation in both shape and expression. Its last section shows a particular concern to redirect the language of Roman culture and values to a Christian perspective. The text followed here is that of Barberini 1642.

Metrical analysis

Strophe = Antistrophe

```
- - v - - - v -              iambic dimeter              Horace Epodes 1.2
- - v - - - v v - v -        Alcaic hendecasyllable      Horace Odes 1.9.1
- - - v v - - v v - v -      Asclepiad                   Horace Odes 1.1.1
- - v - - - v - -            Alcaic enneasyllable        Horace Odes 1.9.3
- v v - v v - v v - - -      hexameter                   Horace Odes 1.7.1, 4.7.1
  v v - -
- - v - - - v - v - -        iambic trimeter catalectic  Horace Odes 1.4.2
- v - - - - v v - v - -      Sapphic hendecasyllable     Horace Odes 1.2.1
- - v - - - v - -            Alcaic enneasyllable        Horace Odes 1.9.3
- - - v v - v -              glyconic                    Horace Odes 1.21.4
- - v - v - v - - - v -      iambic trimeter             Horace Epodes 1.1      S
- - v - - - v -              iambic dimeter              Horace Epodes 1.2      S
- v v - vv - v - -           Alcaic decasyllable         Horace Odes 1.9.4
```

Epode

```
- - v - - - v - - - v -      iambic trimeter             Horace Epodes 1.1
```

Maffeo Barberini (1568-1644; Pope as Urban VIII 1623-44)

- v v - - - v v - -	dactylic tetrameter catalectic	Horace *Epodes* 12.2	
- - - v v - - - v v - v – v - -	greater Archilochean	Horace *Odes* 1.4.1	S
- v – v – v -	trochaic dimeter catalectic	Horace *Odes* 1.4.2, 2.18.1	S
- - v - - - v – v - -	iambic trimeter catalectic	Horace *Odes* 2.18.2	S
- - v - - v - - - v – v -	iambic trimeter	Horace *Epodes* 1.1	
- - - v v – v -	glyconic	Horace *Odes* 1.21.4	
- v v – v v -	hemiepes	Horace *Odes* 4.7.2	S
- vv - - - v v - - - v v - -	hexameter	Horace *Odes* 1.7.1, 4.7.1	S

All the metrical units here form lines in Horace's *Odes* and *Epodes*,[70] but are extracted singly from their original groupings and reassembled to make new longer and mixed stanzas, only occasionally repeating a short Horatian sequence of two or three lines (marked S). The last line of the strophe/antistrophe has the same metrical form as the last line of the Alcaic stanza, perhaps a closural effect, while the last two lines of the epode reverse the constituent dactylic couplet of *Odes* 4.7. It is worth noting that the opening line (iambic dimeter) is the standard metrical line of early Christian hymns, and is used in Prudentius' account of St Laurence in *Peristephanon* 2 (see above).

Text and translation

Strophe 1
Ibera tellus, Austrio
Sub rege felix, aurifero Tagi
Te dicant alii flumine nobilem,
Te classe, te bello ferocem
Oceani dominam celebrent regnisque potentem: 5
Hic Persianis diuitem metallis,
Mexici gazis Arabumque conchis
Et mercibus Goae beatam
Te laudet; fera proelia
Extollat alter et triumphos Caroli, 10
Ac temperatis uiuidum
Consiliis animum Philippi.

Antistrophe 1
Te concinam Laurentii
Sacro Parentem lumine fulgidam;
Non illi facie funeris horrida 15
Immane tortoris repertum
Excussit solida uerae pietatis amorem
E mente: palmis nobiles et ostro
Clarus en inter proceres, decorem
Indutus aeternum, phalangis 20
Addit se comitem Duci
Cui saxa primum post trucem Christi necem
Coniecta probro gloriam,
Interitu peperere uitam.

Epode 1
Acres quid iras aggeras, Rex barbare? 25
Impauidus contemnere nouit
Hispanus iuuenis regum fera iussa. Quid flagellis
Nuda membra saucias

Strophe 1
Iberian land, fortunate
Under an Austrian king, let others
Speak of you as well known for the gold-bearing river of the Tagus,
Celebrate you as fearsome for fleet, for battle
As mistress of the Atlantic and mighty in your realms: 5
Let one praise you as rich in Persian mines,
Wealthy in Mexican treasures and Arabian shells
And the merchandise of Goa;
Let another extol
The fierce battles and triumphs of Charles.   10
And the mind, lively with moderate
Plans, of Philip.

Antistrophe 2
I will sing of you as mother
Of Laurence, as shining with his sacred light:
The monstrous invention of the torturer   15
With its terrible face of death
Did not dash the love of true piety
From his firm mind: behold him bright
Amid the chiefs distinguished by palms and purple,
Clothed in eternal beauty, he joins   20
As comrade that Leader of the band
For whom the first rocks thrown after the grim slaying of Christ.
Brought about glory by means of shame,
Life by means of death.

Epode 1
Why do you heap up your fierce passions, barbarian king?   25
Fearless, this youth of Spain knows well
How to scorn the wild orders of monarchs. Why do you wound
His naked limbs with whips, and pluck at them,

Curuis et hamis lancinata carpis?
Fortis resistit. Heu quid impium struis?   30
Mens haeret, trepidat. Quibus,
Dire Tyranne, feris,
Te quibus exaequem, Colobi saeuissime, monstris?

Strophe 2
Vagas ad undas Tybridis
Lactauit altrix uberibus Lupa   35
Infantes geminos: pinnigero puer
Delphinis in dorso natantis
Saepe Dicarcheo ludens e litore uisus
Et vulnerati pro pedis medela
Hospitem narrant hominis leonem   40
Hunc, inter atroces ferarum
Incursus pauidum, canis
Ut blandiens, adiuit agnitum leo;
Ambosque pubes Romuli
Obstupuit sibi gratulantes.   45

Antistrophe 2
Seu prisca uerum proferat
Seu fingat aetas, aspide saeuior
Hyrcanisque feris mens hominis furit.
Non ursus insectatur ursum,
Non perimit colubrum coluber, non tigrida tigris: 50
Humana uirgas gens rotas et uncos
Intulit terris pedibusque mortis
Aptauit alas. Quid Perilli
Infandum memorem bouem?
Nec sontibus uel hostibus solum minax: 55
Sui ministram gaudii
Perniciem cupit innocentum.

Once mangled, with curved hooks?
He resists courageously. Alas, what impiety do you plot? 30
My mind hesitates, trembles. With what beasts,
Terrible tyrant,
With what monsters shall I compare you, most savage Undershirt?

Strophe 2
By the swirling waters of Tiber
A nurturing she-wolf gave suck with her teats 35
To twin infants; a boy was often seen
Sporting on the fin-bearing back
Of a swimming dolphin from the shore of Puteoli,
And in return for the curing of a wounded foot
They say that a lion, the guest of a man, 40
Knew and came to him in his fear
Amongst the cruel charges of beasts
Like a fawning dog,
And the host of Romulus was amazed
At the pair rejoicing in each other. 45

Antistrophe 2
Whether the ages of old bear truth
Or invention, the mind of man
Rages more furiously than the asp or the beasts of the Caspian:
The bear does not hunt the bear,
The viper does not slay the viper, the tiger the tiger: 50
It was the human race that brought rods, wheels and hooks
To the earth, and fitted wings
To the feet of death. Why should I mention
The unspeakable bull of Perillus?
Nor is it menacing only to the guilty or to enemies: 55
As the medium of its joy
It desires the destruction of the innocent.

Epode 2
Te, matricida, te, lues mortalium,
Incessit tam dira cupido?
Nam facibus passim incensam populatus ignis Urbem   60
Te iubente, fletibus,
Clamore, luctu, cladibus, ruinis
Complens in atri uerterat formam rogi:
Tunc laetus fidibus canens
Diceris excidio   65
Ausus Troiano miseram componere Romam.

Strophe 3
Quo, Musa, Dirces prouehunt
Te uela? ferri per tragicos amas
Terrores? Rutilum sidus Iberiae,
Atlantis emergens ab undis,   70
Te reuocat dira tostus Laurentius olim
In crate: forma nec decor nec aetas
Ferreos flectunt animos, tyrannus
Deridet abstersum cruorem
Caelestis pueri manu.   75
Ludi ne uanis perferam praestigiis?
'I miles', inquit, 'perditus
Det meritas reus igne poenas'.

Antistrophe 3
Et ecce raptim strenuus
Athleta Christi traditur ignibus: 80
Hos inter thalamos uestibus aureis
Compactus excepit iacentem:
Tres o Iordanis pueri decus Isacidarum
Vt uestra flammis emicat probata
Dispari uirtus celebris corona   85
Quos par adegit causa morti

Epode 2
Did such a terrible desire come up on you,
Matricide, plague of mortals?
For fire, having laid waste the City, kindled all over with torches   60
Under your orders, filling it with weeping,
Shouting, mourning, disasters, collapses,
Had turned it into the shape of a dark pyre:
Then, joyously singing with the lyre,
You are said to have dared to compare   65
Miserable Rome to the fall of Troy.

Strophe 3
Where are the sails of Dirce carrying you off,
Muse? Do you wish to be borne away through
Tragic terrors? You are called back by the ruddy star of Iberia,
Emerging from the waves of Atlas,   70
Laurence, long ago roasted on his terrible gridiron:
Neither the beauty of his form nor his youth
Deter a will of iron. The tyrant scoffs
At the blood wiped away
By the hand of the heavenly youth.   75
'Shall I endure being deluded by empty tricks?
Go on, soldier', he said, 'let the desperate offender
Pay the just penalty by fire'.

Antistrophe 3
And behold all of a sudden
The vigorous athlete of Christ is consigned to the flames: 80
Amid those chambers of gold hangings
The framework took his reclining weight:
Just as, o three boys of the Jordan, ornament of the sons of Isaac,
Your courage sparkles, proved by flames,
Famed for its unequal crown,   85
Whom the same cause drove to expose

Vltro exponere pectora?
Non vos Deira militum cohortibus
Equis et armis obstrepens
Terruit aut sonitus tubarum. 90

Epode 3
Non vos furentis Regis atrox commouet
Aspectus: 'Nos', dicitis, 'o Rex,
Non aurum aut statuas colimus; Deus Israel colendus;
Ille solus est Deus.
Frustra catenis alligas lacertos, 95
Et nos in ignes conicis: nam praepotens
Illaesos nos Deus eruet,
Si volet, atra licet
Fluctuet undanti flammarum vertice fornax'.

Strophe 4
Nec uana spes: innoxius 100
Vos lambit ignis vitreus ut liquor,
Non ausus teneram laedere corporum
Cutem, sed infrendens uoraxque
Fertur in adstantes ardenti membra vapore
Hausturus; in vos obsequens, fauenti 105
Dum Deo grates canitis furorem
(Res mira) compescens, aenis
Vinctos nexibus accipit,
Reddit solutos, uinctus ipse, languidus,
Inermis. At Laurentium 110
Letiferis petit acer armis.

Antistrophe 4
Artae coercent compedes
Nudumque prunis concolor os cremat;

Your breasts to death of your own accord?
Babylon, roaring with troops of soldiers,
With horses and arms, did not terrify you
Or the sounding of trumpets.   90

Epode 3
The fierce sight of the furious king did not
Disturb you: 'We', you say, 'o king,
Do not worship gold or statues: it is the God of Israel who should
be worshipped;
He alone is God.
In vain do you bind our arms with chains,   95
And cast us into the fires: for the mighty God
Will draw us out unscathed,
If he wills, though the dark furnace
Heave with a seething whirlpool of flames'.

Strophe 4
Nor was your hope in vain: harmlessly   100
The fire licked you like a glassy liquid,
Not daring to injure the soft skin
Of your bodies, but gnashing and devouring
It moved against the bystanders, seeking to consume
Their limbs with burning heat; acting in your interest,   105
Restraining its rage (a thing of wonder)
As you sang your thanks to God for his favour,
It received you bound with brazen bonds,
And gave you back free from them, but bound itself, powerless,
Disarmed. But it made for Laurence   110
Fierce with its death-dealing weapons.

Antistrophe 4
Close bonds held him fast
And it burned his bare face the colour of a live coal:

Iam corpus celeri corripit impetu,
Iam flamma proserpens adurit, 115
Et carnem uorat, graciles depascitur artus.
Immotus heros, ut doloris expers,
ut rosas inter uiridesque myrtos,
Ferale tormentum uirili
Spernit pectore, dum truci 120
Adipem liquatus igne manat: lumina
Auertit intuentium
Terribili laniena visu.

Epode 4
Assatus ille, gestiens plenus Deo
Solui nexu corporis, infit 125
Ore renidenti: 'Fumant tibi iam, tyranne, cocta haec
Membra: mande, uescere:
En aula Caeli se mihi recludit'.
O quam beate moreris! inclutus magis,
Inuictissime Martyrum, 130
Nullus obire potest:
Hostibus insultas uictor, cadis hostia Christo.

Now it seizes his body with its rapid rush,
Now the flame creeping forward burns him 115
And devours his flesh, feeds on his slender limbs.
The hero, unmoved, like one free from pain,
Like one amid roses and green myrtles,
Scorns the deadly torture
With manly heart, as he flows, his fat 120
Made liquid by the fierce fire:
The butchery made the eyes
Of onlookers turn away,
Terrible to behold.

Epode 4
And he, roasted, desiring, full of God, 125
To be loosed from the bond of the body, said
With smiling mouth: 'These limbs of mine are cooked
And steam for you: eat, consume:
Behold, the palace of heaven opens itself to me'.
O how blessedly you die! None, 130
Most invincible of martyrs,
Can have a more distinguished end:
You mock victoriously at your enemies, and fall as a sacrifice
    to Christ.

Commentary

Strophe 1 (1–12) The poem begins with an address to Spain, diplomatically complimented on its fortune in being ruled by the Habsburg monarch Philip III (reigned 1598–1621), who is invoked by name at the strophe's ring-compositional end (11–12); the rhetorical tactic here of suggesting that another poet will take up a topic which is then briefly recounted recalls the openings of *Odes* 1.6 and *Odes* 1.7 (cf. esp. 1.7.1 *laudabunt alii*). 2–3: *aurifero Tagi / . . . flumine* echoes a topos of Latin poetry on this 'gold-bearing' Iberian river (Catullus 29.19 *aurifer Tagus*, Ovid *Am.*1.15.34 *auriferi . . . Tagi*), while *classe . . . bello ferocem* picks up Horace's descriptions of the Egyptian nation as *classe formidatus* (*Odes* 3.6.15) and of the poet Alcaeus as *ferox bello* (*Odes* 1.32.6). 5: *Oceani dominam* points to Spain's Atlantic fleet and American empire; the 'Persian mines' of line 6 are mysterious. At the time Spain had trading operations in the Persian Gulf (NB the mention of Arabia here; *concha* as often in Roman poetry refers to valuable purple dye from shellfish) and active diplomatic relations with Persia,[71] but no mines there; its great silver mines were in Peru (which would go well with the mention of Spain's further American colony Mexico and its Indian trading settlement at Goa via Portugal),[72] and it would be possible to read *Peruuianis diuitem hic metallis* here to solve the problem (for the postponement of the pronoun cf. *alter* in line 10). 8: *mercibus Goae beatam* recalls *Odes* 3.7.3 *Thyna merce beatum* (a similar reference to profitable imperial trade). 10–12: the many military triumphs of Charles V (which included his forces' sack of Barberini's own Rome in 1527) are contrasted with the more cautious policies of his grandson Philip III, e.g. his then long truce (1609–21) with the rebellious Netherlands; *temperatis . . . consiliis* is a compliment to Philip as moderate ruler, recalling Horace's implicit praise of Augustus at *Odes* 3.4.65–7 *uis consili expers mole ruit sua; / uim temperatam di quoque prouehunt / in maius*.

Antistrophe 1 (13–24) The poem turns to its main subject, the heroic martyrdom of Laurence. 14: *fulgidam* combines the metaphorical light of distinction with a suggestion of Laurence's fiery end. 15–18:

Laurence's resolution in the face of torture recalls that of Horace's Regulus in the same situation in *Odes* 3.5 (see above and 3.5.49–50 *atqui sciebat, quae sibi barbarus / <u>tortor</u> pararet*), and the courage of the wise man at *Odes* 3.3.1–4 *Iustum et tenacem propositi uirum / <u>non civium ardor praua iubentium, / non uultus instantis tyranni / mente quatit solida</u>.* 17–18: *palmis nobiles* transforms Horace's pagan athletic prize (*Odes* 1.1.5 *palmaque nobilis*) into the palm carried by the Christian martyr (e.g. Prudentius *Perist.* 4.77), while *ostro/clarus* applies the smart garb of a Vergilian warrior (*Aeneid* 11.772 *ferrugine clarus et ostro*) to the purple robes of the saints (Prudentius *Perist.* 2.275–6 *purpurantibus stolis / clari*). 21: *Duci* points to St Stephen as the first of Christian martyrs (for his stoning see Acts 7.54–60); note the paradoxical oxymorons *probro gloriam* and *interitu ... vitam* – the notionally shameful executions of Christ and Stephen (like that of Laurence) lead to the glory of eternal life. As noted above, the analogy between Laurence and Stephen is drawn from Prudentius (2.369–72).

Epode 1 (25–33) The poet addresses the wicked 'king' who tortures Laurence, here the emperor Valerian, nicknamed 'undershirt' (*colobium*: cf. *Epitome De Caesaribus* 32.1); in Prudentius' version the oppressor is an anonymous prefect of the city, upgraded here by Barberini following Jacobus de Voragine for a more impressive encounter of saint with supreme ruler (see introduction above). The language here echoes a number of classical passages on cruel tyrants and resisting them. 25: cf. *Aeneid* 4.197 *aggerat iras* (of Iarbas), [Seneca] *Octavia* 649 (of Nero) *principis acres ... iras*. 26–7 (and 32): cf. Valerius Flaccus 5.659–60 <u>*iuuenem*, *qui iussa sui tam dira tyranni / impauidus* maria et nondum qui nota subibat</u>, Seneca *HF* 43 *fera tyranni iussa*. 30: cf. Seneca *Thyestes* 254 (to the tyrant Atreus) *Quid noui rabidus struis?* 31: cf. *Odes* 2.19.5 *mens trepidat*. 32–3: cf. Seneca *HO* 878–9 *ego uos <u>tyrannis regibus monstris feris</u> / saeuisque rapto uindice opposui deis.*

Strophe 2 (34–45) The cruelty of Valerian to his fellow man is unfavourably contrasted with the benevolent behaviour of beasts towards humans; such ethical comparisons or contrasts with the animal world were traditional in Greek and Roman thought.[73] Here Barberini marshals some famous classical examples of animal benevolence to men in the story of the she-wolf suckling the infant Romulu and Remus (Livy 1.4.6), that of the dolphin who loved a boy at Puteoli, for which Dicaearchia was the Greek name (Aulus Gellius 6.8), and that of Androclus and the lion (Aulus Gellius 5.14). These abruptly introduced moralizing stories function like the mythological narratives of Pindar's epinicians (often presented via similar rapid transitions) in illustrating key points in the poem. 34: cf. Lucan 1.381 *Thybridis undas,* Seneca *HO* 779 *undas . . . uagas*. 35: cf. Cicero *Cat*.3.19 [of Romulus] *paruum atque lactantem, uberibus lupinis inhiantem,* Propertius 4.1.38 *sanguinis altricem non pudet esse lupam*. 36: *pinniger* describes the dolphin's dorsal fin (cf. Ovid *Met*.13.963 *pinnigero . . . pisce*), retracted for the boy's comfort in Gellius' version (but not here): note the three alliterative pairs *pinnigero puer, delphinis in dorso* and *ludens e litore* here. 39–45: the story of Androclus and the lion is more fully narrated than the other two and draws on Gellius' language; for the cured foot of 39 compare 5.14.23 *illa tunc mea opera et medela leuatus pede in manibus meis posito*, for the wild beasts of 41–2 compare 5.14.7 *multae ibi saeuientes ferae,* for the canine comparison of 42–3 5.14.12 *tum caudam more atque ritu adulantium canum clementer et blande mouet,* and for the joyous mutual recognition 5.14.14 *quasi mutua recognitione facta laetos. . . . et gratulabundos uideres hominem et leonem*. 44: *pubes Romuli* – cf. *Odes* 4.4.46 *Romana pubes,* Catullus 34.22–4 *Romuli . . . gentem.*

Antistrophe 2 (46–57) 46–7: the truth or falsehood of stories of the distant past are a trope of Augustan poetry: cf. e.g. *Aeneid* 9.79 *prisca fides facto, sed fama perennis,* Propertius 3.1.23 *omnia post obitum fingit maiora uetustas*. 47–50: for the snake as a type of destructiveness cf. *Satires* 2.8.95 *peior serpentibus Afris*. 48: for Hyrcanian tigers (from the region of the Caspian Sea) as pitiless cf. *Aeneid* 4.366–7 *duris genuit te cautibus horrens/ Caucasus Hyrcanaeque admorunt ubera tigres*. 49–50: for the argument that humans are more vicious than wild beasts see

Seneca *Ep*.107.7 *homo perniciosior feris omnibus*, and for the notion that man is monstrous for attacking his own species cf. Seneca *Dial*.5.3.2 *quantum monstri sit homo in hominem furens*; the triple polyptoton of 49-50 recalls the repeated use of this figure in contexts of epic conflict (see Wills 1996: 197-8). 51: recalls Horace's characterization of the human race as bringer of evil to the earth at *Odes* 1.3.25-8 *audax omnia perpeti/ gens humana ruit per uetitum nefas / audax Iapeti genus / ignem fraude mala gentibus intulit*. 51: *uirgas ... rotas ... uncos*: Roman instruments of beating and torture – cf. *Horace Satires* 2.7.58 *uri uirgis*, Tibullus 1.3.74 *uersantur celeri noxia membra rota*, Cicero *Rab*.17 *a uerberibus, ab unco, a crucis denique terrore*. 52: perhaps evokes the winged heels in poetry and art of Mercury/Hermes, escorter of the dead (cf. esp. *Aeneid* 4.239-44). 53-4: refers to the bronze bull devised by the craftsman Perillus for the tyrant Phalaris to torture his victims (Propertius 2.25.11-12, Ovid *Tristia* 5.1.53-4), a metallic technology of torture close to that used for Laurence. For *quid memorem* in a mythological list cf. *Aeneid* 6.601 *quid memorem Lapithas, Ixiona Pirithoumque*? 56: cf. Apuleius *Met*. 4.16.3 *gaudii sui gerulis*. 57: cf. Cicero *Clu*. 129 *perniciem innocentis*, Tacitus *Ann*. 4.33. 3 *perniciem innocentium*, and for this same resonant noun in the same position and case in the same metrical line cf. *Odes* 3.5.16 *perniciem veniens in aevum*.

Epode 2 (58-66) With another Pindaric-style rapid link of thought, Barberini turns to an example of the human depravity just sketched in the preceding antistrophe. This is Nero, another tyrannical Roman emperor associated like Valerian with a fiery outrage, in his case not the roasting of Laurence but the burning of Rome itself (64 CE). Barberini's dramatic and baroque account draws on the accounts of the fire in Tacitus (*Annals* 15.38-41) and Suetonius (*Nero* 38; like Suetonius Barberini presents Nero as the city's deliberate arsonist). 58: for Nero as *matricida* see Suetonius *Nero* 21.3, for *lues* of a pernicious person cf. Seneca *HF* 338 *nostri generis exitium ac lues*. 59: transitive *incedere* of the impact of an emotion is a characteristic expression of Livy (1.56.10

cupido incessit animos, TLL 7.1.857.36–46), while *tam dira cupido* is a hexameter-ending Vergilian phrase (*Georgics* 1.37, *Aeneid* 6.373, 721, the last two similarly in questions). 60: cf. Silius Italicus 10.555–6 *tum face coniecta populatur feruidus ignis / flagrantem molem, Aeneid* 2.327 *incensa . . . in urbe* (of burning Troy, a relevant parallel, see 65–6). 61–2: a melodramatic six-item asyndetic noun-list, redolent of Lucretius in both technique and vocabulary – cf. Lucretius 1.744 *aera solem imbrem terras animalia fruges*, 5.347 *cladem magnasque ruinas*. 64–6: for the shocking story of Nero singing his 'Sack of Troy' poem to the lyre to match the burning ruins of Rome see Tacitus *Ann.* 15.39 *quia peruaserat rumor . . . cecinisse Troianum excidium, praesentia mala uetustis cladibus adsimulantem*; *diceris* picks up Tacitus' *pervaserat rumor, excidio . . . Troiano* his *Troianum excidium, componere* his *adsimulantem*. Note the pointed contrast of the tyrant's joy (64 *laetus*) and his city's misery (66 *miseram*), and the climactic final placing of *Romam* (66).

Strophe 3 (67–78) 67–9: the self-conscious address to the Muse about a potentially inappropriate poetic direction away from lyric imitates Horace's reworking in the *Odes* of the Pindaric technique of the 'break-off formula': cf. *Odes* 3.3.70 *quo, Musa, tendis?, Odes* 2.1.37–8, Pindar *Nemeans* 3.26–7, *Isthmians* 6.56–8. 67: Dirce was a wicked Theban royal stepmother in Greek tragedy who was tied to the horns of a bull by her avenging stepsons (Plautus *Pseud.* 199–200), a death involving cruel bondage like that that of Laurence. Here she stands for tragic drama: *provehunt / . . . uela* (along with *ferri*) suggests the image of a vessel's sails carrying the Muse along in this wrong literary direction, towards a dark genre of fear and suffering (cf. the emphatically alliterative 68–9 *tragicos . . . / terrores*); 69–79 return us to a more triumphant narrative of heroic Christian martyrdom. 69: the ruddy colour (*rutilum*) suggests Laurence's gloriously fiery end, while the star/sun (*sidus*) suggests his good looks (cf. 72 and *Odes* 3.9.21 *sidere pulchrior*) and his heavenly destiny. 70: Laurence is imagined as the bright sun emerging at dawn (symbolizing resurrection) from the waters of Atlas, i.e. the Atlantic Ocean (cf. Pontano *Urania* 2.229 *Atlantis in undis*); this location like

Iberiae (69) points to his Spanish origins. 72-3: cf. Statius *Ach*.1.811 *decor et formae species*, Ovid *Her.* 12.183 *praecordia ferrea*; note the emphatic alliteration *ferreos flectunt*. 75: *caelestis pueri*: the young saint destined for Christian heaven. 76-8: Prudentius gives the prefect an extensive and aggressive speech at this point (2.313-56), radically abbreviated here in Barberini's shorter narrative. 77: *ludi = deludi* - cf. *Odes* 3.27.40-1 *ludit imago / uana*. 78: cf. Ovid *Fasti* 4.239 *meritas do sanguine poenas*.

Antistrophe 3 (79-90) Again in the manner of Pindar, Laurence's fiery torment is illustrated by a traditional story, here from the bible (Daniel 3) rather than Greek myth. The story is that of the three faithful Jews Shadrach, Meshach and Abednego (Hebrew names Hananiah, Mishael and Azariah) put into a burning fiery furnace by king Nebuchadnezzar of Babylon for refusing to worship a golden image and miraculously saved by divine intervention (unlike Laurence, but their heroic defiance is the key point of comparison). The lengthy song of the three in praise of God while still in the furnace (the liturgical canticle *Benedictus*)[74] was commonly referred to as the 'Song of the Three Boys' (*Canticum Trium Puerorum*) and was paraphrased under this title by Barberini himself in another poem (see introduction above); here it is elided in favour of their brief pre-furnace assertion of God's true divinity (see on 92-9 below). In Daniel the three victims are mature senior officials, but their youthful age here (83 *pueri*) matches that of Laurence himself (cf. 72 *aetas*) as well as the 'Three Boys' tradition. 80: the phrase *athleta Christi* seems to be coined by St Ambrose (*TLL* 2.1036.70ff) and by the seventeenth century was an honorific title given to military saints and martyrs; St Paul had famously compared Christian discipleship to athletic training at I Corinthians 9.24-7. 81: recalls the gold-cloth coverings of luxury couches at Apuleius *Met.* 2.19.1 *lecti aureis uestibus intecti*. 83: for the collective *decus Isacidarum* cf. Catullus 64.78 *decus innuptarum*, and for the patronymic *Isacida* see Vida *Christiad* 2.289). 84: the fire-verb *emicat* is an appropriate metaphor here. 85: i.e. the uneven number of three, playing on *par*, 'even' in 86. 88: *Deira* = an alternative spelling of the *Dura* of Daniel 3.1 (cf. Jerome *Commentarii in Danielem* 1.3), the location of the fiery furnace in the Vulgate version. 88–90: the imperturbability of the three before the watching 'princes, governors, and captains' of Nebuchadnezzar (Daniel 3.1) recalls that of the sage at *Odes* 3.3.1–4 *Iustum et tenacem propositi uirum / non ciuium ardor praua iubentium / non uultus instantis tyranni / mente quatit solida*; for 89 cf. Martial 1.49.45 *Equis et armis nobilem* (again of a city), for 90 *Georgics* 4.72 *sonitus imitata tubarum*.

Epode 3 (91–9) A more forceful version of the defiant speech of the three at Daniel 3.17–18: 'If it be so, our God whom we serve is able to deliver us from the burning fiery furnace, and he will deliver us out of thine hand, O king. But if not, be it known unto thee, O king, that we will not serve thy gods, nor worship the golden image which thou hast set up'. 92–3 like 88–90 (see above) echo *Odes* 3.2.1–4 on the imperturbability of the sage before a tyrant; *non uos … commouet* nicely varies *non uos … terruit*, while *atrox … aspectus* makes an elegant alliterative pairing. 95: appropriately recalls the miraculous release of Bacchus from bonds at Ovid *Met*. 3.699–700 *lapsasque lacertis /… catenas* and Horace's allusion to the same episode at *Epistles* 1.16.74–6 '*in manicis et / compedibus saeuo te sub custode tenebo.*' / '*ipse deus, simul atque uolam, me soluet*'. 98–9: cf. Silius 13.836 *fornacibus atris*, Statius *Theb*. 12.431 *uertice flammae*; as often in Latin poetry the language of water is here used to describe fire (see also 101 below). 99: note the forceful alternation of alliteration of f and u in this final hexameter, which also draws attention to the elaborate Vergilian chiastic word order here (ABCBA).

Strophe 4 (100–11) 100–3: the miraculous harmless flames here recall those which mark out Ascanius as under divine protection in the *Aeneid* (2.681–6; 100 *innoxia* = 2.683, 101 *lambit* ~ 2.684 *lambere*); for 102 cf. Seneca *Ep*.123.7 *ne frigus teneram cutem laedat*. 103–6: the consumption of the bystanders by the intense flames is a detail drawn from Daniel (3.46–8). 103–4: cf. Silius 4.685 *flamma uorax*, Apuleius *Met*. 6.31.6 *solis ardentis uaporibus*. 106–9: cf. Martial 7.71.6 *Res mira est*, *Aeneid* 1.295–

6 *centum uinctus aenis / post tergum nodis.* 110: *at* makes a rapid and contrastive move back from the three boys to Laurence, in Pindaric style. 111: uses the language of the attacking warrior from epic – cf. Statius *Theb*.4.676 *ferro petit, Aeneid* 10.169 *letifer arcus,* 12.938 *acer in armis.*

Antistrophe 4 (112–23) By contrast with the strophe, the viciously destructive results of the flames on Laurence are stressed; Barberini has more gory detail here than Prudentius' more euphemistic treatment (2.385–92), using the brutal language of Senecan drama. 112–14: the multiple alliteration of c here (pairs in 112 and 113, a consecutive trio in 114) reinforces the violence of the passage. 115–16: cf. Seneca *Medea* 819 *urat serpens flamma medullas* (another cruel death), *Oedipus* 187 *sacer ignis pascitur artus* (of the plague), Tibullus 2.3.9 *graciles . . . artus* (youthful grace, here sadly destroyed). 117: cf. Ovid *Met.* 4.418–19 *expers / una doloris erat*. 118: roses and myrtle suggest a symposiastic setting, looking to the life of youthful hedonism rejected by Laurence in martyrdom (cf. e.g. *Odes* 1.4.9–10, 1.5.2, 1.38.3–5). 119: *ferale* and *uirili* are pointedly balanced at each line-end – Laurence meets bestial treatment with manly courage. 121: *adipem liquatus* – poetic accusative of respect ('liquified as to his fat'); for the medical *adipes liquatus* cf. Celsus 4.223, Pliny *NH* 32.117. 121–2: cf. Tacitus *Ann.* 2.41 *intuentium visus*. 123: it is possible that *terribilis* should be read here, given the common *terribilis uisu*, 'terrible to behold' (Statius *Theb*. 4.326, Pliny *Pan*. 48.4, Silius 14.385), a more natural use of the ablative than provided by the instrumental *terribili*, found in all editions of this poem.

Epode 4 (124–32) The climactic moment of Laurence's death; his brief final speech (124–8) combines the black humour of the same martyr's words in Prudentius (2.406–8): *tunc ille: 'coctum est, deuora / et experimentum cape, / sit crudum an assum suauius!'* with the protomartyr Stephen's biblical vision of heaven opening as he dies (Acts 7.55 *Ecce video caelos apertos*). This final section of the poem consistently modifies classical elements for Christian ideological purposes, drawing the ethical and theological lessons of Laurence's martyrdom. *plenus Deo*

(124) echoes the pagan *plena deo*, probably referring to Vergil's Sibyl and her inspiration by Apollo (Seneca *Suas*.3.5–6), while *solui nexu corporis* (125) neatly rewrites Ovid *Met.* 9.58 *uix solui duros a corpore nexus* (of a wrestling grip) in terms of Christian release of the soul from the body; 129 *beate mori* inverts the common ancient ethical idea of *beate uiuere*, and *inclutus* is a grand epithet of epic heroes (Ennius *Ann.* 123 Sk, *Aeneid* 6.479), repurposed here for the heroism of a Christian martyr, just as the *inuictissimus* used by Cicero of the Roman military conquerors Scipio and Pompey (*De Rep.* 6.9, *In Pisonem* 34) is applied to a more spiritual victor. In the last line (132) the malicious celebration of Sinon over Troy (*Aeneid* 2.329–30 <u>uictor</u>que Sinon incendia miscet / <u>insultans</u>) is appropriated for the just triumph of the saint over his torturers, while *cadis hostia* reinterprets the death of the sacrificial animal in pagan religion ([Tibullus] 3.7.15 *taurus cadit hostia*, Ovid *Fasti* 1.320 *hostia caelitibus . . . cadit*) as a glorious self-sacrifice to Christ rather than a perverted offering to a pagan deity, as well as reflecting the classical use of *cadere* of falling as a victim in battle, another element of epic warfare here (e.g. *Aeneid* 10.830).

Figure 2 Pope Alexander VII, bust by Melchiore Cafà, photo by Giovanni Piscina. *Source*: Wikimedia Commons/Metropolitan Museum of Art, New York https://commons.wikimedia.org/wiki/File:Pope_Alexander_VII_(1599%E2%80%931667)_MET_DP249454.jpg.

2

Fabio Chigi (1599–1667; Pope as Alexander VII 1655–67)

Chigi's Latin poems were first published in Germany (where he was then papal nuncio)[1] a decade before his papacy (Chigi 1645, printed in Cologne). The title of the collection (retained in all subsequent editions) indicated that they were the work of the author's youth (*Philomathi Musae iuveniles*).[2] The pseudonym 'Philomathus', under which the poems appeared, referred to Chigi's early membership of the literary Accademia de' Filomati in Siena;[3] the poet's true identity was strongly implied in the book's preface presented under the name of its editor Wilhelm van Furstenberg,[4] which was addressed to Chigi's youthful nephew the later cardinal Flavio Chigi (1631–93),[5] praised his uncle and suggested that he would recognize the author. This first edition of 1645 contained seventy-two poems plus the tragedy *Pompeius* (see below); the selection made here uses the fullest third edition of 1656, printed in Paris after the author's election to the papacy the previous year, which contains ninety-three poems and the tragedy.[6]

Like Barberini before him, Chigi favoured Horatian lyric metres; these appear in about a quarter of his poems which form the majority of the items selected for analysis here, since they include much of his most ambitious and richest work. Their subjects range widely, from the praise of poetry (poem 1 = item 1 below) to more Christian themes (e.g. poem 2 = item 2 on the Annunciation, poem 21 = item 6 on Bl. Pietro Petroni, poem 24 = item 4 on the legendary voyage of Bl. Mary Magdalen, poem 56 on the return of Pope Gregory XI from Avignon in 1377 in answer to the prayers of St Catherine of Siena), and commemorations of public and personal events (e.g. poem 7 = item 3 on the election of Urban VIII in 1623, poem 18 = item 5 on the siege of

La Rochelle, poem 29 on the death of Maria de' Medici, former Duchess of Mantua and Siena (1629), poem 64 to a friend on the death of his recent bride, or poem 62 to a friend on the award of a doctorate in law).

He also wrote long hexameter poems describing his journeys in the papal service, following the model of Horace *Satires* 1.5 and other classical poets;[7] only his account of travelling from Rome to Ferrara (1629, poem 11) is included here (as item 5), but there are also similar substantial poems charting journeys from Malta to Rome (1639, poem 40), Ferrara to Cologne (1639, poem 41), Cologne to Münster (1644, poem 87), Münster to Aachen (1649, poem 88), Aachen to Trier (1650, poem 90) and Trier to Aachen (1650, poem 91).[8]

Another set of longer poems is constituted by Chigi's elegiac letters to friends in Rome from his postings abroad. Poem 75 sends back news of his health and the progress of peace talks from Germany, while poem 76 sends a description of Münster to a bishop friend in Rome, and poem 78 marks the writer's fiftieth birthday in another letter from Germany. These poems from Germany where the colder weather was not to Chigi's taste (see poems 20 and 89) echo the long elegiac epistles of Ovid to Roman friends from uncongenial exile in the Black Sea region (*Tristia* and *Ex Ponto*); further Ovidian traces can also be detected in an amusing elegiac letter on the dress and behaviour of the women of Münster (poem 77, cf. the *Ars Amatoria* and the *Medicamina Faciei Femineae*) and an elegiac description of a pilgrimage (poem 92, cf. the *Fasti*). Poem 74 (item 8 below) is another letter from Germany during the peace talks, this time in the hexameters of Horace's *Epistles*.

More than a third of Chigi's poems are epigrams, regularly presented in pairs on the same topic (poems 6 and 7, 22 and 23, 25 and 26, 27 and 28, 36 and 37, 54 and 55, 71 and 73); this is a feature both of Martial's epigrams and the epigrams of the Greek Anthology, both popular in the early modern period.[9] Occasionally these reflect his classical reading or literary life in their subjects (e.g. poems 5 and 6 on the tame lion of Domitian, cf. Martial 1.22 and Statius *Silvae* 2.5, poems 8 and 9 on a mouse-gnawed copy of Caesar's *Commentarii* or poems 54 and 55 on a hare and a lion, picking up Martial 1.6, 1.22, 1.48 and 1.51); others follow ancient types of epigram such as epitaphs (poems 3, 22 and 23, 55, 67, 79, 80, 82, 84) and ekphrases of artworks and the like (15, 17, 25 and 26, 33, 36 and 37, 47–50) as well as Martial-style satire (20, 58, 71, 73); only one epigram is specifically religious (45, a prayer).

Printed with his shorter poems was Chigi's complete Senecan-style tragedy on a Roman historical subject, *Pompeius*. This treats the final episode of the life of Pompey the Great in 48 BCE as the latter, after defeat by Julius Caesar at the battle of Pharsalus, unwisely committed himself to the treacherous young king of Egypt and was deceived and killed.[10] The tragedy was a youthful work, written according to its preface in 1621, when the author was 21 or 22, and follows an established tradition of such Senecanizing tragedies with Roman subjects,[11] not least amongst scholar-poets at the start of their careers: e.g. Marc-Antoine Muret's *Julius Caesar* (1545),[12] and Daniel Heinsius' *Auriacus* on the death of William of Orange (1619).[13]

The predominance of secular over sacred topics in this poetic output is striking for a prominent bishop: the programmatic opening poem is remarkably free of Christian elements (see commentary below), and only around a quarter of the poems have a specifically religious subject, though the Christian morals of the author are consistently on display in the others. There is a clear contrast here with Barberini, in whose poetry religious themes predominate; this may be explicable by the fact that almost all Chigi's 'youthful' collection (see above) belongs to his life before becoming a cardinal (1652),[14] while Barberini's collection includes many poems written as cardinal and pope.

Barberini as Urban VIII is a presence in Chigi's poems, and also provides him with a key recent literary model in the imitation of the great classical poets. Apart from the ode which congratulates Urban on his election to the papacy (poem 7 = item 3 below), we find him mentioned in several other poems, such as two journey-poems which chronicle Chigi's travels in his service (poem 40, Malta to Rome and poem 41, Ferrara to Cologne). Chigi clearly follows Barberini's lead in promoting an austere and moralizing Roman poetic classicism in this period as a counterweight to the vernacular and sensuous mannerism of Giambattista Marino.[15]

The only modern editor of all Chigi's Latin poems admires them for their effective combination of poetry and rhetoric, and sees them as expressing a conservative and classicising spirit akin to the Christian humanism of St François de Sales (a Chigi favourite).[16] It can be added here that their manipulation of classical models, at the lexical, thematic and generic levels, operates with a high degree of skill and presents much of interest for the student of classical reception, while their content can tell us much about the literary, ecclesiastical and diplomatic culture of the seventeenth century. In both these respects Chigi can be well paired with his former papal master Barberini.

1. Ode in praise of poetry (poem 1)

This poem, placed at the head of Chigi's collection, celebrates the commemorative power of poetry. It names Horace as a particular inspiration, natural enough since it is composed in one of Horace's chief lyric metres from the *Odes* (the Alcaic stanza),[17] and contains many Horatian allusions: the commentary below identifies more than twenty in the poem's forty-four lines. As outlined above, alongside epigram, Horatian lyric is the Roman genre most frequently employed in the collection, so the emphasis on Horace here is programmatic for the volume that follows.

The poem can be divided into three sections: an initial characterization of the perpetuating powers of poetry (1–16), a description of everything else in the universe as mutable by comparison (17–26a) and a final address to the Muses recognizing the commemorative capacity of verse, rounded off by Horace as a key example (26b–44). This is a kind of ring-composition, a structure common in Horace's odes,[18] and the address to the gods of poetry and a concern with its perpetuating power is also an Horatian trope (cf. e.g. *Odes* 3.4, 3.25, 4.8, 4.9).

The style and world of the poem is resolutely classical, though the 'Auditoria, wars, generals, rich kingdoms / And whole cities' of lines 20-1 might have historical analogues in baroque Italy. The physical universe described in lines 13-16 draws on ancient cosmography (especially Lucretius) rather than contemporary science; Apollo and the Muses are prominent (lines 8, 23, 26, 27), but there is no mention of the Christian God or saints. That is corrected in the next poem (2 = item 2) with its focus on the Virgin Mary, but what we have here is a strikingly classicizing poetic manifesto.

Text and translation

IN LAVDEM POESEOS

Non tela, rauco percita classico,
Non fluctuantes per mare turgidum
   Gazas, vel immensum patentis
      Arua sequor bene culta ruris.
Me per sonantes tibia riuulos,   5
Me dulce plectrum per iuga montium et
   Antris trahit iocans imago,
      Collis Apollinei inquilinum.
Deuota morti cetera defluunt
Fatoque cedunt irreparabili;   10
   Et, quam dederunt uix, repente
      Abripiunt elementa uitam:
Haec pura mundi semina permanent,
Occasu et ortu alterna, uagantibus
   Vertente natura figuris,   15
      Dum uarius reparatur orbis.
Tempus fugaci uulnerat impetu
Rituque Parthorum feriens ruit
   Versis sagittis: hoc theatra,
      Arma, duces, opulenta regna,   20
Vrbesque totas cuncta silentiis
Immergit altis: nec patitur diu
   Quidquam manere. Vnum Camenis
      Perpetuum dedit esse carmen
Mortale terris lumine dum uago   25
Partitur aeuum Phoebus. Amabili
   Raptus furore, o uestra, Musae,
      Threicia fide notus, antra
Pandam sacerdos, o liceat sacras
Lustrare sedes! Vos lacrimabile   30
   Letum et sepulchrales cupressi
      Et miseri fugiunt dolores.

Fabio Chigi (1599–1667; Pope as Alexander VII 1655–67)

In praise of poetry

It is not weapons, roused by the harsh trumpet,
Nor treasures floating through the swelling sea,
Nor the well-tilled fields of an estate
That stretches immeasurably wide that I seek:
   I am drawn by the pipe through resounding rivulets,   5
By the sweet plectrum through mountain ridges,
And in glens by the playful echo,
A denizen of the hill of Apollo.
   All else is doomed to death and flows to an end
And yields to a fate that cannot be retrieved: 10
And the elements suddenly snatch away
The life they have only just bestowed:
   These pure seeds of the universe are lasting,
Alternating in decline and rise, as nature turns
In its wandering configurations,   15
While the world is renewed in its variety.
   Time wounds with its assault as it flees,
And rushes on, striking us in Parthian mode,
Turning to shoot its arrows: it plunges
Auditoria, wars, generals, rich kingdoms   20
   And whole cities, all of these, into
Deep silence: nor does it permit anything
To last for long. Only song has it granted
To the Muses to be everlasting,
   For as long as Phoebus, with his roaming light,   25
Assigns mortal life to the earth.
Transported by a lovely madness, O may I, Muses,
Famed for your Thracian lyre, reveal your glens
   As your priest, O, may I be allowed
To traverse your sacred home! Before you   30
Dolorous death and funereal cypresses
And wretched pains take flight.

Non cura mordax, non timor anxius,
Non vos inerti pigra tenet gelu
   Senecta, vos et pax quiesque,   35
      Et decor et iocus et iuuentus
Aeterna seruant: aere perennius
Donatis aeuum uos ducibus nouum,
   Et Delphica lauro reuinctis
      Vatibus æthereos honores.   40
Hac arte Flacci Musa, uolucribus
Dum tempus horas praecipitat rotis,
   Orbem pererrat permanetque
      Viuida mobilitate Cæli.

No gnawing care or anxious fear possesses you,
Nor slow old age with its icy inertia:
Peace and quiet, beauty and play,   35
And eternal youth all follow you:
   You bestow on leaders a new life
More lasting than bronze,
And heavenly honours on bards
Bound with the Delphic wreath.   40
   It is by this attainment that the Muse of Horace
While time drives the hours forward on winged wheels,
Ranges through the world, and endures
In full life under the changeability of heaven.

Commentary

1–16 Poetry is the only lasting element in the universe – everything else is mutable. 1–4: this opening priamel (giving a list of alternatives and then choosing one) introduced by repeated *non* recalls that which begins Horace *Odes* 2.18 (lines 1–8, rejecting wealth and choosing virtue) as well as the extended priamel which fills *Odes* 1.1; its specific language also looks back to Horace *Epodes* 2.5–6 *neque excitatur classico miles truci / neque horret iratum mare* and the storm of *Aeneid* 1.119 *Troia gaza per undas* as well as Lucretius 1.957 *immensum pateat* (of the universe). The initial emphatic placement of *me* in 5–6 recalls that at *Odes* 1.1.29 (also in a priamel ending in the choice of poetry), while for *antra* (7, groves) as the territory of the poet cf. 28 below and *Odes* 3.25.3, and for 7 *iocans imago* (= echo) cf. *Odes* 1.12.3–4 *iocosa / . . . imago*. Line 8 recalls Catullus 61.1–2 *Collis o Heliconii / cultor*, while line 9 echoes *Odes* 4.14.18 *deuota morti pectora* and 3.29.33–4 *cetera fluminis / ritu feruntur*, line 10 *Aeneid* 10.467 *irreparabile tempus*. Lines 13–16 present the Epicurean physics of Lucretius' *De Rerum Natura* (cf. 15 *natura*), in which the atoms are everlasting and form temporary combinations to create perishable objects; for *semina* of atoms cf. Lucretius 1.59 *semina rerum*, and for the language of lines 14–16 cf. Cicero *Arat.* 34.230–1 *Sic malunt errare <u>uagae</u> per nubila caeli / atque suos <u>uario</u> motu metirier <u>orbes</u>* and *Odes* 4.7.13 *damna tamen celeres <u>reparant</u> caelestia lunae*.

17–26a Time destroys everything else – only song is perpetual. For *fugax* of time (17) cf. *Odes* 2.14.1–2 *fugaces . . . / . . . anni*, for the backward shots of Parthian cavalry (18) cf. *Georgics* 3.31 *fidentemque fuga Parthum uersisque sagittis*, and for *opulenta regna* cf. Seneca *Phoen.* 54 *opulenta . . . regna*. Chigi here ascribes to time the destructive effects Catullus ascribes to *otium* (leisure) at 51.15–16 *otium et reges prius et beatas / perdidit urbes*. *Theatra* (20) might suggest noisy public assemblies here (dramatic theatre seems out of place with wars and generals, and this list seems to allude to the world of politics in terms which suit both ancient Rome and baroque Italy). For *silentiis . . . altis* (21–2) cf. *Satires* 2.6.58 *altique silenti*, while 23–24 draw on *Odes*

4.6.29-30 *Phoebus artem /carminis nomenque dedit poetae*, on Ovid *Met.*1.4 *perpetuum* ... *carmen*, and on Ovid *Met.*14.29-30 *sacras qui carmine siluas /quique Syracosia resonant Helicona camena*. For 25-6 cf. *Odes* 3.21.24 *dum rediens fugat astra Phoebus*.

26b-44 The poet wishes for access to the commemorative powers of poetry, as so successfully deployed by Horace. *Amabili /... furore* (26-7) of poetic madness recalls *Odes* 3.4.5-6 *amabilis / insania*, with the adjective in the same metrical position, while the description of Orpheus (27-8) looks back to *Odes* 1.24.13-14 *si Threicio blandius Orpheo /... moderere... fidem*, and the poet as priest of the Muses (29 *sacerdos*) picks up *Odes* 3.1.3 *Musarum sacerdos*. *Lacrimabile / Letum* (30-1) presents an elegant alliteration while the funereal cypresses (the tree of graveyards in both ancient Rome and modern Italy) pick up *Epodes* 5.18 *cupressos funebris*, and the idea that negative forces flee before the positive power of the Muses (32) appropriately recalls Lucretius on Venus (1.6 *te, dea, te fugiunt venti*). The initial anaphora of *Non* (33-4) looks back to the same feature in 1-2, while 33 echoes Lucan (2.681 *curis ... mordacibus*) and *Aeneid* 9.89 *timor anxius*, 34 Horace again (*Odes* 2.9.5 *glacies iners*), 34-5 Tibullus (1.10.40 *pigra senecta*). The retinue of divine powers surrounding the Muses (34-6) recalls those surrounding Venus at *Odes* 1.2.34 *quam Iocus circum uolat et Cupido*, while the pair of *decor* and *iuventus* (36) picks up *Odes* 2.11.6 *iuventas et decor*. *Aere perennius* (37) fittingly alludes to Horace's celebrated characterization of his *Odes* as everlasting (*Odes* 3.30.1), 38-40 to his descriptions of how leaders and poets are memorialized in verse (*Odes* 4.8.14-15 *per quae spiritus et uita redit bonis / post mortem ducibus*, *Ars Poetica* 400 *honor et nomen divinis uatibus*); 39-40 look back (once more) to *Odes* 3.30 (3.30.14-15 *Delphica / lauro*), and to *Odes* 2.1.15 *aeternos honores* (similarly of fame). 41-4: these lines focus on Horace, using his *cognomen* Flaccus (as at *Epodes* 15.2 and *Satires* 2.1.18); *hac arte* of an achievement that confers immortality recalls the same phrase at *Odes* 3.3.9, again at the start of an Alcaic stanza. The idea that the immortal poet ranges the world draws on Horace's own description of his global fame at *Odes* 2.20.13–20 as well as picking up *Aeneid* 8.433 *rotasque uolucris* and Petronius fr.20.3–4 Müller *uolucrique Phoebus axe / rapidum pererret orbem*; but the overall image is the Vergilian one of the chariot of poetry (*Georgics* 2.541–2, 3.17–18). The last line looks back to the depiction of the changing physical universe at 14–16.

2. Hymn on the annunciation of the Blessed Virgin Mary (poem 2)

This poem in the Horatian Third Asclepiad stanza[19] is the second in Chigi's collection, and like the first has no indication of date. Its title indicates that it celebrates the feast of the Annunciation to Mary of the coming birth of Jesus (25 March; cf. Luke 1.26–38); its subtitle states that it uses the allegory of the spring season as representing the grace that the coming of Christ will bring to the world. Its metre is that of a celebrated Horatian poem to another female character very different from Mary, the courtesan Pyrrha of *Odes* 1.5, a link which might suggest implicit Christian correction of pagan vice. Its first two words replicate those of the famous spring ode *Odes* 4.7, and there are many Horatian allusions; odes on religious festivals are also a regular feature of Horatian lyric.[20]

It falls into two sections; the first (1–8) is a straightforward description of spring, while the second (9–24) adds the idea of the *hieros gamos* (see below) and its parallels with the Incarnation of Christ through the union of Mary and the Holy Spirit. Its elaborate and musical style makes much use of Horatian lyric language (see commentary) but also suggests the texture of a Marian hymn (see on 17 and 21–2 below); its content draws on traditional elements of Marian liturgy reflecting the Incarnation and its bringing of peace, such as the medieval Alleluia verse used on the feast of the Annunciation in Eastertide (*Virga Jesse floruit: Virgo Deum et hominem genuit: pacem Deus reddit in se reconcilians ima summis. Alleluia*), but combines these with the Roman poets' version of the Greek *hieros gamos*,[21] the 'sacred marriage' of heaven and earth by which the latter as mother is fertilized by the former as father through rain (see commentary for details). The poem is thus a fascinating blend of pagan and Christian in both expression and subject matter.

Text and translation

IN DIEM ANNUNTIATIONIS B.MARIAE. Perpetua allegoria uernum Gratiae tempus concepti in utero Virginis Dei spiritus sancti opera describit.

Diffugere niues, saeuaque turbinum
Tempestas abiit: composuit pater
   Caeli prouidus iram,
     Nec terram iaculis premit
Vltor, nec glaciem pectoris asperat.   5
Mitescunt Zephyris arua tepentibus,
   Puro gratior orbe
     Affulget roseus dies.
Titan purpureo lumine ditior
Ornatur: niueam uernus amabili   10
   Terram luce maritat
     Hospes sidereae domus.
Caelo regnat Amor: feruet amoribus
Caelum, atque impatiens ad thalamos ruit,
   Sese foedere nuptae   15
     Artans in gremium suae.
Terrae exorta salus: spiritus aurea
Terram pace beat, daedala concipit
   Dia fertilis aura
     Tellus atque uterum grauat.   20
Felix, cui superis uernat Amor rosis,
Cui spirat Zephyrus purior aetheris,
   Cui sese ipse minorem
     Ingens insinuat polus!

On the feast of the Annunciation of the Blessed Virgin Mary. He describes by a continuous allegory the springtime of Grace in the form of God conceived in the womb of the Virgin by the operation of the Holy Spirit.

    The snows have fled and the fierce storm of whirling blasts
Has departed: the provident Father
Has calmed the raging of heaven
And does not oppress the earth with missiles
    As avenger, nor does he sharpen the frost of the heart.
The fields soften under the warm Zephyrs,   5
Over a clear world the day
Shines more attractively in rosy light.
    The Sun is decorated with a crimson glow:
The snow-white earth is fertilised
With lovely light by the springtime
Visitor from the starry abode.   10
    In heaven reigns Love: with loving
Heaven seethes, and runs impatiently to the marriage-chamber,
Binding itself in union
Into the lap of its bride.
    For earth salvation has arisen: the Spirit
Blesses the earth with golden peace,
The creative earth conceives, fertilised   15
By the divine breeze, and burdens its womb.
    Happy the one for whom Love is spring-fresh with the roses
        of heaven,
For whom the zephyr of the aether blows more purely,
Into whom the great firmament
Insinuates itself in lesser form!

Commentary

1–8 The poem's two opening words are also those of Horace's spring ode 4.7, marking the departure of snow (see above). This is combined in lines 1–4 with other Horatian weather-scenarios: the initial *saeua ... tempestas* (1–2) recalls the similarly initial *horrida tempestas* of *Epodes* 13.1, while there are several significant echoes of *Odes* 1.2.1–8. There the divine father (there Jupiter as god of the sky, here God the Father, both named as *pater* in the second line of each poem; for *pater caeli* in a pagan context see Cicero *Poet. fr.*17.12 Courtney) has brought bad weather to an end, and divine climatic missiles are no longer thrown at the earth (1.2.1 *terris*, 1.2.3 *iaculatus* ~ 4 *terram iaculis*); the vengeance of line 5 looks both to the biblical rains and flood of Genesis, inflicted on men for their iniquities (Genesis 6.5–7, 7.12), and to the similarly motivated divine flood described at Ovid *Met.* 1.262–312 and alluded to in *Odes* 1.2.5–12. 5 *glaciem pectoris* picks up an Ovidian simile for fear as a metaphor (*Heroides* 1.22 *frigidius glacie pectus*), while 6 again looks back to Horace's spring ode (4.7.10 *frigora mitescunt Zephyris*) and 7–8 to his ode to Augustus (4.5.6–7 *instar ueris enim uultus ubi tuus / adfulsit populo, gratior it dies*); other classical models here are the description of spring and the *hieros gamos* (see below) at *Georgics* 2.330 *Zephyrique tepentibus auris* and Ovid *Amores* 1.8.10 *puro fulget in orbe dies*; *roseus* suggests a rosy-pink dawn sky (OLD s.v. 2b), anticipates the Marian associations of *rosis* (line 21), and begins a sequence of three colour adjectives vertically juxtaposed in lines 8–10 (*roseus, purpureo, niueam*).

9–24 As noted above, the language here describes the Incarnation of Christ through the pagan idea of the *hieros gamos* or 'sacred marriage', the impregnation of the earth by the sky through rain which leads to its fertility (note the marital terms 11 *maritat*, 13 *amoribus*, 14 *thalamos*, 15 *foedere, nuptae*, 16 *gremium*, 18 *concipit*, 19 *fertilis*, and 20 *uterum grauat*). Both Lucretius and Vergil apply this idea to the coming of spring in passages echoed here: Lucretius 1.250–53 *postremo pereunt imbres, ubi eos pater aether / in gremium matris terrai praecipitauit; / at nitidae surgunt fruges ramique uirescunt / arboribus, crescunt ipsae* *fetuque grauantur* and *Georgics* 3.225–30 (330 is recalled at line 6 above; and *in gremium* (line 16) appears at 3.326 as well as in Lucretius). This idea is given a further Christian colour here, with Mary analogous to the earth and the Holy Spirit to the impregnating heaven. 10 *uellus*, which is the reading printed by all editions, 'fleece', is inappropriate here in both sense and syntax: *maritat* would have two unlinked objects and a fleece does not fit the context.[22] *Vellus* might have been suggested by the nearby *niueam* (cf. *Aeneid* 4.459 *uelleribus niueis*); *uernus*, the excellent suggestion here of John Trappes-Lomax, provides an epithet for *hospes* appropriate for the season. 10–11 *niueam ... terram* symbolically suggests the snow-white complexion of the Virgin (cf. Statius *Silv.* 1.2.244 (of the *virgo* Lavinia) *niueos ... uultus*), while *amabilis* is an Horatian adjective (cf. esp. *Odes* 3.13.10 *frigus amabile*), and *maritat* suggests both the generative power of the sun's spring rays and its analogy in the generative operation of the Holy Spirit in the Incarnation. 12: *sidereae domus* = 'heaven', cf. *Aeneid* 10.3 *sideream ... sedem*; the heavenly visitor (*hospes*) is the sun, returning after the winter, representing the Holy Spirit in the allegory. 13: *caelo regnat Amor* echoes Pontano *Eridanus* 1.1.27 *caelo regnat Venus*. 17–18: note the elegant vertical polyptoton of the balancing nouns for 'heaven' and 'earth' at successive stanza starts. The cosmic nature of Love here suggests a Dante-style symbolic theology: cf. *Paradiso* 33.7–9 (in a Marian context) and the famous last line 33.145 *L'amor che muove il sole e l'altre stelle*. 17: compare a thirteenth-century rhyming hymn to Mary (MQDQ *Anonimo Genovese* 24.104–5 *Et tu, uitae cum sis porta / Per quam salus est exorta*); *aurea* suggests a golden age of peace brought on by the divine birth, an idea found at *Eclogues* 4.8–10 (sometimes taken as a prophecy of the coming of Christ). 18–20 *daedala ... tellus* is a Lucretian phrase, fittingly linked with the generative powers of Venus (1.7, 1.228); for *uterum grauat* cf. Statius *Theb.*2.614 *utero ... grauato*. 21 *felix, cui*: the classical traditional form of the *makarismos* or congratulation of a character on their good fortune (cf. e.g. *Odes* 1.13.17, *Georgics* 2.490); in this context it echoes the greeting of Mary by Elizabeth after the Annunciation (Luke 1.42), *Benedicta tu*. 21–2:

earthly natural features are here seen as experienced by Mary in a heavenly form (*superis, aetheris*), marking the presence of the impregnating Holy Spirit, mirrored in the wind of 22 (for the Spirit as wind see e.g. Acts 2.2). Roses are linked with physical love in pagan poetry (cf. Propertius 3.5.22), but with the pure beauty of the Virgin in Christian discourse (see e.g. MQDQ *Anonimo Genovese* 24.28 *fragrans rosa rubicunda*), two ideas brought together here. 23–4: this conceit that the divine power that rules the vast universe (*ingens … polus*) is contained in the narrow space of Mary's womb is found in earlier Marian poetry, e.g. in a late antique hymn sometimes attributed to Venantius Fortunatus (Walsh and Husch 2012, no. 62, 1–4): *Quem terra pontus aethera / colunt adorant praedicant,/ trinam regentem machinam, / claustrum Mariae baiulat.*

3. Ode to Urban VIII on his election to the papacy, 1623 (poem 7)

This lyric poem celebrates the election of Maffeo Barberini as Pope Urban VIII (6 August 1623). The young Chigi, still studying in Siena, was naturally keen to mark the elevation of a fellow Latin poet to the pontificate, no doubt in hope of patronage from the new pope;[23] in similar vein, the great Polish neo-Latin poet Maciej Kasimierz Sarbiewski wrote a brief Horatian epode proclaiming Urban's papacy as an 'age of honey', punning on the Barberini emblem of bees (*Odes* 3.15).[24] This shared status of Urban and Chigi as poets may underlie the poem's echoing of *Epistles* 1.4, in which Horace addresses the poet Tibullus; Urban's status as the ruler of Rome and its territories is also marked by echoes here of Horatian praise of the emperor Augustus.

Chigi's ode is written in Alcaic stanzas,[25] and is modelled on the encomiastic odes to the imperial family to be found in Horace's *Odes*, especially those addressed to Augustus (see commentary below). There is an implicit analogy here between Augustus as bringer of a new age of peace and morality and the new age of Urban's pontificate; the presentation of the supreme ruler as a cosmic force provides an interesting link with the role of the Holy Spirit in poem 2 (item 2 above), while the final suggestion of the harmony of the universe is consistent with the contemporary views of Kepler (see note on line 52 below).

Text and translation

VRBANO VIII PONT.MAX. CREATO. Similitudine uerni solis excitaturum praedicit semina uirtutum ad messem gloriae in orbe Christiano.

Qualis coruscus temporis arbiter
Bis sena qui per signa uolatilis
   Et noctis horis et diei
      Imparibus regit aequus orbem,
Nimbosa postquam saeuiit impete   5
Late maligno bruma, Aquilonibus
   Exasperans imbres, et urna
      Iliacus gelida recessit,
Emensus auri uellera diuitis,
Tauri pererrans terga potentior   10
   Serenat auras et feracem
      Complet humum grauidatque fetu,
Rident odoris gramina floribus,
Arbos renatis luxuriat comis,
   Aues patrem lucis canoro   15
      Murmure conspicuum salutant:
Sic, ut secundo magnus ab æthere
Illuxit orbi, semina suscitat
   Virtutis VRBANUS benigno
      In segetes animata uultu.   20
Regnans beatis tot superum bonis,
Fecunda dii munera pectoris
   Et seruat et terris redundans
      Diuidit in uacuas cateruas.
Hinc Sanctitas, illinc Pudor et Fides   25
Enata robur promouet insitum et
   Augusta maiestas Latino
      Orbe uiget niueusque candor.
Tranquilla vultu Pax redit aureo:

Fabio Chigi (1599–1667; Pope as Alexander VII 1655–67)

To Urban VIII on his election to the papacy. By means of the comparison of the sun in spring he predicts that Urban will encourage the seeds of virtue towards a harvest of glory in the Christian world.

>Just like the flashing arbiter of time
>Who, flying through the twelve constellations
>Over the unequal hours of both day and night
>Rules the world with equality,
>>After the cloudy winter has raged 5
>
>With its widely malign onset, sharpening
>The showers with north winds, and the Trojan boy
>Has departed with his chilly urn, after
>>Traversing the fleece of rich gold,
>
>Wandering over the hide of the Bull 10
>Calms the breezes with greater power and fills
>The fertile earth and impregnates it with issue,
>>The grass-fields smile with fragrant flowers,
>
>The tree luxuriates in its reborn locks,
>The birds greet the illustrious 15
>Father of light with tuneful noise:
>>Just so does Urban, once he has shone
>
>On the world in his greatness from the favouring heaven,
>Arouse the seeds of virtue, given life
>By his kindly glance over their fields. 20
>>Reigning through so many rich qualities from the gods,
>
>He both preserves the fertile gifts of his divine heart,
>And, overflowing, distributes them to the earth
>For the benefit of its deprived masses.
>>On one side Holiness, on another Modesty and Loyalty 25
>
>Spring up and advance their inborn strength,
>And august majesty flourishes in the Latin world
>And a snow-white purity.
>>Tranquil Peace returns with golden face:

Concors potentem dat Pietas manum, 30
   Vindexque probrorum et salubris
     Iustitiae metuenda praeses
Fraudis repellit nequitiam Themis
Semperque hiantis monstra Cupidinis.
   Quicumque mores imperantis 35
     Ad genium excoluisse gaudet,
Sollers honestum praeferat utili,
Humana temnens: mente adeat Deum,
   Ex quo perobscuris renidet
     Lux animis fugiuntque nubes: 40
Doctusque naturam omnigenam soli
Caelique vires quaeque beatitas
   Manet supernos quaeque cuncta
     Ore Deus retegit benigno,
Mox rebus aequa dextera in arduis 45
Prudens habenas flectat amabiles,
   Quies ut extremis ab usque
     Fluctibus Oceani triumphet.
Sic, prima caelum dum mouet, altera
edocta motu mens trahit aemulo: 50
   Stant ima summis et canoro
     Aura sonat modulata cursu.

Harmonious Piety lends its powerful hand,   30
And Themis, avenger of evil deeds and formidable
Guardian of salutary justice,
   Repels the wickedness of crime
And the monstrosities of ever-gaping Desire.
Whoever joys to shape his character   35
In accordance with the spirit of the ruler,
   Let him skilfully prefer the honourable
To the useful, spurning human things: in his mind
Let him approach God, from whom light shines
On the darkest of souls and clouds flee: 40
   And, instructed on the multiple nature of the earth
And the forces of the heavens, and the felicity
That awaits us above, and all that God
Reveals from his kindly mouth,
   Soon, with balanced hand in difficult times,   45
Let him wisely wield the reins of love
So that peace may triumph
From the furthest waves of the Atlantic.
   Just so, as the first mind moves the heaven,
The second, thus instructed, drags it with imitating motion: 50
The lowest stands with the highest, and the air
Resounds, playing music with its singing course.

Commentary

1–16 The ode begins with a long four-stanza simile, comparing the newly elected Urban to the sun returning to the earth in spring: this formal feature echoes the opening of Horace *Odes* 4.4 (1–16), where the young prince Drusus is compared to an eagle or a lion, matching it in metre, length and opening adjective introducing a comparison (1 *Qualis*, 4.4.1 *Qualem*): the comparison of the sovereign to the sun and the idea that he brings peace and fertility to the countryside are also features from Horace's encomiastic fourth book of *Odes* – cf. *Odes* 4.2.46–7 (sun), 4.5.5–32 (peace and fertility), both referring to Augustus, an apt parallel for the new pope as ruler of Rome. Line 2 picks up Manilius 1.309 *bis sena . . . nitentia signa* (similarly referring to the twelve astronomical signs), line 4 another Horatian description of Augustus in *Odes* 1 (1.12.57 *te minor latum reget aequus orbem*), *impete* in line 5 is an archaic form of *impetu* favoured by Lucretius (13×), the combination *nimbosa . . . bruma* (5–6) is from Statius (*Silvae* 1.3.89) while the adverb *late* qualifying an adjective (6) is Horatian (*Odes* 3.16.19 *late conspicuum*). *Iliacus* (8) refers to the Trojan prince Ganymede, seen as the mythological origin of the astronomical sign of Aquarius (the water-carrier) as at Hyginus *Astronomica* 2.16.1 (the urn is chilly since Aquarius is a winter sign), while line 9 refers to the sign of Aries (the ram), commonly identified with the ram of the mythological Golden Fleece (Hyginus *Astronomica* 2.20.1). 9 *auri uellera* provides a balance in sound, sense and phrasal shape with the matching poetic plural 10 *tauri terga* (for the phrase see Catullus 63.10 *terga tauri*) – note also the alternating alliteration here *Tauri pererrans terga potentior*; for 11 *serenat auras* see *Aeneid* 1.255 *tempestatesque serenat*, and for the anthropomorphic smile of line 13 cf. Catullus 64.284 *domus iucundo risit odore* and *Eclogues* 4.20 *ridenti . . . acantho*. For the leaves of a tree as its hair (13) cf. *Odes* 4.7.1–2 *redeunt iam gramina campis / arboribusque comae*, another spring context (*redeunt* also underlies *renatis*); *patrem lucis* (15) recalls Gellius' etymology of Jupiter as *lucis pater* (5.12.16), though the reference here is clearly to the sun as the source of light (cf. Statius *Achilleid* 2.2–3 *genitorque coruscae /lucis*).

17-34 Urban's beneficial spiritual impact on humanity, the comparandum of the opening simile, is lavishly celebrated in the poem's central section. It uses the same imagery of fertility and abundance, but now in a metaphorical sense (*semina, segetes, fecunda, redundans, enata* and *uiget*); *illuxit* once again compares him to the sun. All this looks back to Horace's praise of Augustus as the sun in spring in *Odes* 4.5 (see above), especially 4.5.5-8: *Lucem redde tuae, dux bone, patriae; / instar ueris enim uultus ubi tuus / adfulsit populo, gratior it dies / et soles melius nitent.* 17 *secundo . . . aethere* suggests divine approval of Urban's election, 19-20 *benigno . . . uultu* his own quasi-divine benevolence (cf. similarly *dii . . . pectoris* below); note the vertical juxtaposition of noun and adjective here, and for the *benignitas* of the gods see *Odes* 3.29.52, 4.2.52, 4.4.74 and line 44 below). 21 *regnans* points to the supreme power of the pontificate; *superum* suggests an interestingly pagan plurality of gods, and recalls such compliments as *Epistles* 1.4.5-6 (to Tibullus) *di tibi formam, / di tibi diuitias dederunt artemque fruendi* (similarly from one poet to another). 22 *dii . . . pectoris* draws doubly on Lucretius, recalling his evocation of his fellow poet (again) Empedocles at 1.731 *divini pectoris* and his use of the archaic adjective *dius* (2.172 *dia uoluptas*), while 23-4 suggest benevolent distribution of spiritual gifts to the needy. 25: the personified abstracts here (as in line 29-34) recall Horace's use of similar lists in the *Odes*, especially 1.24.6-7 (*cui Pudor et Iustitiae soror, / incorrupta Fides, nudaque Veritas*; cf. also 1.2.34 *quam Iocus circum volat et Cupido*). Line 26 recalls *Odes* 4.4.33 *vim promovet insitam*, while 27 *Augusta maiestas* reminds the reader of the parallels between Chigi's praise of Urban and Horace's praise of Augustus (see above), 27-8 *Latino . . . orbe* points similarly to the continuity between Augustus' rule of the Roman world and Urban's role as head of the Roman church and its lands, and 28 *niueusque* plays on the literal sense of *candor* (whiteness) as well as its figurative sense (moral purity). The return of Peace (29) is a theme drawn from Horace's *Carmen Saeculare* (57-9 *iam Fides et Pax et Honos Pudorque / priscus et neglecta redire Virtus / audet*, an analogous list of personifications); her epithet *tranquilla* looks back to Lucan 1.171 *pax tranquilla*. Peace's golden face suggests a Golden Age, associated with Augustus by Vergil (*Aeneid* 6.792-3), and the list of moral benefits of Urban's election (29–34) recalls those ascribed to the principate of Augustus in *Odes* 4.5 (17–28) and the *Carmen Saeculare* (53–60) as well as Horatian lyric lists of abstract deities (see above, especially for *Cupido*): in line 30 *manum potentem* picks up *Carmen Saeculare* 53 *manus potentes*, while the pairing *concors Pietas* comes from the pseudo-Ovidian *Consolatio Ad Liviam* (84 *concors pietas*). 31 *uindexque probrorum* recalls another encomiastic Horatian ode (4.9.37 *uindex auarae fraudis*), 31–2 *salubris / iustitiae* imitates both the phrase and its enjambement at *Ars Poetica* 198–9 *salubrem / iustitiam*, while the image of ever-gaping desire recalls Cicero (*In Verrem* 2.134 *auaritia semper hiante*), and *monstra* suggests the mythical monsters symbolically associated with low desires by Plato (*Republic* 588c).

35–52 The poem's final section points to the specific lessons that humanity can learn from Urban's example. It opens with strongly Horatian language: for the moralizing and generalizing *quicumque* (35) cf. *Odes* 3.14.25–6 o *quisquis volet inpias / caedis et rabiem tollere ciuicam*, for line 36 cf. *Odes* 1.34.16 *hic posuisse gaudet* (in the same metrical position) and for line 37 cf. *Odes* 4.9.41 *honestum praetulit utili* (in the same metrical position). The imagery of sunlight in lines 39–40 looks back to the poem's earlier sun comparisons, suggesting an analogy between the illumination offered by God and that offered by Urban as his divinely inspired representative; *Deum* is no doubt Christian here, though Horace can use *deus* quasi-monotheistically of divine power (cf. *Odes* 1.3.21, 1.34.13, 3.16.43, 3.29.30, and note that *superum* at line 21 above is polytheistic). In line 39 *perobscuris renidet* is a neat juxtaposition of opposite ideas, while in line 40 *fugiuntque nubes* exactly echoes the same phrase at *Odes* 1.12.30. The reference in lines 41–4 to proper knowledge of the universe reflects Urban's interest in maintaining orthodox views of astronomy (see the Introduction to this volume); the poem urges its readers to follow the new pope's doctrine in this controversial area. 41 *omnigenam* (like 22 *dii*) picks up an archaizing adjective from Lucretius (5.440), while 42 *caelique uires* echoes *Aeneid* 7.301 *uires caelique marisque*, and *Beatitas* (though a Ciceronian word) looks to Christian ideas of eternal felicity; for *manet* of a fate awaiting all after death cf. *Odes* 1.28.15 *omnis una manet nox*. For the divine benevolence of *ore* . . . *benigno* (44), also a feature of the quasi-divine Urban, see on line 17 above. Line 45 recalls *Odes* 2.3.1 *aequam memento rebus in arduis*, while *habenas flectat* (46) recalls the out-of-control Phaethon at Ovid *Met*.2.169 *flectat habenas*; the suggestion is that the Christian who takes due notice of the new pope will do better than his doomed pagan counterpart (who disobeyed the Sun's instructions). *amabiles* (46) points to Christian love as a force for peace, while *quies* (47) is paradoxically the subject of the military *triumphet* (48); here as in Horace the stormy Atlantic is seen as a far-distant boundary of civilization (cf. *Odes* 1.35.32, 4.14.48). Lines 49–50 refer to the Aristotelian doctrine in the *Metaphysics* (Book 12.7) that the first mover in the universe is the mind of God; this had been emphasized in the Catholic tradition by Thomas Aquinas. The point is that Urban is like the divine first mover, whose initiatives can be followed by his subordinates in the pursuit of world harmony. 51 *stant ima summis* similarly combines pagan and Christian theology: in Horace divine power can exchange the top for the bottom (*Odes* 1.34.12–13 *valet ima summis / mutare . . . deus*), while a medieval liturgical text (*Virga Jesse floruit*) suggests that God brought about peace in the form of the Incarnation by combining the highest divinity with humble mortality in the form of Christ (*pacem Deus reddidit, / in se reconcilians ima summis*). The poem's last line perhaps evokes the classical idea of the harmony of the cosmos (*musica universalis*), recently reasserted by Kepler in his *Harmonices Mundi* (1619), which argued for a divine creator and for musical harmony as a central force in the universe.

4. Hexameter poem recounting a journey from Rome to Ferrara, 1629 (poem 11)

This lengthy poem (91 lines) is the first of a series of substantial hexameter works[26] chronicling Chigi's journeys in the papal service (see introductory section above), in this case from Rome to Ferrara, where

Chigi had been papal legate since 1627 (see the Introduction to this volume). The subtitle claims it to be a travelling diary kept at the time,[27] though it seems likely that it was revised later. In metre, length, topic and expression it draws on Horace *Satires* 1.5, the poet's account of a journey from Rome to Brindisi in 104 hexameters, also a real trip taken in the context of political service (in Horace's case, accompanying his patron Maecenas and others on a diplomatic mission from the young Caesar in Rome to Mark Antony, probably in 37 BCE).[28] Horace's journey heads south from the great city while Chigi's goes north, but both poems give a humorous travelogue which describes the places visited en route and refer to the details and discomforts of pre-modern travel; Chigi's text has more about meals and their quality (6, 13, 21, 25, 33, 74, 87–8). Chigi's poem reports no direct speech, while Horace's presents the words of boatmen (12–13) and the major set piece of the comic verbal duel of Sarmentus and Messius (51–70).

As in Horace's poem, the role of friends on the journey is emphasized: both narrators travel with friends, meet other friends on the road, and stay at houses provided by friends as well as at inns. Horace names all his contacts, which include the distinguished diplomats Maecenas and Cocceius, but Chigi does not, providing inviting hints: the grand friend with a carriage who sees him off from Prima Porta (3) is no doubt meant to be imagined as a major clerical figure, while it is an unnamed (but identifiable) absent bishop who provides accommodation at Faenza (80–1). Both poets thus point to their high-level social contacts.

Both journeys use major Roman roads: Horace's route followed the via Appia from the city (*Satires* 1.5.6), while Chigi's follows the via Flaminia much of the way to Rimini on the Adriatic coast, and then a little of the via Aemilia to Cesena and Forli before finally turning north to Ferrara. Both use short-distance water travel as well as long-distance roads: Horace is carried by a boat on the canal across the Pomptine marshes (*Satires* 1.5.11–22), while Chigi crosses rivers on rafts (84–5). The two proceed at much the same pace though more than sixteen centuries apart: Horace's trip to Brindisi (some 540 kilometres) takes about fifteen days in his narrative (36 kilometres/day), while Chigi's to Ferrara (some

420 kilometres) takes about thirteen days in his (32 kilometres/day), unsurprising as modes of transport (horse-drawn vehicles) were still much the same.

Chigi's poem naturally uses Latin place names like Horace's, but it also imitates the Roman poet's indirect namings of locations: both allude jokingly to place names which cannot be fitted into the hexameter metre (*Satires* 1.5.87, cf. lines 19–20 below), and both present elaborate periphrases from which the reader can derive a relatively familiar place name (*Satires* 1.5.37, cf. lines 13–14 and 66 below).

A non-Horatian element is the respectful emphasis on Christian sanctuaries and worship, unsurprising in a poem by a high-ranking cleric, though in general the poem uses the pagan 'god for thing' metonymy (*Phoebus* = the sun, *Lyaeus* = wine) familiar from classical Latin poetry and normal in neo-Latin. Visiting churches is a regular feature: Chigi and his companions attend a church service early on at Borghetto (12–13), and there are descriptions of the miracles associated with the Basilica di San Nicola at Tolentino (36–8) and the celebrated sanctuary of the Santa Casa at Loreto (41–8), two major pilgrimage sites on the route; the poet's professed belief in these wonders is a pointed correction to Horace's scepticism in a similar case (see 35–48n.). This pair of religious digressive descriptions is nicely balanced by the two lighter animal anecdotes of lines 50–8, the falling mule and the accompanying prophetic dolphin.

Much of the territory of the Marche covered in the main part of the journey, east of the Apennines (32–91), belonged to the Duchy of Urbino, which had recently (1626) been incorporated into the papal territories following the abdication of the last della Rovere ruler. This can be seen partly as a celebration of that major acquisition (the last major expansion of the Papal States) by a loyal papal servant, just as lines 80–1 compliment the pope's recent promotion of his brother to the role of Grand Inquisitor (see commentary). Chigi's poem is an attractive travelogue with entertaining detail and narrative; but it is also a skilful and learned reworking of its Horatian model for an alert contemporary readership.

Text and translation

ITER ROMA FERRARIAM anno MDCXXIX in pugillaribus quolibet die, ut agebatur, plumbo adnotatum, obstetricantibus poemati (ut auctor dicere solitus) non aliis Musis quam nautis, stabulariis, cauponibus.

Libra ter Autumno Phoebi cum luce niteret,
Egressus Roma Primae quod nomine Portae
Dicitur hospitio, eximii comitantis amici
Officia et raedam linquo gratoque sodali
Adiunctus uector lectica moenia Castri 5
Vsque Noui: hic parcus uix prandia contulit hospes,
Et Castellanam noctu peruenimus urbem,
Improba ubi culicum legio torrentis et ingens
Inde fragor tenuem lassis fecere soporem.
Aufugimus primos nebula condente nitores: 10
Quattuor emensi postquam iam milia sacris
Adsumus ad tenuem Borghetti pauperis aram.
Tum mensa excipimur, celsam qua nominat urbem
Sulphureis Nar albus aquis. hic plurimus imber
Nos tenet in noctem: ueterum simulacra uirorum 15
Inspicimus, circa famosum picta lacunar,
Narnia quos genuit. molli requiescere lecto
Iuuit et aurora campos surgente uidere,
Vitiferasque ulmos, et quae mihi dicere uersu
Difficile est, amnes inter sita moenia. Posthaec 20
Sexta nos reficit Stricturae caupo benignus:
Summaque transgressi fastigia, nona priusquam
Hora diem ferret, Spoletum venimus: illic
Aedibus inspectis diuorum, munera cenæ
Accipimus, uinum testa fundente niuali. 25

Fabio Chigi (1599–1667; Pope as Alexander VII 1655–67)

A journey from Rome to Ferrara, 1629, noted down in pencil on writing tablets on the various days of its action, with no other Muses as midwives for the poem (as an author commonly says) than boatmen, ostlers and inn-keepers.

When in Autumn Libra was shining out for the third time
   with the light of the sun,
Departing from Rome, from the guest-house which is called
   by the name
Of Prima Porta, I leave behind the kind attentions of an
   illustrious associate
And his carriage, and in company with a dear friend
I am carried in a waggon as far as Castrum Novum;   5
Here a stingy host barely provided a meal,
And we came through to the city of Castellana by night,
Where an evil legion of mosquitos and then the mighty crashing
Of a rushing stream provided slim sleep for the tired.
We escaped as mist hid the sun's first rays: 10
After covering four miles we are present for the sacred rites
At the mean altar of the poor Borghetto.
Then we are welcomed by a meal, where the white Nar
With its sulphurous waters names a lofty city; here a strong shower
Keeps us until night: we gaze at the representations   15
Of men of old that Narni has produced, depicted all over
A celebrated ceiling: it was a pleasure to rest in a soft bed
And to see as dawn arose the fields and wine-bearing elms,
And the walls that it is difficult for me to say
In poetry, sited between the rivers. After this   20
At the sixth hour a kindly innkeeper refreshed us at Strettura:
And having crossed some lofty peaks before the ninth hour
Brought the daylight, we came to Spoleto: there
After inspecting the house of the saints, we received
The gift of dinner, with a snow-cool jar pouring our wine.   25

Fulginiam mane hinc egressi ad tecta maligni
Hospitis appulimus, qui turpi et paupere mensa
Extorsit nummos. Apenninum inde subimus,
Posthabitis Vmbris, clausa qua ualle fluentum
Fertur in Adriacum, cursu mox ditius, aequor, 30
Ac laterum obiectu montis uix cernit auari
Sidera pauca poli. Ad sonitum requieuimus undae
Post molles epulas: transiuimus inde Cluentum,
Liquimus et Vissi montes collesque Camertum.
Picenum ingressos nona nos excipit hora 35
Vrbs Tolentini: celebrem hic ueneramur ad aram
Post tot lustra sacro manantia sanguine diui
Ossa uiri, humanis praesagia certa periclis.
Tum Maceratae complexus lux postera amici
Restituit ueteris dapibusque et fronte benigna, 40
Lauretumque dedit luna spectare nitente:
Cara Deo sedes, mortales cum induit artus,
Et matri dilecta domus, quae barbara quondam
Regna Palestinae fugit regionis et agris
Institit Illyricis, caelestum et uecta per auras 45
Remigio alituum Piceni colle resedit.
Hic puri sceleris diuino et pane refecti,
Excolimus Diuam et iam quarta exsoluimus hora
Auspiciis faustis Anconae ad litora cursum.
Namque pede extremo labens de ponte ruensque 50
Mulus lecticae casum nobisque parabat
Funera: continuo egredimur cum concidit undis,
Et rediit rursus uectandi ad munera sospes.

Early next day we left there and put in at the house
Of a mean host at Foligno, who extorted our money for a foul
And poor meal. Then we approached the Apennine massif,
Leaving Umbria behind us, by the enclosed valley in which
A flowing stream, now richer in its course, rushes to the Adriatic,   30
And can barely see the few stars of the ungenerous sky
For a barrier of mountainsides. We rested by the sound of the water
After an agreeable supper: then we crossed the Chienti,
And left behind us the mountains of Visso and the hills of Camerino.
Entering Picenum, the city of Tolentino received us at the ninth hour: 35
Here we worshipped at the famous altar the bones of the saint
Which still after so many years drip with sacred blood,
Sure predictors in time of human peril.
Then the next day at Macerata brought back to us the embrace
Of an old friend with feasting and friendly brow,   40
And allowed us to see Loreto as the moon shone:
A home dear to God, when he put on mortal limbs,
And a house beloved of his Mother, which long ago
Fled the barbarian kingdom of the region of Palestine
And stopped in the lands of Illyria, and borne through the air   45
By the rowing of the wings of celestial flyers, settled on a hill in Picenum.
Here free from sin and refreshed by divine bread,
We worshipped the holy lady, and already at the fourth hour
We completed our course to the shores of Ancona with good omens.
For a mule, wobbling on its back leg and slipping and falling   50
From a bridge, was about to cause a crash to our conveyance and death
To us, but we alighted at the very moment it fell in the water,
And it returned safe once more to its duties of carriage.

Pone sequens tum delphinus, dum fluctuat aequor,
Sponte sua, nullis uexantibus aëra uentis, 55
Dat comitem sese et curuo nunc Nerea dorso
Stat super et nunc illudens immergitur undis.
Praedixit uero nimbos delphinus et aestum:
Nam simul Aesino transmisso ponte tabernam
Ad litus positam (Ambustam dixere coloni) 60
Attigimus, taetra tempestas nocte profundum
Turbauit, caenoque uias corrupit et imbri.
Sed Phoebo nascente dies redit ore sereno,
Ac tuto spectare datur uicina frementis
Litora Neptuni, spumantibus acta procellis, 65
Ac Senonum dictos Gallorum nomine muros,
Et detestatum Poenis transire Metaurum,
Sublicio longoque recens a ponte subactum,
Nec non Fortunae Fanum, noctemque Pisauri
Sedibus exigere et tabulis insignia templa, 70
Roboreumque decus magni spectare palati.
Picenum exiguo pontis coniunximus arcu
Dehinc et Flaminiam properamus Arimini ad urbem
Pransuri, et membris dulcem indulsere soporem
Arua Sabignani, felici culta Lyaeo. 75
Tum praetergressi Caesenam Pompiliique
Tecta Forum Liui deuenimus: hic, ubi amici
Plausibus excipiunt gratis et diuite mensa,
Nos mora grata iuuat, paruaque Fauentia nocte
Praesulis hospitium praestat, quem purpura Senis 80
Abstulit illustrem meritis: tum, sole tenente
Vix medium caeli, stetimus, dum pabula mulis

Then a dolphin, following behind as the sea seethed
Of its own accord, without winds stirring the air, 55
Made itself our companion and now stood above the sea
With its curved back, now dived playfully into the waves.
But the dolphin predicted clouds and a swell:
For as soon as we had crossed the bridge over the Aesis
And reached the inn located on the shore (the inhabitants 60
call it Ambusta), a filthy storm stirred up the deep at night,
And made the roads rotten with mud and rain.
But as Phoebus rose day returned with unclouded face,
And it was granted us safely to see the nearby shores
Of seething Neptune, beaten by foaming gales, 65
And the walls of the Senones called with a Gallic name,
And to pass by the Metaurus so hated by the Carthaginians,
Recently mastered by a long bridge of wooden piles,
And the Shrine of Fortune, and spend the night in lodgings
    at Pesaro,
and gaze on the churches remarkable for paintings 70
And the oak-panelled glory of the great palace.
From there we connected with Picenum over the arch of a
    small bridge
And hurried to the city of Flaminian Rimini
To dine: and our limbs were given the pleasure of sweet sleep
By the territory of Savignano, planted with fertile wine. 75
Then, going past Cesena and the houses of Pompilium,
We came to Forlì: here, where friends receive us
With pleasant clapping and rich dining,
The stay was pleasing and delightful, and over a short night
Faventia provided the guest-house of the bishop, whom
    the purple 80
Had taken away from Senigallia, famed for his merits: then,
    when the sun
Was barely in mid-heaven, we stopped at the settlement by quiet
    Sancternum

Sufficerent uires, Sancterni ad tecta quieti.
Hunc rate transnamus parua celerique fluentem
Eridanum cursu superamus, et ultima Phoebi   85
Linea cum flamma tenui uix spargeret orbem,
Argentae gratis epulis mollique sopore
Perfruimur noctu et lauti data copia piscis.
Mane hinc dum nebulis uicinas inficit auras
Flumen, ad octauam accepit Ferraria tandem   90
Incolumes, placidam lassis factura quietem.

Until fodder should give sufficient strength to the mules.
That river we crossed on a small raft, and traversed the Po,
Flowing with swift current, and as the last ray of sun 85
Was barely scattering the world with its thin flame,
At Argenta we enjoyed a welcome feast and soft sleep
At night, and we were given an abundance of rich fish.
From there next morning, as the river spread
The nearby air with mist, Ferrara received us safe at the eighth hour, 90
Destined to bring peaceful rest to the tired.

Commentary

1-9 The first day of travel, from north of Rome to Civita Castellana (45 kilometres). The opening line refers to 25 September, the third day after the autumnal equinox (for Libra used poetically for the time of equinox cf. *Georgics* 1.208); poem 74 (item 8 below) also opens with an astronomical date. Lines 2-3 recall the opening of Horace's *Satires* 1.5 (1 <u>Egressum</u> *magna me accepit Aricia* <u>Roma</u> /<u>hospitio</u> *modico; rhetor* <u>comes</u> *Heliodorus*); Prima Porta was a settlement on the Via Flaminia some 10 kilometres north of early modern Rome (it is now part of the city, just outside the modern Grande Raccordo Annulare), while *eximii . . . amici* suggests a friend of high rank (see above), contrasting with the more intimate *sodali* (4). 5 *lectica*: in classical Latin this usually indicates a litter carried by slaves, but here it is clearly a more long-distance vehicle drawn by mules (cf. lines 51 and 83 below). 5–6 Castrum Novum is the usual ancient name for the port of Civitavecchia in Lazio, but here designates a town on the Via Flaminia between Rome and Civita Castellana (the *urbs Castellana* of line 7), perhaps Fiano Romano with its Orsini castle of 1489; the *parcus . . . hospes* here (6) recalls the *cauponibus . . . malignis* of *Satires* 1.5.4 and is the opposite of the *sedulus hospes* of *Satires* 1.5.71. For the complaint about mosquitoes and insomnia (8: *legio* nicely expresses the insects' quasi-military aggression) see *Satires* 1.5.14–15 *mali culices ranaeque palustres / auertunt somnos*; the noisy stream here might be the modern Treja, a tributary of the Tiber.

10-17 The second day, from Civita Castellana to Narni (33 kilometres). Borghetto must be a minor stop on the way to Narni with a small church; *sacris adesse* is a classical phrase for attending the worship of a god (Seneca *Medea* 770). The high-style periphrasis for Narni in lines 13–14 recalls the elaborate description of Canusium at *Satires* 1.5.92 *qui locus a forti Diomede est conditus olim*; 14 echoes *Aeneid* 7.517 *sulphurea Nar albus aqua* and *Eclogues* 7.60 **plurimus imbri* (this is the modern river Nera). The images of ancient heroes at Narni (15 echoes Ovid *Fasti* 5.621 *priscorum . . . *simulacra uirorum*) are the frescoes of local worthies (including the Emperor Nerva) once visible in the council chamber of the Palazzo del Podestà.[29]

18–25 The third day, from Narni to Spoleto (45 kilometres). 19 *uitiferasque ulmos* points to the continuation of the Roman agricultural technique of using elm trees to support vines (*Eclogues* 2.70, *Georgics* 1.2), while 19–20 echoes *Satires* 1.5.87 *oppidulo quod uersu dicere non est* in suggesting a place-name which does not fit into the hexameter metre (here revealed in the next line as ancient Interamna = modern Terni; the identity of Horace's place is still debated).[30] The small hill-town of Strettura (21) stands roughly at the half-way point of this stage as the road rises to Spoleto from Narni; its *caupo benignus* (21) neatly inverts Horace's *cauponibus ... malignis* on the via Appia (*Satires* 1.5.4). 22–3 the hour-indication here (cf. also 48 and 90) is an element also found in Horace's poem (*Satires* 1.5.23). 24 *aedibus ... diuorum* describes the various churches in Spoleto dedicated to different saints (*diui*), while 25 *testa ... niuali* seems to refer to (refreshing) wine from the cooled amphorae of Spoleto's rocky cellars.

26–34 The fourth and fifth days, probably a slow mountainous stage from Spoleto to Foligno (31 kilometres), with mid-day stop, then a night on the road between Foligno and Tolentino (another 70 kilometres further), moving along the valley of the river Chienti (with high mountains on both sides and a restricted view of the sky and stars at night (31–2); note the striking personification of *auari*). 26–7 *maligni / hospitis* recalls *Satires* 1.5.4 *cauponibus ... malignis*, 27 *paupere mensa* the same phrase at *Tibullus 1.1.37, while 29 *clausa ... ualle* puns on the local name Serravalle di Chienti. In 31 for *laterum obiectu* cf. *Aeneid* 1.160 *obiectu laterum*, for 32 *sidera pauca poli* cf. Lucan 5.424 **sidera prima poli*. Visso is the main town of the Monti Sibillini some 10 kilometres south of the road, while Camerino is a hill-town a few kilometres north of it. In 33–4 note how the alliterating, rhyming and prosodically identical topographical names *Cluentum* and *Camertum* stand in elegant vertical juxtaposition at consecutive line-ends, an Horatian technique (see note on item 7 lines 9–14 below).

35–48 The sixth day, spent at Tolentino and the seventh, travelling on to Macerata (26 kilometres) and Loreto (another 20 kilometres). This section is one of pilgrimage: the party stops at Tolentino to visit the relics of the thirteenth-century saint Nicola di Tolentino, whose corpse was supposed to bleed miraculously and prophetically long after his death and who is honoured in a fine fourteenth-century painted chapel in the Basilica di S. Nicola, and at Loreto to visit the great Marian sanctuary of the Basilica della Santa Casa, home of the so-called childhood house of Jesus traditionally carried there from Palestine by angels. The poet's professed pious belief in these Christian miracles is a pointed correction to Horace's Epicurean scepticism about the miraculous liquefying of incense at a temple near Bari (*Satires* 1.5.97–103). In 35 *Picenum* is the Roman name for the modern Marche region; for 37 *manantia sanguine/ossa* cf. Livy 40.39.9 *manantia sanguine spolia*, and for 39 *lux postera* cf. Valerius Flaccus 2.664 **lux postera*. 42 echoes both *Eclogues* 4.49* *cara deum suboles* and Statius *Ach.* 1.262 **induit artus*. 43–4 *barbara / regna*: the supposed house of Jesus, genuinely from Nazareth but probably later in origin, was shipped to Loreto via Dalmatia after the final Muslim occupation of Palestine in 1294 and formed the core of a great pilgrim sanctuary. The legend that it was carried there by angels (45–6) seems to reflect the role of the Angeli family in its move to Italy as part of a dowry.[31] 46 *remigio alituum* echoes *Aeneid* 1.301 **remigio alarum*, the common classical metaphor of flying as aerial rowing. 47 *puri sceleris* Christianizes Horace's *sceleris . . . purus* (*Odes* 1.22.1), pointing to the normal confession before communion.

48–62 The eighth day, first from Loreto to Ancona (30 kilometres) and then north along the coast towards Rimini, ending at an inn where the coastal road crosses the river Esino (cf. 59) close to the fortress of Rocca Priora (another 15 kilometres). 48 echoes the only hour-reference in Horace's journey, *Satires* 1.5.23 *quarta . . . exponimur *hora* (see the introductory section above), while the story of a mule impacting the journey (50–3) recalls *Satires* 1.5.17–23, and the consequent near-disaster the kitchen fire of *Satires* 1.5.71–5; 51–2 *nobisque parabat / funera* makes comically bathetic use of Horace's elevated phrase at *Odes* 1.37.8 *funus et imperio parabat* (of Cleopatra); the comic exaggeration of *funera* here is marked by the single-word enjambment. The dolphin anecdote of lines 54–8 is realistic, but also generally reminiscent of the Roman 'friendly dolphin' stories of Pliny *Ep.* 9.33, Gellius 6.8 and Gellius 16.19; at 54 *pone sequens* wittily echoes *pone sequens of the sea-goddess Cymodocea at *Aeneid* 10.226, while at 57 *immergitur undis* picks up *mergitur undis at Lucan 8.174. The parenthesis in 60 echoes *Aeneid* 1.12 (*Tyrii tenuere coloni*); 61 *taetra tempestas nocte* recalls Lucretius 4.172 *taetra nimborum nocte*; note the forceful alliteration matching the sense, continued by 62 *turbauit* and (with another letter) in 63 *caenoque . . . corrupit*.

63–71 The ninth day, from the Esino to Pesaro. This is a very long stage of 65 kilometres, but the flat coastal road may have enabled rapid progress here (the route picks up the via Flaminia again between Fano and Rimini, 73). 63 echoes Lucan 3.231 *nascenti . . . Phoebo* and Statius *Theb.* 11.459 *ore sereno, while the sight of the raging sea from the safety of the shore (64–5) evokes the famous opening of Lucretius Book 2 (1–2) *Suave, mari magno turbantibus aequora uentis / e terra magnum alterius spectare laborem*, and the end of 65 echoes Silius 3.228 *acta procellis*. 66 like lines 13–14 paraphrase a place name, Sena Gallica (modern Senigallia, half-way between Ancona and Pesaro), while the river Metaurus, site of a key victory of Rome over Carthage in the Second Punic War (207 BCE) in which Hannibal's brother Hasdrubal was killed (cf. Livy 27.46-9), enters the sea 14 kilometres south of Pesaro; for *detestatum Poenis* cf. *Odes* 1.1.24–5 *bellaque matribus / detestata*. 69 *Fortunae Fanum* is the Roman name for the city of Fano, 12 kilometres south of Pesaro, which had an ancient temple of Fortune (Pliny *Nat.* 3.113). 70–1 refer to paintings in the various churches in Pesaro (e.g. the cathedral of Santa Maria Assunta and Sant'Agostino) and to the magnificent coffered ceiling of the Salone Metaurense of its Palazzo Ducale, constructed by the last della Rovere ruler in 1616 (*roboreum* puns on their name = 'of the oak-tree' as well as indicating material).[32]

72–81 The tenth and eleventh days, from Pesaro to Savignano (50 kilometres) then to Faenza (another 50 kilometres), on the via Flaminia until Rimini, then turning further inland on the via Aemilia to Faenza. 72 *Flaminiam*: Rimini (Ariminium) was well known as the end-point of the via Flaminia (e.g. Livy 39.2.10). 74 – cf. Juvenal 13.217–18 *nocte breuem si forte indulsit cura soporem /et toto uersata toro iam membra quiescunt*, Epodes 5.56 *dulci sopore*. The places named in 75–6 are all stations on the via Aemilia going north-west: Savignano (16 kilometres from Rimini), Cesena (35 kilometres) Forlimpopoli (42 kilometres) and Forlì (50 kilometres); from Forlì to Faenza ia another 15 kilometres. 80 *praesulis hospitium* is the Palazzo Vescovile at Faenza, now the home of the Museo diocesano d'arte sacra; 80–1 are a subtle compliment to Urban VIII's brother Cardinal Antonio Marcello Barberini (1569–1646), bishop of Senigallia 1625–8, who had been recently appointed as Grand Inquisitor at Rome.

81–91 The twelfth and thirteenth days, from Faenza to Ferrara, with a mid-day stop at Imola (16 kilometres) by the river Sancternus (modern Santerno), turning north off the Via Aemilia to Argenta, the last overnight stop (44 kilometres), followed by a last stage to Ferrara (another 33 kilometres). The Eridanus here is not the river Po proper (as usually in Latin) but its tributary the Reno, crossed by the Ferrara road in the broad Po valley a few kilometres south of Argenta. The time indications of 81–2 and 85–6 are in the grand Vergilian epic style (cf. *Aeneid* 8.97 *sol medium caeli conscenderat igneus orbem*, 9.459–60 *Et iam prima nouo spargebat lumine terras/* . . . *Aurora*); this is also a feature of *Satires* 1.5 (cf. 1.5.9–10 *iam nox inducere terris /umbras et caelo diffundere signa parabat*). 88 *copia piscis* is also in Vergilian high style (cf. *Georgics* 3.308 *largi copia lactis*), while the personification of *accepit Ferraria* (90) neatly echoes the start of Horace's poem at the end of Chigi's (cf. *Satires* 1.5.1 *me accepit Aricia*), stressing its key model status. Likewise, 91 *quietem* wittily provides a word of rest at the moment that the poem stops, a piece of self-conscious poetic closure echoing that at the end of *Satires* 1.5 (104 *Brundisium longae finis chartaeque uiaeque est*[33]) and resembling the use of the closural *exitus* as the last word of the *Epodes* (17.81).

5. Ode on the capture of La Rochelle, 1628 (poem 18)

This Horatian ode in twenty Alcaic stanzas[34] celebrates the capture by Louis XIII's forces of La Rochelle, the Huguenot Protestant stronghold on the French Atlantic coast, in October 1628, after a siege of more than a year in which Cardinal Richelieu, Louis XIII's chief minister, had taken personal command. The poem stresses the triumph of the Catholic cause in France, and the advisory role in France of Cardinal Francesco Barberini, nephew of Urban VIII and his chief diplomat;[35] this is natural given Chigi's then position in Urban's service as papal legate in Ferrara. It is appropriately addressed to Cassiano dal Pozzo (1588-1657), chamberlain to Urban and a scholar, connoisseur and collector who had accompanied Francesco Barberini on his mission to France.[36]

This ode follows Barberini's ode on the capture of Antwerp (analysed above in this volume) in celebrating a triumph for European Catholicism through the medium of an encomiastic Horatian ode. It echoes the victory poems of *Odes* 4 and Horace's celebration of the Battle of Actium (1.37, imitated at lines 1 and 31); it also echoes Tibullus' poem for the triumph of his patron Messalla for his victories in Aquitaine (1.7), fittingly since La Rochelle is in roughly the same region of France. In overall form it is part of a tradition of neo-Latin Horatianizing victory odes in Alcaics celebrating similar triumphs over the English in the French recapture of Calais in 1558 (by e.g. George Buchanan and Jean Dorat) and over the Muslim forces at Lepanto in 1571.[37]

It falls into a clear structure of four parts, announcing and celebrating the victory (1-16), praising the courage and determination of Louis XIII (17-48), praising Cardinal Richelieu (49-52) and praising and exhorting Cardinal Barberini (53-80); the monarch and the pope's nephew thus get most of the space and the most emphatic positions in the middle and at the end, with a cameo part for the monarch's minister, reflecting their relative status for the writer.

Text and translation

DE RVPELLAE EXPVGNATIONE AD CASSIANVM PVTEVM EQVITEM. Regis constantiam in obsidenda laudat, uictoremque ad rebelles reliquos persequendos animans, in partem laudis uocat consiliarium et cardinalem sacrae sedis legatum, qui ea bella suaserat.

Nunc o uetustis sume superbiam
Fastis nitentem, Gallia nobilis,
   Virtute bellorum redemptam
     Atque nouis geminam triumphis.
Te nunc cruento Marte ferocior   5
Lux una terris et pelago uidet
   Hostem domantem, pertinaci
     Quae Dominum renuebat arce.
Lux una cultus fanaque iam diu
Direpta summo restituit Deo,   10
   Et prisca ceruices rebelles
     In iuga supposuit regendas.
Frustra Britanni regia construit
Vrbes natantes per mare deuium,
   Victuque et armis, ne perirent,   15
     Suppetias tulit usque belli.
Non aestus alti gurgitis impotens,
Non ore latrans Sirius igneo,
   Hiberna nequidquam niuali
     Bruma gelu subitiue nimbi,   20
Aut multa diris machina moenibus
Excussa Regem terruit, ardua
   Quo sorte cedens, ad quieta
     Otia et imperium rediret.
Senile menti consilium uiget,   25
Et grande robur pectoris aspera
   Belli capessens: infidelem
     Stat populum, latebris proteruum
Hucusque, sceptris reddere Gallicis,

On the capture of La Rochelle, to the knight Cassiano del Pozzo. He praises the resolution of the king in the siege, and, stirring the victor to pursue the remaining rebels, he hails for their share of praise the counsellor and cardinal legate of the Holy See, who had urged the campaign.

    Now take up the pride which shines
In your annals of old, noble France,
Now regained by courage in warring,
And redoubled by these recent triumphs.
    Now a single day, made more ferocious 5
By bloody Mars, sees you mastering the foe
On land and ocean, in the stubborn citadel
Which used to deny the Lord.
    A single day has restored services and shrines
Long since plundered to the supreme God, 10
And placed rebel necks to be steered
Under the yoke they knew of old.
    In vain did the royal power of Britain build
Cities floating through the distant sea,
And often bring the defenders aid of war 15
In food and arms, lest they perish.
    Not the wild surge of the deep sea,
Nor the dog-star barking with fiery mouth,
Nor in any way the winter's cold with its
Snowy frost or the sudden clouds, 20
    Or the repelling of many a siege-engine
From the accursed walls could frighten the king
Into yielding when fortune was against him
And returning to peaceful leisure and rule.
    The sense of an old man thrives in his mind, 25
And a mighty strength of heart which takes on
The tribulations of war: it is his firm purpose to return
A faithless people, thus far made impudent
    By their lair, to the rule of France,

> Et euagatam saepe licentiam 30
> Frenasse. Iam fatale monstrum
> Impietas cecidit, furenti
> Enata Auerno, quae male perderet
> Vt regna sedem legerat aequore
> Terraque mixtam: pertimendos 35
> Sed superi uetuere casus,
> Et magna Regis dextera contudit
> Infame uulgus, neue colonias
> Deducat errorum per orbem
> Edomitum didicit timere. 40
> Haec signa rex o deferat undique,
> Assuetus acri militiae, Deo
> Tutante: praescriptum parentum
> Et celebres titulos auorum
> Christum colentum uictor adorea 45
> Semper recenti ditior impleat,
> Seruata quo tandem redonet
> Religio sine labe pacem.
> Comes pericli laudis et integrae,
> Nitens galero et purpureo comas, 50
> Armandus, his pergat potentem
> Sensibus implicuisse regem.
> Tuque o beati spes Capitolii,
> Regi sacrorum proxime, fulgido
> Insignis ostro, Barberinae 55
> Gentis et Ausoniae renidens
> Francisce lumen, cui Latium refert
> Quod Mars recessit bis procul Italis,
> Et quod piis parcens in hostes
> Arma tulit metuenda Gallus: 60
> Impelle rectos proelia in exitus,
> Ducemque adurge castra sodalium
> Vt barbarorum persequatur,
> Reliquias graue olentis Orci.
> Pestem latentem corpore Galliae 65
> Scelusque gentis sedulus expiet,

And to bridle their oft-straying licence.   30
Now the deadly monster of impiety,
Born of raging Avernus, has fallen,
    Which, in order to wickedly destroy
The kingdom, had chosen a home
Of sea and water mixed together;   35
But the gods forbade that fearsome mischance,
    And the mighty right hand of the king subdued
The infamous mob, and taught it once mastered
To fear, so that it should not found
Colonies of errors throughout the world.   40
    O may the king bear these standards everywhere,
Grown used to fierce soldiering, with God
As protector: may he fulfil the precepts
Of his fathers and the famous achievements
    Of his Christian ancestors as a victor   45
Even more richly with ever-fresh glory,
So that true religion, at last preserved,
Can bring back peace without taint.
    And may his comrade in peril and full praise,
His hair shining with a scarlet cap,   50
Armand, continue to wrap his powerful king
In these very sentiments.
    And you, o hope of the blessed Capitol,
Who stand next to the ruler of things sacred,
Distinguished by glowing scarlet,   55
The shining light of Italy and the Barberini race,
    Francesco, to whom Latium owes the fact
That Mars has twice retreated from the Italians,
And that the Frenchman has spared the pious
And borne his fearful arms against the enemy,   60
    Drive these battles to the right issue,
And press the general to follow the camp
Of the infidels who are the enemy's friends,
The remains of foul-smelling Hell.
    Let him take care to expiate the plague   65
That lurks in the body of France and the crime of its race,

Delubra diuorum reponat,
    Iusque pium Themidisque leges.
Huc obsequentem flectere tu potes,
Francisce, regem, quem tibi Sequana   70
    Debet triumphantem, quod olim
        Eloquio ac pietate uictum
Probata caelo haec bella coegeris
Gessisse uictorem. Eia, Quiritium
    Et urbis heros purpurate,   75
        Cara Deo referens tropaea
Suspende templis; nec tibi carmina
Lesboa tentet dicere barbitos,
    Quando alta Virtus, quas meretur,
        Spernit adhuc inimica laudes.   80

Let him restore the shrines of the saints,
And holy justice and the laws of Themis.
   This is the way you can direct, Francesco,
The duty of the king, whose triumph 70
The Seine owes to you, since earlier
you compelled him, overcome
   By your eloquence and piety, to wage victoriously
This war approved by heaven. O, hero
In scarlet of the Romans and their city, 75
Bring back those trophies dear to God
   And hang them in sanctuaries: and let
The Lesbian lyre not attempt songs for you,
Since your lofty virtue yet spurns
With emnity the glories that it merits. 80

Commentary

1-16 celebrate the surrender. In line 1 the initial *nunc* echoes first word of Horace *Odes* 1.37, in the same metre and similarly celebrating a victory in a civil war (the battle of Actium against Antony and Cleopatra), while *sume superbiam* cites *Odes* 3.30.14 (modifying Horace's literary pride into France's military honour), and the reference to the calendar's record of the past in celebrating an occasion (1-2) also has Horatian encomiastic colour (cf. *Odes* 4.14.4, on Augustus). 3 *redemptam* and 4 *geminam* may look back to the failed siege of La Rochelle two generations earlier in 1572-3 by the future Henri III as Duke of Anjou, while 4 *nouis . . . triumphis* recalls the poem of Tibullus for Messalla's victory in the same area (1.7.5 *nouos . . . triumphos*; see the introductory section above) as well as *Odes* 2.9.18-19 *noua / . . . Augusti tropaea*. 5 cf. *Odes* 2.14.13 **cruento Marte* (similarly figurative); for the causal ablative cf. *Odes* 1.37.29 *deliberata morte ferocior*. 6 For *lux una* of a single crucial day in battle see Silius 10.587, while *terris et pelago* varies *terra marique* in another victory poem, *Epodes* 9.27; at coastal La Rochelle both land and sea were strategically crucial. 8 *Dominum renuebat* – i.e. denying the true nature of Christ, e.g. in the Protestant view of the Eucharist. 9-10 refer to the iconoclasm carried out by Protestants in La Rochelle in 1560-1, casting them as Horace's impious enemy Carthaginians and Parthians by drawing on the imagery of *Odes* 4.4.46-8 *impio / uastata Poenorum tumultu / fana* and 4.15.6-8 *signa nostro restituit Iovi / derepta Parthorum superbis /postibus*, while 11-12 echo the animal-taming language of *Odes* 3.9.17-18 *quid si prisca redit Venus / diductosque iugo cogit aeneo*, replacing erotic subjugation with its political form. 13-16 refer to the various English attempts to relieve La Rochelle by sea in 1627-8; for *frustra* placed emphatically at the start of both a sentence and an Alcaic stanza cf. *Odes* 2.14.13 (a line recalled at 5, see above). 16 *suppetias* ferre is a phrase from Plautus (5×), a little low for this elevated context, while *usque belli* placed in this position at the end of a sentence and an Alcaic stanza recalls *Odes* 2.19.28 *mediusque belli*.

17-48 praise the virtues of the young Louis XIII (b. 1601); the image of the hero unterrified by multiple external forces (17-24) recalls *Odes* 3.2.1-6 *Iustum et tenacem propositi uirum /non civium ardor praua iubentium, / non uultus instantis tyranni / mente quatit solida neque Auster, / dux inquieti turbidus Hadriae,/nec fulminantis magna manus Iovis*; cf. also *Odes* 3.30.3-4 *quod non imber edax, non Aquilo impotens/ possit diruere*; 18 *latrans* ('barking') puns on the identity of Sirius as the summer Dog-star, as at Statius *Silv.* 1.3.5 *nec calido latrauit Sirius astro*. 19-20 *nequidquam = nequicquam* in classical Latin; for the combination *hiberna . . . bruma* cf. Tibullus 1.4.5, Propertius 1.8a.9, for *niuali . . . gelu* cf. Seneca *Medea* 716, for *subiti . . . nimbi* cf. Silius 1.134. 21 – cf. Ennius *Ann.* fr.620 Sk. *Machina multa minax minitatur maxima muris*. 22-3 *ardua . . . sorte* recalls *rebus in arduis* at *Odes* 2.3.1; 23-4 *quieta / otia et imperium* recalls *Satires* 1.1.30 *ut in otia tuta recedant* and suggests the safe pleasures of the distant French court in Paris. 24 *senile consilium* – a compliment to the youthful Louis, presented as wise beyond his years; for *consilium* as a monarchical virtue cf. *Odes* 3.4.65; for 25 *robur pectoris* cf. *Aeneid* 11.368 *pectore robur*, and for 25-6 *aspera / belli capessens* cf. *Odes* 4.4.76 *acuta belli, Satires* 2.7.7 *recta capessens*. 29 *sceptris . . . Gallicis* – cf. Lucan 10.87 *sceptris . . . paternis* (in similar transferred sense); 30-1 recall the praises of Augustus at *Odes* 4.5.10-11 *euaganti frena licentiae / iniecit* and 3.24.28-9 *indomitam audeat / refrenare licentiam* and the description of Cleopatra at *Odes* 1.37.21 *fatale monstrum* (for the animal-taming metaphor of *frenasse* cf. 11-12). 33 *male perderet* – cf. Catullus 14.5 *male perderes*, a rather colloquial phrase for this elevated context; *ut* appears immediately after its verb as at *Odes* 1.37.20. 35-6 cf. Cicero *Arat.* 34.191 *metuendos . . . casus*, Ovid *Met.* 4.61 *sed uetuere patres*. 37 for the heroic *magna dext(e)ra* cf. Statius *Theb.* 10.662, Silius 7.371 and for *contudit* of forceful suppression of evil enemies *Epistles* 2.1.10 (Hercules) *diram qui contudit Hydram*; 38 for *infame uulgus* cf. *Odes* 1.35.5 *uulgus infidum*. 38-9 *colonias / deducat* is the standard language for founding settlements, here Protestant offshoots of La Rochelle spreading its heresies, while 39-40 *orbem / edomitum* looks back to Silius 9.201 *edomitum . . . orbem*. 41 neatly literalises the erotic soldiering of the similarly young Paullus Fabius Maximus at *Odes* 4.1.15–16 *et centum puer artium / late <u>signa feret militiae</u> tuae*, while 42 recalls the Augustan youth of *Odes* 3.2.1–3 *Angustam amice pauperiem pati / robustus <u>acri militia</u> puer/ condiscat*. 43–8 seem to encourage a return to the non-toleration of Protestants in France before the Edict of Nantes of 1598, which was indeed to be revoked by Louis' son Louis XIV in 1685; 43 *praescriptum parentum* might look back to the Edict of Saint-Maur (1568) banning Protestant worship, while 45 *Christum colentum* and 48 suggest 'correct' Catholic faith (cf. on line 8 above and *sine labe* in 48); both phrases are forcefully alliterative. 44 echoes Lucan 8.73 *titulis insignis auorum*, while *semper recens* (46) is a Vergilian phrase (3x), *sine labe* (48) an Ovidian one (9×).

49–52 praise Cardinal Richelieu, who is here presented as the king's companion in battle (as the similar adviser Maecenas is of Augustus at *Epodes* 1.3–4) and glory; for 49 cf. *Odes* 4.4.66–7 *integrum / cum laude uictorem*. Line 50 refers to the cardinal's scarlet skullcap,[38] while 51 names Richelieu by his first name (Armand Jean du Plessis), and *sensibus ... implicuisse* suggests the subtle approach of the older adviser (b. 1585) to the young king.

53–80 turn to Cardinal Barberini, the youthful (b. 1597) representative of papal Rome in France; 53 *beati spes Capitolii* suitably compares him to Aeneas' young heir Iulus at *Aeneid* 12.168 *magnae spes altera Romae* (for the Capitol in such contexts see commentary on poem 23.39, item 7 below) while *regi sacrorum* likens the papal office of his uncle Urban VIII to one of the highest Roman pagan priesthoods. 54 *fulgido* is a rare Lucretian adjective (3.363), while for *insignis ostro* (54) cf. *Aeneid* 4.134 *ostroque insignis* (here *ostro* refers to Barberini's cardinal's scarlet, matching Richelieu's at 50), and for the encomiastic *Ausoniae ... lumen* (56–7) cf. *Aeneid* 2.281 *lux Dardaniae*; the first name *Francisce* (57) matches that of *Armandus* (50), pairing the two cardinals again. 58 refers to two recent escapes of Italy from war owed to Barberini, probably referring to his negotiations with Spain over the Valtellina and with France over the Mantuan succession, while 59–60 point to his current support for French war against Protestants rather than other Catholics (*piis parcens*: note the emphatic alliteration and cf. *Aeneid* 1.526 *parce pio generi*). 62–4 press Barberini to urge Louis to further attacks on remaining Protestant strongholds: *barbarus* invidiously compares Protestants with foreign 'infidels' such as Muslims, while for *reliquiae* (64) of a surviving body of men cf. *Aeneid* 1.30 *reliquias Danaum*, and for *graue olentis Orci* cf. *Aeneid* 6.201 *graue olentis Auerni*. 65 cf. Valerius Flaccus 7.252 *pestemque latentem*; 66 recalls *Odes* 1.2.29 *scelus expiandi* in another context of civil strife, while 67 echoes *Satires* 1.6.35 *delubra deorum* (changing pagan gods for Catholic saints, *diui*), and echoes *Odes* 3.6.1–4 in the idea of temple restoration as a symbol of national renewal. 68 Themis is a classical goddess of justice and order (cf. e.g. Catullus 68.153). 69–74 – a very hopeful characterization of Barberini's past and future influence on Louis (who did not need papal urging to attack La Rochelle); the Seine, the river of Paris, stands by synecdoche for France, while 72 recalls Ovid *Ars* 1.462 *eloquio uicta* and Lucan 8.718 *uictum pietate* and *eia* (74) is a colloquial exclamation not found in the *Odes* (but in the *Satires*). 75 *heros purpurate* again points to the cardinal's red, while the hanging of spoils in Rome's temples (76–7) is a Roman custom (cf. e.g. *Aeneid* 6.859, Propertius 4.10.45). 77–80 the poem ends with an honouring of Barberini's modest virtue, by which he declines the recognition in poetry of his achievements. This is in essence a rhetorical *praeteritio* or treatment of a theme by claiming not to treat it, an encomiastic technique used by Horace in the *Odes* (e.g. 1.6 and 4.15), since the last few stanzas have in fact been lyric praise of the cardinal, even if the poem is addressed to one of his subordinates. 78 *Lesboa . . . barbitos* – cf. *Odes* 1.1.34 *Lesboum . . . barbiton*; Chigi uses Horace's adjective but Ovid's feminine gender (*Her.*15.8 *barbitos ulla*). 79–80 – cf. Silius 10.68-9 *altae / uirtutis*, and *Odes* 3.2.21–4 *Virtus . . . spernit humum*. The last word of the poem (*laudes*) emphasizes its praise of Barberini which the closing rhetoric denies.

6. Ode on the humble courage of the Carthusian Blessed Pietro Petroni (poem 21)

This short ode in seven Alcaic stanzas[39] praises the humility and courage of the monk, prophet and miracle-worker the Blessed Pietro Petroni (1311–61),[40] who cut off his left index finger to deny himself the honour of becoming a priest and celebrating the mass; such deliberate self-mutilation was a disqualification for the priesthood under canon law.[41] This act is explicitly compared to those of self-sacrificing Roman heroes, the early Republican Mucius Scaevola ('left-handed'), who burned his right hand to show his Roman courage to the invading Etruscans under Porsenna, and Pompey the Great, who saved Rome from a destructive battle in Italy by crossing the stormy sea to Illyria at the start of the Civil War against Caesar. Petroni's self-mutilation surpasses that of Scaevola because of its motivation of humility, and ensures his salvation and glory. The date of composition is unclear: Petroni was a major religious figure in Chigi's home city of Siena, and the poem may be stimulated by a biography of him published there in 1619.[42]

The poem thus suggests a new model of Christian heroism which transcends the traditional Roman form. Courage linked to humility is even more long-lasting than the glory ascribed to the mere physical courage of the Romans, even if the latter was unselfishly exercised for the benefit of Rome. This evolution in moral values is matched by the adaptation and reworking of elements of Horace's odes celebrating Roman virtues, the Roman Odes (*Odes* 3.1–6) in which even more dramatic examples of self-sacrifice are presented (e.g. Regulus in *Odes* 3.5); the new Christian form of ode will ensure the perennial fame of the new Christian ideology of courage.

Text and translation

DE B. PETRO PETRONIO CARTHUSIANO. *A pietate laudat atque ab humilitate, qua permotus sinistrae manus indicem sibi absciderat, ne sacerdos promoueretur.*

> Virtus, ad imum nescia deprimi,
> Velox citatis fertur ad aethera
>   Pennis, nec umquam aeui fugacis
>   Fata nocent, dubiisue praeceps
> Fortuna telis. Hac petiit polum   5
> Vectus curuli nube per aerem
>   Diuinus heros, hac triumphans
>   Fama canit, geminumque uiuax
> Praecurrit axem; nec sibi terminos
> Praescribit ullos, cum meritis neque   10
>   Sit meta summis. Vidit olim Sena
>   parens humilem Tonantis
> Sacrum negantem tangere corporis,
> Laeuae resecta parte: sed interim
>   Sinus decora sede cordis   15
>   Ara Deum rutilans fouebat.
> Prudens remoto qui indice semitam
> Signauit orbi, qua medium mare
>   Mortemque transgressus minacem
>   Astra petat placidumque litus.   20
> Huic postferendus Mucius et tenax
> Pompeius acrem missus ad Illyrin:
>   Vtroque maior spreuit ignes
>   Tartareos, aliena soluens
> Delicta poenis. Ergo perennibus   25
> Obliuiones laudibus inuidas
>   Vitabit, et mutum superstes
>   Gloria post cinerem uigebit.

Fabio Chigi (1599–1667; Pope as Alexander VII 1655–67)

On the Blessed Pietro Petroni, a Carthusian. He praises him for his piety and for his humility, motivated by which he cut off the index finger of his left hand, so that he could not be promoted to priest.

> Courage, incapable of being pressed down to the depths,
> Is carried swiftly on hastened wings to the aether,
> Nor does the destiny of fleeting time harm it,
> Or headlong Fortune with its unreliable weapons.
>   By this route the divine hero made for heaven,   5
> Borne on a chariot of cloud through the air,
> By this route; this quality is the song of triumphant Fame,
> And, full of life, outruns the twin poles;
>   Nor does this quality set itself any boundaries,
> Since there is no limit for highest merit.   10
> Siena, his mother-city, once saw him
> In humility, declining to touch
>   The holy element of the Body, having cut off
> A part of his left hand: but meanwhile
> In the fine home of the heart of his bosom   15
> A ruddy altar cherished God.
>   Intelligent was he, who marked out his path for the world
> By removing his index-finger, a path by which,
> Crossing the midst of the ocean and the threats of death,
> He could seek the stars and the shore of peace.   20
>   To him Mucius is to be subordinated, and Pompey,
> Tenacious when dispatched to fierce Illyria:
> Greater than both, he scorned the fires of Hell,
> Paying for the sins of others by his penalties.
>   So he will escape envious forgetfulness   25
> Through the means of eternal praise,
> And his glory will live on in survival
> Long after his speechless ashes.

Commentary

1–11a This opening encomiastic description of courage draws on Horace, especially *Odes* 3.2: line 1 closely recalls 3.2.17 *Virtus repulsae nescia sordidae*, with the word *Virtus* placed with similar emphasis at the start of an Alcaic stanza, while the idea that courage leaves the earth behind on swift wings and opens up the way to heaven for those who show it picks up 3.2.21-4 *Virtus, recludens inmeritis mori / caelum, negata temptat iter uia / coetusque uulgaris et udam / spernit humum fugiente pinna*, and the theme that its glory cannot be harmed by the flight of time in *aeui fugacis* (3) recalls *Odes* 3.30.5 *fuga temporum*. Lines 5–7 on the route to heaven for heroes echo *Odes* 3.3.9–10 <u>hac</u> *arte Pollux et uagus Hercules / enisus artes attigit igneas*, and the repetition *hac/hanc* (5, 7) picks up that of *hac/hac/hac* in the same context (3.3.9, 13, 15); for the metaphor of Fortune's weapons cf. Cicero *Pis.* 43, *Fam.* 5.16.2, Seneca *Ep.* 18.12, 85, 25, 104.22. Horace's Roman heroes, however, are here replaced by their Christian counterpart through the proclamation of the Gospel, which has triumphed in the modern world (7–8 *triumphans / Fama*): 6 *curuli nube*, i.e. with a cloud replacing the Roman triumphal chariot (*curulis* is here in effect the adjective from *currus*, as at Suetonius *Aug.* 22 *curulis triumphos*). This looks to the Ascension of Christ (for *heros* of Christ and the saints see *TLL* 6.2664.14–31), taken up by a cloud (Acts 1.9 *et nubes suscepit eum ab oculis eorum*), with an echo of the 'chariot of fire' in Elijah's translation to heaven (2 (4) Kings 2.11 *currus igneus*). 7: I read *hanc*, John Trappes-Lomax's excellent suggestion for *hac*, an easy error, which is hard to translate here: Fama proclaims Christian virtue. Virtue's progress beyond the twin poles recalls and outdoes Lucan's characterization of the expansion of the Roman empire (7.422 *te* <u>geminum</u> *Titan procedere uidit in* <u>axem</u>), while the denial of limits to virtue (9–11) recalls both Isaiah's prophecy of Christ's kingdom (9.7 *multiplicabitur eius imperium, et pacis non erit finis*) and Vergil's Jupiter's characterization of the limitless rule of Rome (*Aeneid* 1.278–9 *his ego nec metas rerum nec tempora pono: / imperium sine fine dedi*). Roman dominion is now firmly surpassed by that of Christ.

11b-20 The central section of the poem narrates the story of Petroni himself; the act seems to have taken place not in Siena (11 *Sena*) as claimed here but in the Certosa di Parma (see Pellegrini 2015). 12 *Tonantis* (= *Iouis*) is a striking paganism for Christ in this eucharistic context. 13–14 for the issue of canon law here see the introductory section above (the reference is to handling the sacred bread as part of the mass). 14–16 the point is that Petroni's heart becomes an alternative for the altar of the mass in honouring God (for the heart as the seat of love for God cf. e.g. 1 Peter 3.15): the ruddy colour is that of its flesh, anticipating the later depictions of the Sacred Heart of Jesus. 15 *decora sede* recalls *Odes* 1.30.3–4 *decoram* / . . . *aedem*. 17–19 cf. *Odes* 1.3.21–3 *nequiquam deus abscidit* / *prudens Oceano dissociabili* / *terras* (note the metaphor of severing); there is a play here on the word *index*, meaning both 'index-finger' and 'sign'. The reference to the dangers of the sea in 18–20 is figurative, referring to navigating the dangerous ocean of life (Petroni never left Italy), and looks forward to the mention of Pompey's literal voyage in the next section. These lines have three classicising alliterative pairings – cf. Statius *Theb.* 11.4 *signauit* . . . *semita*, *Eclogues* 8.58 *medium* . . . *mare* and Lucan 2.26 *morte minaces*. 20 *astra petat* recalls Lucan's anticipation of the deification of Nero (1.46 *astra petes serus*), here adapted for a Christian context; for *placidumque litus* cf. Statius *Ach.*1.696–7 *placidique* . . . / *litoris* (the metaphor is that of the peaceful harbour of death, cf. e.g. *Aeneid* 7.598–9).

21–8 The final section makes explicit what the earlier sections have expressed implicitly by multiple intertextuality: Petroni's Christian and humble courage is superior to that of traditional Roman military heroes. 21 *Mucius* is Q. Mucius Scaevola, who burned his right hand in front of the Etruscan king Porsenna as a sign of his courage (Livy 2.12), while 22 *missus ad Illyrin* recalls the episode in Lucan where Pompey in 49 BCE decides not to engage in a major battle in Italy but to escape to Illyrian Dyrrachium (Lucan 2.525–627, cf. especially 2.624 *Illyris*). Pompey's self-sacrifice here in the public interest seems to be a loss of personal reputation through flight from Italy in order to avoid a major internecine conflict there (*acrem* points to the later battle at Dyrrachium in 48 BCE). This is a very generous view of Pompey's motives; Chigi's tragedy *Pompeius* (see introductory section above) shows his interest in and sympathy with Pompey. 23–4 *Tartareos ... ignes* defines the Christian Hell in terms of pagan epic topography (on the flames of Tartarus cf. *Aeneid* 5.548–51), while 24–5 rewrites the pagan punishment of offenders for their own offences in terms of Christian atonement for others as a route to salvation (cf. *Aeneid* 6.739 *exercentur poenis*, 743 *quisque suos patimur manis*). 25–6 *perennibus ... laudibus* recalls Silius 15.392 *laus ... perennis, obliuiones ... inuidas Odes* 4.8.23–4 *taciturnitas ... inuida*, while 27–8 appropriately recall the reflections of Horace and Ovid on the immortality of their work (*Odes* 3.30.5–6 *non omnis moriar multaque pars mei / uitabit Libitinam, Ex Ponto* 4.16.3 *famaque post cineres maior uenit*). The ending is a self-fulfilling prophecy: Petroni, though dumb in death (cf. Catullus 101.3 *mutam ... cinerem*), has achieved his posthumous glory partly through the voice of this ode, like Horace's *fons Bandusiae* (*Odes* 3.13.13 *fies nobilium tu quoque fontium*).

7. Ode on Mary Magdalen's legendary voyage to Marseille (poem 24)

This lyric poem in the Horatian Fourth Asclepiad metre[43] refers to the apocryphal story that St Mary Magdalen sailed safely to Marseille from Palestine with some of Jesus' followers including members of her family and household, having been placed on a leaky ship by the local authorities who hoped to get rid of her, and had a subsequent career as a preacher of the Gospel in Roman Gaul. A version of this narrative is found in the life of Mary Magdalen in the *Golden Legend*, the widely read thirteenth-century collection of saints' lives by Jacobus de Voragine.[44]

Mary's voyage is also illustrated in a famous work of art, the fine fifteenth-century painted altarpiece in the church dedicated to St Mary

Magdalen at Tiefenbronn near Stuttgart (the Magdalenenaltar), which Chigi might have visited in his travels between Italy and northern Germany in the 1640s (see e.g. poem 41, where he travels from Ferrara to Cologne, passing within 50 kilometres or so of Tiefenbronn). The name Ekhard/Erhard appears in an inscription on the altar describing its dedicatee saints (alongside Mary and St Antony; the inscription reads BEATUS VENERABILIS EKHARDUS, referring to the eighth-century Erhard of Regensburg).[45] This has been speculatively linked with the first name of the dedicatee of Chigi's poem.[46]

The poem is dedicated to a mysterious Eherardus Saracenus, knight. The surname looks like a Latinization of Saraceno/Sarrazini (Italian) or Sarazin (French), and *eques* here may refer to a papal knight (as it does in the dedication to poem 18 = item 5 above). The major French sculptor Jacques Sarazin (1592–60), Saracenus in Latin, spent the years 1610–28 in Rome, and may have known Chigi there; this figure could conceivably have been a relative of his.

The poem's metre is that of Horace *Odes* 1.3, and the opening eight lines of Chigi's poem are very close to the same lines of Horace's poem; this comes close to the baroque practice of *parodia*, in which a poem kept as close as possible to the words of its classical model, while treating a modern, often Christian subject.[47] Chigi's subject is a neat transposition of Horace's, which is a *propempticon* (send-off poem) for his friend the poet Vergil as he sails east to Greece; here Mary is given a farewell as a beloved saint as she sails west to Europe.

The poet imagines himself dispatching Mary on her journey, and looks forward to her future religious activities in Gaul. This reprises the prophetic role of the sea-god Nereus in Horace *Odes* 1.15, who prophesies the future Trojan War as Paris sails away from Sparta with Helen (the naming of Nereus in ths last line of this poem is a hint at this intertextual relationship); Chigi's poem foretells a different kind of foreign war (18 *proelia*), that of converting the heathen in Gaul. Mary's weathering of a storm to make a successful westwards voyage in pursuit of a new beginning also recalls Aeneas' similar survival at the start of the *Aeneid* (1.34–158).

This poem is thus a sophisticated adaptation of two Horatian odes concerned with voyaging, modifying their Roman historical and Greek mythological content for the context of an imagined voyage from the earliest days of Christianity celebrated in hagiography and cult. Its concern with an improving anecdote from church history links it with Chigi's ode about Pietro Petroni (poem 21, item 6 above), while its interest in a story tracing a European connection with the Palestine of Christ's lifetime recalls the house of the Holy Family at Loreto in poem 11 (item 4 above).

Text and translation

DE DIVA MARIA MAGDALENA, IN GRATIAM EHERARDI SARACENI EQUITIS. Fluctibus expositae in solutili cumba[48] *faustum iter precatur ac praedicit, quæ post appulsum in Galliam euentura erant, propagato baptismo. Ex illo: Et spiritus Domini ferebatur super aquas.*[49]

    Sic te diua Dei parens,
Sic caeli proceres, lucida sidera,
        Sic ponti regat arbiter
Immensi, sacer et numinis halitus,
    Nauis, quae tibi creditam   5
Debes Magdalidem cum socia manu,
    Reddas incolumem precor,
Et serues animae praesidium meae.
    Frustra saeuior aequoris
Vnda rex Solymus, fraude solutili   10
    Cumbae composuit dolos.
Euincet leuior cuncta pericula
    Inconcussa minacibus
Neptuni fragilis cumbula uiribus.
    Felix remigio, feris   15
I constantior exercita fluctibus;
    Perfer, nobilior nouo
Teque accinge operi, proelia classibus
    Motura indomitae Stygis.
Non sic tot feret in Tartara portitor   20
    Praedas, dum rate paruula
Transcribi superos cernat in ordines
    Tot magnas animas, gemens
Addi ludibrio turpius otium.
    O quantum Oceani natat   25
Vndis diuitiarum! Emicat aureum
    Vellus, quod pretio mala

Fabio Chigi (1599–1667; Pope as Alexander VII 1655–67)

On St Mary Magdalen, to please Eherard Saraceno, knight. He prays for a fortunate voyage for her when she was exposed to the waves in a collapsible ship, and predicts what was to happen after her landing in Gaul, spreading baptism. The poem derives from that well-known text 'And the spirit of God moved upon the face of the waters'.

    So may the blessed mother of God,
  So may the leaders of heaven, those shining stars,
    So may the ruler of the vast deep
Direct you, and the sacred breath of divine power,
  O ship, who owes the debt of the lady of Magdala   5
Entrusted to you with her band of companions,
    May you give her back unharmed,
I pray, and preserve the half of my soul.
    In vain did the king of Jerusalem,
Crueller than the waves of the sea, set up a deception   10
    In the dissolving trap of a boat:
The rather light fragile little vessel will overcome
    All perils unshaken by
The threatening powers of Neptune.
    Fortunate in your crew, go on   15
More firmly for being harassed by the fierce waves:
    Endure, and, become more noble,
Gird yourself for a new task, destined to stir up
    Battles against the hosts of untamed Hell.
Not so will the ferryman carry so many victims   20
    To Tartarus, while he can see
In this small craft so many great souls
    Enlisted into the ranks of heaven, and he complains
That the greater shame of inactivity is added to ridicule.
    O, what a great amount of riches   25
Is afloat on the waves of the ocean! A golden fleece
    Gleams, which with its great price takes away

Tollit degeneris crimina saeculi.
  Haec Argo melioribus
Mox afflata modis, carmine concinet, 30
  Angustam in Cererem, Deus
Qua duci cupiat sub prece mobilis:
  Elatum fidei genus,
Auctorisque Dei dogma recentius.
  'Istaec uos, socii, manet 35
Sors, ut Massiliae gens (trabe sutili
  Emenso maris impetu)
Vestro addicta nouis munere legibus
  Addatur Capitolio,
Heroum numero inserta decentior. 40
  Me saxa et vacuum nemus,
Et desueta feris antra fugacibus,
  Siluae mensa beatior,
Et somnus gelidi me lapidis iuuet.
  Idem non decor omnium est: 45
Vos maiora vocant: quîque tenet ratem
  Quassam Spiritus integer
Formabat tenerum sic ab origine
  Mundum ex Oceani uadis.
Idem nostra pius crimina diluat, 50
  Et lustret genus impium
Post mollita patris fulmina sanguine.'
  Sacris Magdala uocibus
Dum facunda trahit corda sodalium,
  Seruent mite silentium 55
Edixit rapidis flatibus Aeolus
  Nec nauis mare sorbuit,
Et tranquilla dedit murmura Nereus.

The evil crimes of our degenerate age.
   This Argo, now blown forward in a better way
To a scarce nourishment, 30
   Will sing in prophecy of where
God, responsive to prayer, might wish to be taken,
   Of the elevated mode of faith
And the more recent teaching of God the creator.
   'This lot is in store for you, companions, 35
That the people of Marseille, when you have traversed
   The sea's force in a stitched craft,
Attached to new laws owing to your gift,
   Is to be added to the Capitol,
A more attractive insertion into the band of heroes. 40
   Let the rocks and the empty grove
And the caves disused by fugitive beasts,
   The richer table of the forest, be my pleasure,
And the sleeping-place of a cold stone.
   Not all have the same distinction: 45
You are called by higher things, and the unimpaired
   Spirit that possesses the shaken ship
Was already thus at the beginning shaping
   The still-tender world from the ocean's waters.
May the same pious spirit wash away our crimes, 50
   And purify our impious race,
After the Father's thunderbolts have been softened by blood.'
   As the Magdalen with her holy words
Eloquently influenced the hearts of her companions,
   Aeolus commanded the rapacious winds 55
To keep a gentle silence, nor did the ship
   Swallow the sea, and Nereus
Uttered peaceful whispers.

Commentary

1–8 are an opening prayer for the safety of the saint imagined as already voyaging, plunging the reader into the midst of the drama. As noted above, this passage is closely based on *Odes* 1.3.1–8 *Sic te diua potens Cypri,/ sic fratres Helenae, lucida sidera, / uentorumque regat pater / obstrictis aliis praeter Iapyga, / nauis, quae tibi creditum / debes Vergilium; finibus Atticis / reddas incolumem precor /et serues animae dimidium meae*, where Horace imagines his friend Vergil's voyage to Greece. Note the Christian modifications: Venus (1) is changed to the Virgin Mary, the Dioscuri (2) to angels or saints in heaven, Aeolus (3) to the vague 'ruler of the sea', and the Holy Spirit is added at the end of the list (4), recalling its presence over the waters at Genesis 1.2 as quoted in the subtitle; Chigi also changes *dimidium* for *praesidium*, pairing Mary Magdalen with Maecenas as a protector (cf. *Odes* 1.1.2 *o et praesidium . . . meum*).

9–14 detail events before and after the voyage. The 'king of Jerusalem' (potentially the Herod Antipas of the Gospels) does not appear in the *Golden Legend* account, where Mary is forced to leave by unspecified wicked men, and may be Chigi's specification here: the king's typically tyrannical strategy against Mary recalls Nero's equally unsuccessful attempt to kill his mother Agrippina by devising a similar collapsible boat (Suetonius *Nero* 34 <u>solutilem</u> *nauem . . . commentus est*). 14 *fragilis cumbula* recalls the boat which carries Vergil at *Odes* 1.3.10–11 *fragilem . . . / . . . ratem*; note the vertical juxtaposition of rhyming and prosodically matching noun and adjective pair at the ends of lines 13 and 14, an Horatian technique (cf. e.g. *Odes* 1.6.17–18 and note on item 4, lines 26–34 above).

15–19 turn to address Mary herself. 15 *felix remigio* – according to the *Golden Legend* she was accompanied by her sister Martha, her brother Lazarus, her steward the future St Maximinus and others. 17 *nobilior* – i.e. made more noble by suffering; note the emphatic alliteration with *nouo*. 18–19: cf. *Aeneid* 2.235 *accingunt omnes operi*, Lucan 4.211 *moturas proelia uoces*, *Aeneid* 7.716 *Ortinae classes* ('forces'), *Odes*

2.14.4 *indomitaeque morti*. *Stygis* is a notably pagan metonymy for Hell, here representing the paganism which Mary is to combat in her future missionary work in Gaul.

20-4 Charon is disappointed that he cannot take these important souls in his boat to Hell since they are preserved for life by another vessel (Mary's brother Lazarus supposedly became the first bishop of Marseille, her companion Maximinus the first bishop of Aix-en-Provence and a saint). 20 *in Tartara* is a Vergilian phrase, especially at *Aeneid* 4.446, while *portitor* is used of Charon at *Aeneid* 6.298 and 326. 21 *rate paruula* – cf. Ovid *Met*.1.319 *parua rate* (of the boat carrying the similarly righteous Deucalion and Pyrrha). 23-4 are very Horatian in expression: cf. *Odes* 1.12.37 *animaeque magnae*, *Odes* 3.5.26-7 *flagitio addis / damnum*, and for *gemo* with infinitive cf. *Epistles* 1.15.7, 1.20.4.

25-34 A comparison between Mary's boat and the Argo of classical mythology which sailed in search of the Golden Fleece. 25-6 cf. Statius *Silv.* 2.7.26 *Oceani ... in undis*. In 26-8 the pagan Golden Fleece is neatly transformed into Christ the Lamb of God, who takes away the sins of the world (28 *tollit ... crimina*) – cf. John 1.29 *ecce agnus Dei, ecce qui tollit peccatum mundi*, while in 29-30 Mary's boat is the new Argo sailing with better purpose (not robbery but conversion) and will foretell a better future than the prophetic Argo, which spoke to urge the Argonauts onward to Colchis (Apollonius 1.524-6). 31 *angustam in Cererem* looks forward to the virtuous destination of the voyage in Mary's ascetic life in Gaul (41-4; *Ceres* = 'bread, food' as often, *OLD* s.u. 2b), a contrast with the rich kingdon sought by the Argonauts in Colchis. 33-4 refer to the established bible and post-biblical Christian teachings (a nice touch from a poet interested in theology); *dogma* need not be dogma in the technical Catholic sense (it can mean just 'teaching' in classical Latin, cf. e.g. Juvenal 13.121).

35-52 Mary's speech of encouragement to her companions is marked by a typical opening speech-address (35 *socii* – cf. *Aeneid* 1.198 *o socii*) and is followed by a typical concluding speech-formula (53). It resembles the prophetic speech of Nereus in *Odes* 1.15 (see introductory section above) in being delivered in mid-ocean, and that of Aeneas at *Aeneid* 1.198–207 in comforting the speaker's companions with reassurances about the future. 35 *istaec* is an archaic/prosaic form of *iste* not found in Augustan poetry. 36 *trabe sutili* recalls Charon's boat at *Aeneid* 6.414 *cumba sutilis*, appropriately given its mention at line 22 above, while 38 *uestro munere* recalls and reverses the same phrase of the gift of pagan gods at *Georgics* 1.7. 39 *Capitolio* = the power/domain of Roman Catholic Christianity, as at poem 18.53 (item 5 above), reusing Vergil's use of the Capitol as a symbol of Roman dominion (*Aeneid* 9.448–9). 40 *heroum* – i.e. heroic early Christians (for the usage see poem 21 line 7, item 6 above, and note there). 40 *decentior* perhaps stresses the poet's view of the prestige for the early church of this supposed first expansion into Western Europe, beyond the Eastern communities evangelized by St Paul. 41–4 appropriate the wild landscape of Horatian poetic inspiration for the wilderness of Christian asceticism: cf. *Odes* 3.25.1–2 *quae nemora aut quos agor in specus / uelox mente nova? quibus / antris* . . ., .13 *uacuum nemus*, *Odes* 1.1.30 *gelidum nemus*; according to the *Golden Legend*, Mary spent thirty years in the desert in contemplation. In 45–6 Mary's desert retreat is contrasted with the more active proselytizing of her companions (*maiora*) in these years, recounted in the *Golden Legend*; 45 echoes gnomic statements such as *Eclogues* 8.63 *non omnia possumus omnes*, while 46–7 echo Statius *Theb.* 5.37 *uos arma uocant* (similarly allierative), id.ib. 6.483 *rates tenet aestus*, and *Aeneid* 4.53 *quassataeque rates*). 47 *spiritus integer* – both a favourable wind and the Holy Spirit, looking back to Genesis 1.2 as cited in the subtitle above, *et spiritus Domini ferebatur super aquas*, a biblical context then evoked in 48–9. 48–9 also recall the classical creation narratives of *Eclogues* 6.34 *ipse tener mundi concreuerit orbis* and Ovid *Met.* 1.3 *prima ab origine mundi*, alongside the formation of the earth from the waters of Genesis 1.6–7. 50 *crimina diluat* is a Ciceronian phrase (12×), here enlisted for the Christian concept of atonement through the blood of Christ (cf. 52 *sanguine*); the watery context here fits the washing metaphor. 51 echoes [Seneca]

Oct.393 *premat genus impium*, inverting its pagan punishment into Christian salvation, while 52 uses the thunderbolt of Jupiter (cf. Statius *Silv*.3.1.186 *fulmina patris*) to characterize the wrath of God the Father.

53-8 The elements react favourably to Mary's words. Here again the divine forces named are pagan, though the context is clearly Christian, and have an intertextual force: the mention of Aeolus looks back to the storm he directed in *Aeneid* 1, while that of Nereus reminds the reader of *Odes* 1.15 (for both of these as models here see the introductory section above). Aeolus' intervention to still the winds inverts his action of rousing them in *Aeneid* 1 (81-3). 55: for the alliterative *seruent . . . silentium* cf. Statius *Theb.* 4.423 *silentia seruat*; *mite* suggests the reversal of their previous unrelenting nature (cf. Tibullus 1.1.45 *immites uentos*). 56: cf. Statius *Silv*. 2.2.118 *rapidi . . . flatus*. 57 recalls the Argo (appropriately, see on 25-34 above) at Valerius Flaccus 1.638 *uasto puppis mare sorbet hiatu*, while for *dare* = 'utter' of sounds cf. *Aeneid* 1.485 *gemitum dat*. Note how the prosodically identical names of the gods Aeolus and Nereus both appear at the end of alternate lines in an elegant vertical juxtaposition; the mention of Nereus may look back to *Odes* 1.15 (see introduction above).

8. Hexameter letter to a friend from Germany to Italy, 1648 (poem 74)

This hexameter poem,[50] dated to August 1648, sets out Chigi's frustrations with his role as papal representative at the years of negotiations (on and off since 1636) which were shortly to lead to the formal end of the Thirty Years War in the Treaty of Westphalia (October 1648), and (especially) his dismay at the massive devastation he had seen in a Germany now war-torn for a generation. The conditions of the final treaty (not yet clear at the time of writing) were far from satisfactory to the then Pope Innocent X, Chigi's master, who had succeeded Urban VIII in 1644.

This poetic letter is one of several sent during Chigi's years in Westphalia (1643-8) to friends back in Italy; they form a group in his

1656 collection (poems 74–7). Poem 75 is an elegiac letter also from 1648, similarly frustrated at the delay in negotiations at what was in effect the first major international summit meeting; 76 is another elegiac letter from the same year, eloquently describing the city of Münster, while 77 is yet another elegiac epistle which presents a humorous account of the elaborate headdress of Münster's ladies.

Its addressee is a noble friend in Ferrara, where Chigi had spent a period in the papal service some years before (1627–34; cf. poem 11, item 4 above). His friendship with Ascanio Pio di Savoia may well have dated back to that point: the Pio di Savoia family were members of the elite of Ferrara, and descendants of the lords of Carpi near Bologna. Ascanio himself (1586–1649) was a man of letters and dramatic poet,[51] and his brother Carlo (1585–1641) had been a cardinal.

In terms of classical literary models, this hexameter epistle looks back in outer form to Horace's first book of *Epistles* sent to friends, though its content is darker than any of the poems in that book; its tone of lamentation and its sending home to Italy as a letter from a place of foreign exile rather evoke the exilic elegies of Ovid, while its main theme of the devastation inflicted on a country by disastrous civil war recalls both Vergil's depiction of Italy at the end of *Georgics* 1 (471–97) and (especially) Lucan's epic on the civil war between Caesar and Pompey, marked by the feature (exceptional in Chigi's work) of the literal re-use of Lucan 3.55–8 as lines 23–6 (see commentary below). The close of the poem (65–78) echoes both the climactic prayer for peace in time of civil war at *Georgics* 1.498–501 and the opening address to the Holy Spirit in Girolamo Vida's sixteenth-century neo-Latin epic on the life of Christ (see commentary), a rich pagan/Christian combination.

Text and translation

D. ASCANIO PIO DE SABAUDIA FERRARIAM. *Moram suam in Westphalia ad quinque annos ac pacis frustrationem dolens, Italiae motus, Germaniae uastitatem amico ob oculos ponit, ac tranquillitatem uouens, Deo amoris spiritui sancto commendat, Augusto mense anni MDCXLVIII.*

> *Ergo deuexum caelo quae terminat annum,*
> *Vltima sidereos ostentans semita pisces,*
> *Iam quintum rediit, totiens redit ordine libra,*
> *Phoebi aequans noctisque uices, me Saxonis ex quo*
> *Inferior tellus Vbiis excepit ab oris?* 5
> *Nec tamen ulla uenit populorum candida uotis*
> *Pax optata diu? lacrimisque et sanguine rursus,*
> *Et ferro flammaque uorax producitur aeuum?*
> *Hunc mihi da calamo saltem lenire dolorem,*
> *Quaeso, Pii genus Aeneae, solare gementem* 10
> *Eridani decus, Ascani, seu libera uinclis*
> *Musa fluat, metrica seu stringat compede gressus.*
> *Tu patriam seruas immunem Martis aperti:*
> *Imminet ille tamen uicinoque aestuat igne.*
> *Nec deest Italiae minitans discrimen, egestas* 15
> *Infelix frugum. Siculas uacua horrea primum*
> *Turbarunt urbes: simili mox concita fato*
> *Parthenope casura fuit Latiumque, paterna*
> *Dextera Pontificis quod muniit. Vmbria clamat,*
> *Piceni armantur, rabies Firmana trucidat* 20
> *Rectorem uesana suum, diraque cruentat*
> *Caede manus, fore quod cecinit Pharsalidos auctor:*
> *'Gnarus et irarum causas et summa fauoris*

To Lord Ascanio Pio di Savoia, at Ferrara. Lamenting his lingering in Westphalia for as much as five years and the frustration of the peace process, he sets the disturbances in Italy and the devastation of Germany before the eyes of his friend, and, praying for peace, he commends him to the God of Love, the Holy Spirit, in August 1648.

> And so has the sign in the heaven which ends the decline of the year,
> The last path displaying the stars of Pisces,
> Returned for the fifth time, and is Libra returning as many times in order,
> Equalising the interchange of sun and night, since the lower land
> Of the Saxon has received me from the shores of the Ubii?   5
> And does no bright peace come through the voting of the nations,
> Peace so long desired? And is this devouring age still to be lengthened
> With tears and blood, and with sword and flame?
> Allow me at least to lighten this pain with my pen,
> I beseech you, Ascanio, scion of Enea Pio, console me as I groan,   10
> You glory of the Po, whether your Muse flows free of bonds
> Or constrains its steps with the fetters of metre.
> You keep to your native land free from open war:
> But that threatens, however, and seeths with a fire that is close.
> Nor is there a lack of peril threatening Italy, a miserable lack   15
> Of corn. It was the cities of Sicily that were first troubled
> By empty granaries, then, driven on by a similar fate, Naples
> Was set to fall, and Latium, which the paternal hand
> Of the Pontiff protected. Umbria cries aloud,
> The men of the Marche are armed, Fermo's raging madness   20
> Slaughters its governor, and bloodies its hands with accursed gore:
> This is what the author of the Pharsalia prophesied would come:
> 'Well aware that the causes of resentment and the greatest motivations of popularity

> *Annona momenta trahi: namque asserit urbes*
> *Sola fames emiturque metus; cum segne potentes*   25
> *Vulgus alunt, nescit plebes ieiuna timere.'*
> *Hinc Astraea dolet labem, hinc exempla malorum.*
> *Sed placidas hominum mentes bella, horrida bella,*
> *Corrupere magis. Toto Pax exulat orbe,*
> *Et maeret calcata Fides; temeratur eodem*   30
> *Crimine Nobilitas, et auiti stemmatis exlex*
> *Degenerat Virtus, uitiisque oppressa rebellat.*
> *Ast ego quas uideo (decimus iam uoluitur annus)*
> *Damnorum segetes Germanis surgere campis!*
> *Si cupiam lingua calamoque referre fideli*   35
> *Excidium gentis lati quae finibus orbis*
> *Terror erat, clades animus miseratus acerbas*
> *Vix queat, auersas auditor praebeat aures,*
> *Et ueri lucem media de luce requirat.*
> *Vsque adeo praedura fidem et praegrandia uincunt.*   40
> *Infernis emissa plagis nostro orbe uagatur*
> *Eumenidum funesta cohors, comitesque sequuntur*
> *Et dolus et furor insidiaeque et flebile letum.*
> *Nulla uiget regio, uiduatae ciuibus urbes,*
> *Tecta euersa, arae incensae, spoliata colonis*   45
> *Squalent arua, calent cognato sanguine riui:*
> *Effrenis nec adhuc scelere exsatiata libido*
> *Bellandi nec adhuc rabiem compescit Erinys.*
> *His ego nocturnis lacrimis gemituque diurno*
> *Immoror. Haec utinam gentes, quas Rhenus inundat,*   50
> *Quas Rhodanus praeceps, quas torrens ambit Iberus,*

Are induced by the price of corn: hunger alone controls cities,
And veneration is purchased when the powerful feed 25
the inactive mob, while a starving people knows no terror.'
Astraea laments the disaster, the models of evil that flow from
   this.
But the peaceful minds of men have been perverted by war,
Terrible war. Peace is in exile from the whole world
And Fidelity is trampled and mourns; the nobility 30
Is desecrated by the same crime, and virtue degenerates,
No longer bound by its ancestral pedigree, and rebels, oppressed
   by vices.
But I, what crops of calamity (for the tenth year passing now)
Do I see growing in the fields of Germany!
If I desired to report with faithful tongue and pen 35
The destruction of that race which was the terror
Of the ends of the wide world, my mind in pity at its bitter
   calamities
Could barely do so, my listener would turn their ears away,
And would miss the light of truth in the midst of that light,
So far do extraordinarily cruel and enormous things surpass
   belief. 40
The deadly troop of the Furies, dispatched from the infernal
   regions,
Wanders over our world, and there follow as their comrades
Deceit and madness and surprise attack and lamentable Death.
No area flourishes, cities are bereaved of their citizens,
Houses are wrecked, altars burned, the fields, robbed of their
   cultivators, 45
Are overgrown, the streams are warm with the blood of relatives;
The unbridled passion for warring is not yet sated by crime,
Nor does the Fury yet restrain her madness.
I linger with these nightly tears and daily groaning.
Would that the peoples, who are watered by the Rhine, 50
Whom the hurtling Rhone and the streaming Hebro surround,

Secum animo reputent, et amicas foedere certo
Coniungant dextras et fessus pondere belli
Miles et exhausti ciues populique quiescant!
Iura magistratus repetat sua, nobilis artes 55
Ingenuas pubes, desertaque rura colonus,
Securas quoque pastor oues, ad litora merces
Nostra uehat nigris auidus mercator ab Indis,
Et sua tranquillo redeat pax aurea saeclo!
Sed rapuere Noti tum spes tum uerba proterui 60
Per mare, per Syrtes. Toto haec collegia lustro
Tot legatorum decumana uolumina uerbis
Opplerunt pacis nec adhuc concordia constat:
Sed maiore fremens saeuit Bellona tumultu.
Te rogo, qui caelum, qui terras numine comples, 65
Quo sine frondosa folium non decidit ulmo,
Cuius ad arbitrium flectuntur corda potentum,
Spiritus alme Patris Natique aeterna uoluptas,
Tu miseris assiste pius, tu frange rebelles,
Tu Romanum orbem caelesti pace serena, 70
Tu magni quintum geniali hac luce corona
Praesulis Innocui annum; tu delubra reponens
Discordes conuerte animos, populumque tuorum,
Sancte Amor, hic seruans actae post nubila uitae
Aethereas olli sedes et regna beata 75
Indulge ambrosiasque epulas quibus usque fruatur
Pronus ad obsequium. Dignis tibi gloria fastis
Crescat et aeternis nectatur adorea sertis.

Think on these things, and join hands in friendship and sure
    agreement,
And that the soldiery, tired by the burden of war,
And the exhausted inhabitants and peoples could rest!
Would that the authority could recover its rights, the noble host   55
Their inborn qualities, and the tiller his deserted farmlands,
The shepherd his sheep in peace, that the greedy merchant
Could carry his goods to our shores from swarthy India,
And that its own peace should return to our age made tranquil:
But the violent storm-winds have snatched away both hopes
    and words   60
Over the sea, over the sandbanks. For this whole five years
So many of these teams of delegates have filled vast volumes
With words of peace, and agreement is not yet established,
But Bellona rages, roaring with greater tumult.
You I beg, who fill the heaven and the earth with your power,   65
Without whom a leaf does not fall from a luxuriant elm,
By whose will the hearts of the mighty are turned,
Kindly spirit of the Father and eternal delight of the Son,
Stand with pity by the suffering, crush those who rebel,
Make the Roman world calm with heavenly peace,   70
Crown with that cheerful light the fifth year
Of Innocent the great bishop: restore the shrines,
Turn around the spirits of discord, and, holy Love,
Saving here the race of your people, bestow on him
After the clouds of life are done a home in heaven   75
And the blessed realm and feasts immortal for him to enjoy for
    ever,
Responsive in compliance. For you, may the glory of your worthy
    family annals
Grow, and your distinction be crowned with everlasting garlands.

Commentary

1–8 The poem opens with a series of three increasingly impassioned rhetorical questions, setting its high emotional tone. 1–3: the opening astronomical dating with the mention of the equinox recalls that at the start of poem 11 (item 4 above). This type of time calibration by constellation and the mention of repeated years passing in a place of exile together evoke the world of Ovid's exile poetry: cf. *Ex Ponto* 1.8.27–8 *Vt careo uobis, Stygias detrusus in oras, / quattuor autumnos Pleias orta facit*, 4.7.1–2 (again at the start of a poem and involving Pisces) *Bis me sol adiit gelidae post frigora brumae, / bisque suum tacto Pisce peregit iter*. Chigi had been at the negotiations since the spring of 1643, and is here referring in August 1648 to the spring that has passed some months ago; Pisces is the last of the twelve signs of the zodiac (*terminat, ultima*), governing the period 19 February to 20 March, while line 3 refers to the autumnal equinox which is soon to happen 'on 23 September, followed by the domination of the sign of Libra (23 September to 22 October). 1: for a similar poem opening with *Ergo* introducing a rhetorical question see Ovid *Am.* 2.7.1 *Ergo sufficiam reus in noua crimina semper?* 3: for *totiens redit* cf. Statius *Silv.* 3.3.55. 4: for *noctis . . . uices* cf. Seneca *Ag.*53. 4–5 *Saxonis . . . inferior tellus* – i.e. Lower Saxony, then including the modern Westphalia. 5: *Vbiis . . . ab oris* – i.e. Cologne/Köln (*Colonia Agrippina/Ara Ubiorum*), where Chigi had previously been based as papal nuncio (1639–43). 6: *populorum uotis*: sixteen European countries were represented at the negotiations as well as over 100 of the constituent mini-states of the Empire. 6–7 *candida . . . / pax* – for the phrase cf. Tibullus 1.10.45, Ovid *Ars* 3.502. 8: for the alliterative pairing *ferro flammaque* cf. Cicero *Cat.*2.1, Livy 1.29.3; note the striking personification *uorax . . . aeuum*.

9–14 Address to Ascanio Pio. 9: cf. *Aeneid* 7.331 **hunc mihi da*, *Epistles* 1.1.35 *sunt verba et voces, quibus hunc *lenire dolorem /possis*. 10: cf. Statius *Theb.* 9.885 **solare parentem*. 10–11: these lines bring out the Vergilian origins of the addressee's family names; in the *Aeneid* as in Ferrara Ascanius is the son of Aeneas who has the name/epithet 'pious'

(*Aeneid* 1.220 *pius Aeneas*). For *genus* = 'scion, descendant' in a similar context cf. *Satires* 2.5.62–3 *ab alto / demissum genus Aenea*. 11 *Eridani decus* – cf. *Aeneid* 11.508 *o decus Italiae uirgo*, a similar complimentary address; Ferrara is just south of the Po. Note the vertical juxtaposition here of two pairs of words linked by rhyme and assonance (*genus Aeneae, decus Ascani*). 11–12 i.e. in prose or verse: Pio's most noted work was his libretto for the opera *Andromeda* by Michelangelo Rossi, performed in 1638; the phrases *libera uinclis* and *stringat compede* balance each other in sense, while *metrica* points to the pun (regular in classical Latin poetry) on metrical foot (*pes*) in com*pede*. 13: cf. *Epistles* 1.10.6 *tu nidum servas (again in a letter to a distant friend), Ovid *Met*.13.208 *aperti copia Martis*. 14 *imminet ille* echoes *Ilias Latina* 809 (but there at line end not line start), while for *aestuat igne* cf. Ovid *Met*.4.64 *aestuat ignis.

15–26 Disorder in Italy owing to grain shortages, a situation closely parallel to that at the start of the third book of Lucan's civil war epic, from which 3.55–8 are cited without modification as lines 23–6. This kind of exact reproduction of a classical model over more than a short phrase is exceptional in Chigi's work (the opening of item 7 is another example), and given *cecinit* (22) here seems to echo the biblical technique by which an Old Testament prophecy is quoted at its moment of New Testament fulfilment, e.g. 1 Corinthians 15.54 'then shall be brought to pass the saying that is written, Death is swallowed up in victory', citing Isaiah 25.8. Lucan is a highly appropriate author to cite here given the focus of his epic on the miseries of civil war. 15–16: cf. Statius *Theb*. 10.236 *nec deest, Tacitus *Ann*. 12.43 *frugum ... egestas*; there is a play here on the double sense of *infelix* ('unhappy' and 'unfertile'). 16–17: cf. Ovid *Fasti* 2.93 *Siculas ... urbes*, Ovid *Her*. 19.21 *concita uento, and for Parthenope = Naples cf. *Georgics* 4.564 *Parthenope. 18–19 *paterna / dextera* – cf. Catullus 68.143 *dextra ... paterna*; *muniit* points to Innocent X's 'fatherly' strengthening of the defences of the papal territories in the 1640s. 20 *Firmana*: poetic adjective for genitive, cf. *Aeneid* 1.200 *Scyllaeam rabiem*; cf. also Lucan

5.190 *rabies uaesana*. The reference is to the very recent so-called 'bread revolt' of July–August 1648 in Fermo in the Marche, in which the inhabitants refused to send the usual grain to Rome; the city's governor was killed and the papal authority had difficulty reestablishing order.[52] 20-1: prosodically matching and rhyming verbs of similar sense appear in elegant vertical juxtaposition at consecutive line-ends (*trucidat, cruentat*). 21-2: for *diraque . . . caede* cf. Ovid *Met.* 3.625 *dira pro caede* – *dirus* refers to the 'accursed' slaying of fellow citizens. *Pharsalidos auctor* = Lucan, from whom the next four lines (23-6) are reproduced without variation (see on 15-26 above); *Pharsalidos* varies the unmetrical genitive *Pharsaliae* (*Pharsalia* is the usual neo-Latin title of Lucan's poem), and is also a form established in neo-Latin (found e.g. in Coluccio Salutati *De Laboribus Herculis* 27.3). 23 *gnarus* agrees with *auctor*, neatly inserting the quotation into Chigi's syntax (the subject is Caesar in the original).

27-32 The evils of war in general; the list of abstract personifications here is in the grand Horatian manner (cf. e.g. *Odes* 1.35.16-20). 27 *Astraea* – the pagan goddess of justice (e.g. Ovid *Met.* 1.150); lines 27 and 28 both have emphatic repetitions, of which the second aptly recalls a famous Vergilian prophecy of war in Italy (*Aeneid* 6.86 *bella, horrida bella*), while line 28 echoes Lucretius 2.14 *o miseras *hominum mentes*. 29: cf. *Georgics* 1.511 *saeuit *toto Mars impius *orbe*, a context important for this poem (see introductory section above). 30: for the metaphor cf. Statius *Ach.*1.403 *iura, fidem, superos una calcata rapina*. The striking phrase *auiti stemmatis exlex* (31) reverses the praise of *Aeneid* 10.752 *haud* expers *. . . uirtutis* auitae, while in 32 *degenerat Virtus* recalls Silius 10.68-9 *pro* degener *altae /* uirtutis *patrum* and *uitiisque oppressa* echoes Seneca *Dial.* 3.8.3 *oppressa uitiis*.

33-49 The sufferings of Germany in particular. 33 *Ast ego* – a grand Vergilian archaism here (cf. *Aeneid* *1.46, *7.308, both diuine speeches); cf. also *Georgics* 2.402 **uoluitur annus* and *Aeneid* 5.626 *septima . . . iam uertitur aestas* (Chigi first went to Germany in 1639, see Introduction). 34: the metaphor of the disastrous harvest of civil war looks back to

Georgics 1.491-2 *bis sanguine nostro / Emathiam et latos* Haemi pinguescere campis (an important context here, see introductory section above) and Lucan 7.851 (another civil war context) *quae* seges *infecta* surget *non decolor herba*? 35-9 is a version of the the classical trope where the poet claims incapacity to narrate something particularly impressive or fearsome (cf. especially *Aeneid* 6.625-7, of the unspeakable horrors of Tartarus). 36-7: the unity and international formidability of Germany (i.e. the Holy Roman Empire) before the war are exaggerated here for pathos and for comparison with ancient Rome; the tragedy of a great world power destroying itself by internecine strife rather than attacking foreign enemies is similarly the theme of Lucan 1.8-20. 36: cf. Tacitus *Hist.*5.25 *excidium gentis*. 37: cf. Silius 6.589 *cladis acerbae*, *Aeneid* 6.332 *sortemque *animo miseratus iniquam*. 38: cf. [Tibullus] 3.3.28 *audiat auersa non meus aure deus*, with similar initial assonance, Ovid *Ars* 2.347 **praebeat aures*. 39: for the rhetorical paradox and polyptoton cf. e.g. *Aeneid* 2.354 *una* salus *uictis nullam sperare* salutem (similar polyptoton), for the paradox alone Ovid *Am.* 3.12.30 *proditor in medio Tantalus amne sitit*. 40: a Lucretian-style one-line conclusion to an argument: cf. Lucretius 1.497 **usque adeo in rebus solidi nihil esse uidetur*, 4.1120 **usque adeo incerti tabescunt uulnere caeco*. 40 *praedurus* is Vergilian (*Aeneid* 10.748), *praegrandis* from Persius (1.124); note the emphatic initial alliteration of matching intensifiying prefixes. 41: cf. *Georgics* 3.551-2 *in lucem* Stygiis emissa tenebris *) pallida Tisiphone*, Seneca *HO* 1975-6 *me iam decet subire caelestem* plagam: / inferna *uici rursus Alcides loca*, *Georgics* 1.511 *saeuit toto Mars impius orbe* (another link with that civil war context). 42: cf. Seneca *Thy.* 250-1 *dira Furiarum cohors / discorsque Erinys*, [Seneca] *Octauia* 161 *Erinys saeua funesto pede*. 42-3: high-style use of abstract personifications again (cf. on 27- 32 above); cf. the retinue of Mars at *Aeneid* 12.335-6 *circumque atrae Formidinis ora / Iraeque* Insidiaeque, dei comitatus, *aguntur*; for *flebile letum* cf. Seneca *Ph.* 997 *flebile leto*. 44: cf. *Aeneid* 8.571 *tam multis uiduasset ciuibus urbem*. 45: *arae incensae* is a dramatic perversion of the conventional burnt offerings at altars (*Aeneid* 3.279 *uotisque incendimus aras*). 44-5 echo *Georgics* 1.507 *squalent abductis arua* *colonis*, an important context of civil war here (see introductory section above). 46: cf. Lucan 4.554 (another civil war) *cognato tantos inplerunt sanguine sulcos*. 47 *effrenis . . . libido* (note the line-enclosing hyperbaton of noun and epithet, an elegant and classical feature) varies the Ciceronian *libido effrenata* (7×) with the late antique form *effrenis* (cf. e.g. Prudentius *Psych.* 179); cf. also Catullus 64.147 *cupidae mentis satiata libidost*. In 47–8 words of matching sense (*scelere/rabiem, exsatiata/compescit*) are vertically juxtaposed, as is the rhetorically forceful anaphoric *nec adhuc/nec adhuc*; *bellandi . . . rabiem* (48) varies *Aeneid* 8.237 *belli rabies*, while for *compescit* cf. Ovid *Ars* 3.501 *rabidos compescere mores*. 49: cf. Statius *Theb*.3.692 **lacrimis gemituque propinquo*, and for this polar pair of adjectives (here in an elegant chiasmus) cf. *Epistles* 1.19.11 *nocturno certare mero, putere *diurno*.

50–64 The poet wishes for peace in this time of war. Lines 50–1 refer to the great powers of Germany/the Holy Roman Empire, France and Spain, the major actors in the peace negotiations, by means of their rivers, whose descriptions here draw on classical poetry – cf. Lucan 6.475–6 *Rhodanumque morantem / praecipitauit Arar*, Seneca *Phoen.* 604–5 *Pactolus / inundat auro rura*, Lucan 7.15 *gentes quas torrens ambit Hiberus*. 52: cf. *Aeneid* 6.157–8 *caecosque uolutat / euentus animo secum*, *1.62 *foedere certo*. 53: cf. *Aeneid* 1.514 *coniungere dextras*, Lucan 5.354 *iam pondere fessis*, Statius *Theb*. 4.196 **pondere belli*. 55–6: cf. *Aeneid* 1.426 **iura magistratusque*; *artes ingenuae* is an Ovidian phrase (4×), while for deserted farmland as a symbol of civil war see *Georgics* 1.507 *squalent abductis arua colonis*, from an important context here (see introductory section above). 57: for the safe grazing of sheep as a mark of peace cf. Tibullus 1.10.10 <u>securus</u> *sparsas dux gregis inter* <u>oves</u>. 58: cf. Ovid *Ars* 1.53 *nigris portarit ab Indis*, *Epistles* 1.1.45 *inpiger extremos curris *mercator ad Indos*. 59: cf. Calpurnius 1.42 *aurea secura cum pace renascitur aetas*. 60: cf. Propertius 4.7.21–2 *uerba / non audituri diripuere Noti*, Ovid *Fasti* 5.321 *uenti nocuere *proterui*. 61: cf. Ovid *Her*. 7.88 *per mare, per terras*, *Odes* 1.22.5 *per Syrtes . . . aestuosas*; *lustro* refers to the five years Chigi has spent at the negotiations since 1643. 62 *tot*: for the large number of delegations see on line 6 above;

Fabio Chigi (1599-1667; Pope as Alexander VII 1655-67)   177

decumana = 'massive' since the tenth item in a list was thought the largest, an archaic usage of Lucilius (*OLD* s.u. 1b) – in 63 *opplerunt* is another archaic word (6× in Plautus), while the alliterative repetition of the same prefix in *concordia constat* is highly emphatic, stressing the key idea of togetherness. 64: for Bellona (Roman goddess of war) in a similar context of civil conflict cf. *Aeneid* 7.319, 8.703; *fremens* recalls the roaring of Furor (the spirit of civil war) at *Aeneid* 1.294-6 *Furor impius intus / saeua sedens super arma ... /... fremet horridus ore cruento*, while *saeuit* recalls *Georgics* 1.511 *saeuit toto Mars impius orbe* (echoed at line 41 above, see note there).

65-78 The poet prays to God for peace and to bestow eternal life on the pope, with a final brief return to his addressee. This concluding prayer matches that to the *di patrii* for the future victory of the young Caesar in time of civil war at the end of *Georgics* 1 (498-501), but is strongly Christian in language; line 65 echoes Vida's opening address to the Holy Spirit at *Christias* 1.2 *Qui mare, qui terras, qui coelum numine comples / Spiritus alme,* also imitated in 68. 66: a modification of Matthew 10.29 *Nonne duo passeres asse ueneunt? et unus ex illis non cadet super terram sine Patre uestro?,* using *Eclogues* 2.70 *frondosa ... ulmo* and perhaps Seneca *Ep.*104.11 *decidant folia.* 67: cf. Lucretius 2.281-2 **cuius ad arbitrium quoque copia materiai / cogitur interdum flecti per membra per artus,* Statius *Theb.*3.281 *flectere corda, Aeneid* 12.519 **potentum.* 68: cf. Bargeo *Syrias* 1.13-14 *(MQDQ,* 16C) *Verus amor patris, natique aeterna uoluptas / Spiritus.* 69-71: each of these three lines of prayer begins with *tu* (the classical *Du-stil* for addressing a god), just as the three stanzas of Horace's mock prayer to the wine-jar begin with *tu, tu* and *te* (*Odes* 3.21.13-24). 69: cf. Fulbert of Chartres' hymn *Sancta Maria, succurre miseris* (tenth to eleventh century) and Statius *Ach.*1.355 **tu frange regendo.* 70: cf. Lucan 8.441-2 *orbem / Romanum,* Irenaeus 3.1.1 *caelestem pacem* (for the imperative *serena* cf. e.g. Seneca *Ag.* 521). 70-71: note how *luce corona* is in vertical juxtaposition at line-end with *pace serena,* similar in shape, sound and grammar (*corona* like *serena* is imperative). 71-2 *quintum ... / ... annum*: Innocent X was elected pope in September 1644 (*praesul* can mean 'pope' as well as 'bishop' – cf.

TLL 10.2.949.69–72); *Innocuus* is used for the name Innocent in earlier neo-Latin poetry (e.g. Celtis *Epigrammata* 6.6.6, of Innocent VIII), while *delubra reponens*, referring to repairing the many Catholic shrines destroyed in the Thirty Years War, recalls Horace's claim that restoring the temples at Rome will be an act of moral progress (*Odes* 3.6.2 *donec templa refeceris*). 73: cf. 9.688 *animis discordibus*, Catullus 62.17 *animos . . . conuertite uestros*. 75: cf. Ovid *Met.* 5.348 *aetherias . . . sedes*; *olli* is an archaizing poetic form, while *regna beata* (a regular phrase in previous neo-Latin poetry) comes originally from Ovid *Her.* 12.24. 76: cf. Ovid *Ex Ponto* 1.10.11 *nectar et ambrosiam, latices epulasque deorum*. Pope Innocent's future life in heaven with its privileged consumption of celestial fare looks back to that prophesied for Augustus by Horace in *Odes* 3.3.12 (*purpureo bibet ore nectar*). 77–8: a somewhat abrupt return to the poem's formal addressee. *Dignis . . . fastis* and *aeternis sertis* pay matching compliments to Pio's ancient and distinguished family (*fasti* here means '(family) history, annals': cf. *TLL* 6.1.328.57–70), while *aeternis sertis* recalls the everlasting triumphal garlands of Pollio at *Odes* 2.1.15–16 *cui laurus aeternos honores / Delmatico peperit triumpho* and *nectatur* the garlands of poetic distinction at *Epistles* 2.2.96 *qua re sibi nectat uterque coronam*. Note the vertical juxtaposition at rhyming line-ends of the parallel phrases *gloria fastis* and *adorea sertis*, which adds (rhyme-like) to the closural effect here.

Figure 3 Pope Leo XIII, photograph by Francesco De Federicis, 1898. *Source*: Wikimedia Commons/Library of Congress https://commons.wikimedia.org/wiki/Leo_XIII#/media/File:Papa_Leone_XIII_(1898).jpg.

3

Vincenzo Pecci (1810–1903; Pope as Leo XIII 1878–1903)

Pecci wrote Latin poetry throughout his long life from the time of his schooldays, though he was nothing like as prolific a versifier as either of his fellow popes, Barberini and Chigi. Most of his major poems were written during his papacy, and collections of them appeared in Italy, Germany and the United States in that period.[1] The Latin texts here are taken from the 1902 US edition, which also presents a parallel English verse translation and adds some useful explanatory notes (Pecci 1902).

The complete collection contains some seventy poems, varying in length from brief epigrams and inscriptions to more substantial works, and in date from 1822 to 1901. My selection here has largely focussed on poems that imitate those of Horace, which for me represent his most enterprising work. Like Barberini and Chigi, Pecci wrote some major Horatian-style odes for public occasions: included here are two substantial commemorative lyric odes, that written in 1896 for the 1400th anniversary of the conversion of the Frankish king Clovis in 496 CE (in nineteen Sapphic stanzas; item 3) and that marking the new millennium of 1900 (in fourteen Alcaic stanzas, item 5). As pope, Pecci seems to have regarded such public compositions as an important form of international outreach. Less public poems include a hexameter epistle to a friend on moderate diet (in eighty-five lines, item 4), which clearly imitates Horatian *sermo* in both form and content, a substantial Propertian-style elegy (fifty-four lines) on the key role of the Virgin Mary in two historical conflicts (item 2) and hymns to saints such as Constantius of Perugia in the form both of Horatian odes and of Ambrose's early Christian hymnography (item 1). These less public items also belong to the years of his papacy.

The 1902 collection contains several thematic groupings of poems which further reflect Pecci's life and his literary and theological interests.

There are further hymns to saints in addition to those to Constantius (above), especially to the Virgin Mary and the Holy Family,[2] which similarly mix Horatian and early Christian lyric forms. There are also poems to his fellow members of the Accademia degli Arcadi, a prestigious literary academy at Rome under papal patronage[3] which the young Pecci joined in 1832,[4] and obituary poems for his brother Cardinal Giuseppe Pecci (1807–90) and other friends.

The context of Pecci's poetry in the late nineteenth century presents some significant cultural differences from those of Barberini and Chigi in the baroque period. First, Pecci's approach to Latin verse composition is more recognizably like the discipline as practised as a linguistic exercise in educational contexts in the modern period, relying especially on the close and detailed imitation of prominent classical sources, as the commentary consistently shows. Second, by this time Latin, though still the language of Catholic liturgy worldwide, was not so freely understood internationally as it had been in the early modern period,[5] and it is significant that Pecci's poetry was rendered into English already in his own lifetime for worldwide diffusion to the Catholic faithful;[6] it was partly through such translations that he achieved some fame as a practising papal poet.[7] Third, some of the more modern subject matter presents especially interesting technical challenges for poets in the language of ancient Rome, for example in Pecci's brief 1867 poem on the new technology of photography;[8] these challenges were often ingeniously confronted in the contemporary virtuoso Latin verse compositions submitted for the international *Certamen Poeticum Hoeufftianum*, which began in 1844.[9]

1. Pair of hymns to St Constantius (San Costanzo) of Perugia

These hymns, written in 1878 and 1879, belong to the earliest years of Pecci's papacy in which he was still formally bishop of Perugia (1878–80).[10] They celebrate the city's saint Constantius (San Costanzo), said to have lived in the second century and to have been the first of Pecci's episcopal predecessors. Pecci provided a prose biography of Constantius to accompany the poem (Pecci 1902: 82) which gives a useful summary of the traditions about the saint's life and death:[11]

> Constantius Perusiae christianis parentibus natus, uirtute aetatem antegressus, Episcopus patriae suae factus est. Is propter studium christiani numinis multa dictu grauia, perpessu aspera inuicto animo pertulit. Nam primum pugnis contundi iussus, deinde in thermis includi septuplo uehementius accensis; sed aquis Dei nutu repente tepefactis, e summo discrimine euasit incolumis. Mox prunarum cruciatu fortissime perfunctus, coniicitur in custodiam: unde christianorum opera extractum satellites imperatorii comprehendunt, et ui uulnerum prope conficiunt. Continuo tamen ille diuinitus conualuit: tunc Assisium in carcerem rapitur. Paullo post illinc eductus, cum quamlibet carnificinam subire mallet, quam a proposito disseminandae catholicae religionis desistere, idcirco in triuio apud Fuliginium nobile martyrium fecit, Marco Aurelio Vero Imperatore, Sotere Pontifice maximo. Sacrum eius corpus inhumatum proiectum Leuianus, magna pietate uir, domo Fulginio, ab Angelo in somnis admonitus, uenerabundus feretro composuit. Quod cum Perusiam deduceretur, ea res miraculo fuit, quod sacrarum reliquiarum uectores repente lumen oculorum, quo antea carebant, recepere. Martyrem fortissimum Perusini summa religione colunt, eiusque memoriam, templo extructo, consecrarunt.

Constantius was born in Perugia, of Christian parents. Achieving a virtue that outran his years, he was elected Bishop of his fatherland. He was persecuted because of his zeal for Christianity, and endured with unflinching courage much grievous suffering. First of all he was ordered to be beaten, then to be shut up in the baths, which were heated sevenfold more than usual. God willed, however, that the water should suddenly become lukewarm; and thus he escaped unharmed. Forced to walk over live coals, he bore the torment with the greatest fortitude, and was then cast into prison. Thanks to the efforts of some Christians, he escaped, only to fall again into the hands of the Emperor's satellites, who wounded him nigh unto death. By divine help, however, he immediately recovered, and was then hurried off to Assisi and again cast into prison. Shortly afterwards he was led forth to trial; but declaring that he preferred to suffer any kind of death rather than give up his purpose of spreading the Catholic religion, he achieved a noble martyrdom at the cross-roads of Foligno, during the reign of the emperor Marcus Aurelius Verus and the pontificate of Soter.[12] His body, which had been cast forth unburied, was reverently placed on a bier by Leuianus of Foligno, a man of great piety, who had received in sleep an angelic admonition to that effect. While the body was being carried back to Perugia, a wonderful thing happened. The bearers of the sacred relics, who were blind, suddenly received their sight. The people of Perugia entertain the greatest reverence for the mighty Martyr, and have dedicated a church to his memory.[13]

Metrically, the first poem uses the four-line stanza of iambic dimeters associated with St Ambrose and used in several hymns to martyrs in the *Peristephanon* by the late antique Christian poet Prudentius, a poet also imitated by Barberini in his ode to St Laurence (*Peristephanon* 2, see Barberini item 5 above). The second uses Horace's Sapphic stanza,[14] which was also employed by Prudentius in his hymn to the martyrs of Saragossa (*Peristephanon* 4). The first poem is set on the eve of San Costanzo's feast day of 29 January in 1878, the second marks the day itself in 1879, a chronological progression.

The first poem presents a dramatic recreation of the procession of the inhabitants of Perugia, heading to the church of San Costanzo just outside the medieval city walls, where the saint was traditionally buried, a church that Pecci himself had restored as bishop of Perugia.[15] It falls into three parts: an initial announcement of the sacred occasion and invocation of the saint (1–12), a description of the severe winter weather which cannot deter the joyful procession of the citizens of Perugia (13–20) and an account of the nocturnal procession itself (21–36).

Though, as noted above, the poem is not in an Horatian metre, its content is strongly reminiscent of Horace. Its opening clearly echoes that of the Roman Odes (3.1.1–2; see notes on I:1–2 below), while its situation in which the return of a revered saviour figure to his city is desiderated and imagined recalls *Odes* 4.5, which both expresses the poet's longing for Augustus' return and anticipates popular celebration of the same, and *Odes* 3.14, which presents the return of Augustus to Rome from Spain with 'eye-witness' commentary. The honouring of the quasi-divine figure of the ruler of Rome is thus neatly transmuted into that of the saint of Perugia, a modification which is explicitly indicated in I.11.

The second poem also points to a specific occasion, the marking of the saint's day in 1879 at the church itself, the location reached at the end of the first poem. An introductory stanza (1–4) is followed by the dramatic martyrdom narrative (5–32), its miraculous aftermath (33–48) and a final section which combines invocation of the saint with a personal allusion to writer and his papacy (49–64). The main section, the martyrdom narrative, follows the traditional pattern of the stories of Prudentius' *Peristephanon* with a cruel and persecuting government official, a defiant and fearless martyr, gory description, miraculous divine intervention, direct speech and a crowd of impressed onlookers,[16] while its closing section alludes prominently to Horace with the self-naming of the poet (62) and the conscious repetition in its last line of the last line of the *Carmen Saeculare* (64).

Text and translation

IN HONOREM S. CONSTANTII

I AN. MDCCCLXXVIII

Fauete linguis; hinc procul
Este, o profani: crastinus
Sollemnibus Constantii
Sacer dies est martyris.

O diue, praesens o tuae   5
Salus decusque patriae!
Redi auspicatus, iam redi
Umbris colendus gentibus.

Te heroa, te fortissimum
Efferre caelo martyrem,   10
Oblita laudes Caesarum,
Tyrrhena gestit canticis.

Hiems rigescit asperis
Montes pruinis albicant,
Solisque crines frigido   15
Irrorat imbre Aquarius.

At bruma non desaeuiens,
Non atra caeli nubila
Cives morantur annuis
Rite exsilire gaudiis.   20

Nox en propinquat: cerneres
Feruere turbis compita,
Late per umbram cerneres
Ardere colles ignibus,

Urbisque ferri ad moenia   25
Incessu et ore supplici

Vincenzo Pecci (1810-1903; Pope as Leo XIII 1878-1903)

IN HONOUR OF SAINT CONSTANTIUS

I: 1878

Hold your tongues in silence, be far
From here, you uninitiated: tomorrow
Is the holy day for the rituals of
The martyr Constantius.

O Saint, present to help,   5
O salvation and glory of your birthland!
Return with good auspices, return now
To be worshipped by the peoples of Umbria.

To exalt you to heaven as hero,
You as the most courageous of martyrs,   10
Forgetting the praise of Caesars,
Is the desire of Tuscany in its songs.

The winter stiffens, and the hills
Are white with rough frosts,
And the Sun's locks are bedewed   15
By the cold shower of Aquarius.

But neither the winter venting its rage,
Nor the dark clouds of the sky
Holds back the citizens from due leaping
In their annual rejoicing.   20

Behold, the night approaches: you might see
The crossroads seethe with crowds,
You might see the hills alight
Far and wide with bonfires,

And the flocking to the city's walls   25
With humble gait and expression

Senes, uiros, cum matribus
Longo puellas agmine.

Ut uentum ubi ara martyris
Corusca lychnis emicat, 30
Festiua turba ciuium
Irrumpit ardens, clamitat:

'O Pastor e caelo, o parens
Constanti, adesto filiis',
Pressis sepulcro dulcia 35
Figit labellis oscula.

II AN. MDCCCLXXIX

Panditur templum, facibus renidet
Ara Constanti: celebrate nomen
Dulce pastoris, memoresque fastos
Dicite cantu.
Impios ritus et inane fulmen 5
Risit indignans Iouis et Quirini;
Obtulit ferro iuvenile pectus,
Obtulit igni.
Aestuant thermae saliente flamma;
Densa plebs circumstat anhela; praetor 10
Clamat: 'i, lictor, calida rebellem
Merge sub unda'.
Mergitur: plantas simul unda tinxit,
Frigidus ceu fons per amoena florum
Defluens, blando recreata mulcet 15
Membra lauacro.
Vulgus immoto stupet ore; praetor
Frendet elusus; scelerum ministris
Mandat, obstrictum manicis recondant
Carceris antro. 20
Vincla nil terrent: fidei magister

Of old men, men in their prime,
And girls in a long column with their mothers.

When they come to where the martyr's altar
Shines out glittering with lanterns, 30
The festive crowd of citizens
Breaks in with burning zeal, repeatedly shouting:

'O shepherd, o father Constantius,
Come from heaven and be with your children',
And with lips together 35
Presses sweet kisses on his tomb.

II: 1879

The shrine is opened up, the altar of Constantius
Shines with torches: celebrate the sweet name
Of the shepherd, and recite the annals' memories
By your singing.
He laughed disdainfully at the unholy rites 5
And the empty thunderbolt of Jupiter and Quirinus:
He offered his youthful breast to the sword,
Offered it to the fire.
The baths are glowing with leaping flame:
The people stand about close-packed and breathless: 10
The praetor shouts 'Go on, lictor, plunge the rebel
Under the boiling water'.
He is plunged: as soon as the water wet his feet,
Like a spring flowing through lovely flowers,
It refreshes and caresses his limbs 15
With a soothing wash.
The crowd gaped with fixed faces: the praetor
Grinds his teeth, thwarted, and bids the agents
Of his crime to hold the man bound in manacles
In the prison's cavern. 20
The bonds bring no fear: as teacher of faith

Liber effaris, uigilum docendo
Pectora emollis, Stygiusque cedit
Mentibus error.
Saeuior contra rabies tyranni   25
Flagrat; insontem lacerat flagellis,
Sauciat ferro, rigidaque plantas
Compede torquet.
Nec datum immani sat adhuc furori;
Hostiam diris agit, et deorum   30
Numini spreto uouet immolandam
Caede cruenta.
Corpus in limo iacet interemptum:
At pius forti celebrandus auso
Luce pallenti uigilans ad umbram   35
Carceris, ima
Saepta pervadit Leuianus; artus
Colligit sparsos, caput ense truncum
Rite componens fouet, et beata
Condit in urna.   40
Grande portentum! sacra membra in urbem
Quattuor latis umeris reportant
Lucis expertes, subitoque uisus
Munere gaudent.
Redditur pastor patriae, refulgens   45
Aureis uittis et honore palmae,
Saeptus aeterna superum corona
Redditur heros.
Diue, quem templis ueneramur
Umbris, Umbriae fines placido reuisens   50
Lumine, exoptata reduc opimae
Gaudia pacis.
Diue, pastorem tua in urbe quondam
Infula cinctum, socium et laborum,
Quem pius tutum per iter superna   55

You speak freely, and soften by instruction
The hearts of your guards, and infernal error
Leaves their minds.
In response the madness of the tyrant burns 25
More cruelly: he cuts the innocent man with whips,
Wounds him with iron, and tortures his feet
With unyielding fetters.
Nor was satiety yet given to his monstrous raging:
He assails his victim with curses and vows him 30
To be sacrificed to the mocked majesty of his gods
In bloody slaughter.
The murdered body lies in the mud:
But a holy man, to be lauded for his daring deed,
Staying awake in the pale light beside the shadow 35
Of the prison,
Levianus, penetrated that deepest of enclosures,
Gathered the scattered limbs, cherished the head,
Cut off by the sword, duly laying it out, and put it all
In a blessed urn. 40
Such a great portent! Four blind men
Carry the sacred limbs into the city
On broad shoulders, and rejoice in the sudden
Gift of sight.
The shepherd is returned to his fatherland, 45
Shining with golden headgear and the honour of the palm,
Girded with the eternal crown of those above
The hero is returned.
Saint, whom we revere in the Umbrian shrines,
Visit once more the land of Umbria with your peaceful light 50
And bring back the longed-for joys of
The riches of peace.
Saint, the man whom, as shepherd wearing the headband
And as sharer in your labours, you used loyally
To guide on a safe path by the 55

Luce regebas,
Nunc Petri cumbam tumidum per aequor
Ducere, et pugnae per acuta cernis
Spe bona certaque leuare in altos
Lumina montes. 60
Possit o tandem, domitis procellis,
Visere optatas Leo uictor oras;
Occupet tandem uaga cumba portum
Sospite cursu.

Vincenzo Pecci (1810–1903; Pope as Leo XIII 1878–1903)

Light of heaven,
You now see steering Peter's bark through
Swollen seas, and raising in the sharp times of battle
his eyes in good and certain hope
To the lofty hills. 60
May Leo at last, having tamed the storms,
See the longed-for shores in victory,
May his wandering bark gain the harbour
In safe passage.

Commentary

I

1–12 An initial announcement of the sacred occasion and invocation of the saint. 1–2: cf. Horace *Odes* 3.1.1–2 *Odi profanum uulgus et arceo. / favete linguis*, *Aeneid* 6.258 *procul, o procul este, profani*, both similarly the words of a dramatized priestly figure warning the 'uninitiated'; in the context of the late 1870s this points to 'unbelievers' in an increasingly secular Italy. 2–4 *crastinus / . . . / dies* – cf. *Aeneid* 10.244 *crastina lux*, Horace *Epistles* 1.5.9 *cras nato Caesare festus* (a similar celebratory anniversary for Augustus); *sollemnia* = 'regular religious ritual' as at *Aeneid* 8.185. 5 *Diue*: stanza-initial address as at Horace *Odes* 4.6.1 *Diue* (Apollo, here transmuted into the saint); *praesens* is used as often of the active presence of a pagan god (*OLD* s.u. 3). 6: for *patriae decus* of an individual cf. *Ilias Latina* 273 *o patriae, germane, decus*, and Ovid's address to Augustus at *Tristia* 2.574 *o patriae cura salusque tuae*. 7: compare Horace's address to Augustus at *Odes* 4.5.4 *redi*; *auspicatus* uses the language of pagan auspices (favourable divinatory signs) for the Christian saint (see note on item 2 line 1 below). 8: cf. Ovid *Tristia* 5.10.48 *Scythicis . . . gentibus* (similarly poetic plural for singular). 9–10: cf. *Aeneid* 6.169 *fortissimus heros*, Augustine *Serm.* 65.2 *fortissimus martyr* (again combining pagan and Christian encomium; for *heros* of martyrs cf. *TLL* 6.3.2664.14ff); *caelo* is dative of motion as in the Vergilian *it caelo* (*Aeneid* 5.451, 11.192, 12.283), while *efferre caelo* varies the Ciceronian phrase *ad/in caelum efferre* (8×). 11 *oblita laudes Caesarum* looks back pointedly to the praises of Augustus echoed in lines 1–7 (see notes above and introductory section above): this encomium of the Christian saint surpasses morally that of the pagan emperors which it echoes verbally. 12 *Tyrrhena* is a post-classical form of the noun *Tyrrhenia* (Ovid *Met.* 14.452), found widely in neo-Latin poetry; here by poetic exaggeration the neighbouring region of Tuscany is added to Umbria in praise of the saint. For *canticis* after *efferre caelo* cf. Catullus 6.17 *ad caelum lepido uocare uersu*.

13-20 The severe winter weather cannot deter the joyful procession of the citizens of Perugia. 13-16 recall Horatian and Vergilian descriptions of winter (cf. *Georgics* 3.363 *rigescunt*, Horace *Odes* 1.4.1 *acris hiems*, 4 *nec prata canis albicant pruinis*, *Georgics* 1.259 *frigidus . . . imber*, *Aeneid* 3.304 *extremoque irrorat Aquarius anno*). and the effective alliteration of Columella 10.1.147-8 *imbres / . . . irrorans*. 17-18: cf. *Aeneid* 4.52 *desaeuit hiems*, 5.512 *atra . . . in nubila*, *Georgics* 4.166 *nubila caeli*. 19-20: cf. *Aeneid* 5.53 *annua uota*, Cicero *Fam.* 16.16.2 *exsilui gaudio*; note how rhyming and metrically matching noun and epithet are vertically juxtaposed at line-end here (*annuis / . . . gaudiis*).

21-36 The nocturnal procession to the church of San Costanzo. 21: cf. *Aeneid* 9.7 *dies en attulit*, 9.355 *lux . . . propinquat*. 21-3: for the emphatic anaphora of the same verb of sight cf. Horace *Epodes* 2.63-4 *uidere . . . / uidere*; these lines recall the wedding-procession at Statius *Siluae* 1.2.230-1 *iam festa feruet domus utraque pompa./ fronde uirent postes, effulgent compita flammis*, here converted to sacred Christian use. The plural form *turbis* occurs only once in classical Latin poetry (*Ilias Latina* 1014) but is frequent in neo-Latin verse, while *per umbram* is a Vergilian phrase (5×, rare otherwise); *ignibus* suggests celebratory beacons on the surrounding hills. 25: cf. *Aeneid* 11.900 *ad moenia ferri*; the church of San Costanzo lies just outside the ancient city walls. 26: cf. Silius 15.29-30 *ore / incessuque*, Ovid *Met.* 2.396 *supplice uoce*. 27-8: compare the family groups in the procession to receive Augustus at *Odes* 3.14.9-10 *uirginum matres . . . / . . . pueri et puellae*; *longo . . . agmine* inverts the formula *agmine longo* (3× Vergil, 2× Statius). 29-30: cf. *Aeneid* 8.362 *ut uentum ad sedes*, Statius *Theb.* 5.572-3 *capitisque insigne corusci / emicat*, Lucretius 5.295-6 *pendentes lychni claraeque coruscis / fulguribus taedae*. 33-4: the enthusiastic words of the crowd are quoted in dramatic direct speech, as in the imagined acclamation of Augustus at *Odes* 4.5.37-8 *longas o utinam, dux bone, ferias / praestes Hesperiae!*; *pastor* is used in the Christian sense of 'caring religious leader', found in the Vulgate (Isaiah 63.11) and in patristic writers from Tertullian on (*TLL* 10.1.640.79ff), while *parens* is employed in its classical sense of a god or mortal acting with father-like benevolence, here as a local saint (*TLL* 10.1.362.34ff., 363.5ff.). For the rare subjunctive form *adesto* in an invocation of divine power cf. Ovid *Met*.2.45; it is here treated as an imperative as often in neo-Latin (e.g. Petrarch *Africa* 5.734), and *adsum* is common of the helpful presence of a pagan deity (see on item 2 line 11 below). Note the vertical juxtaposition in final position of the related words *parens* and *filiis*. 35–6 Christianize the erotic kisses of Ovid *Am*.1.7.41 *impressis* ... *labellis* and *Her*.11.117 *oscula frigida* (on a lover's tomb); cf. also *Aeneid* 1.687 *oscula dulcia figet*. Note the vertical juxtaposition of rhyming and metrically equivalent noun and epithet at line-end in the last two lines, resembling a final rhyme in a vernacular language (for a similar effect at the close of a poem see note on Chigi item 8 lines 77–8 above).

II

1–4 Scene-setting introduction at the church of San Costanzo. 1: cf. *panditur* ... *domus* of the opening of the divine palace of Olympus at *Aeneid* 10.1, and Lucretius 2.27 *auroque renidet*. 2–3: cf. Lucretius 4.1062 *nomen dulce* (an erotic context Christianised here); for *pastor* see note on I.33–4 above, and cf. Horace *Odes* 4.14.4 *memoresque fastos*. 4: cf. *Georgics* 2.95 *carmine dicam*.

5–32 Narrative of the saint's martyrdom. 5–8 suggest his refusal of the opportunity to abjure Christian faith in favour of the established pagan religion, and his consequent choice to face torture and death, traditional features of martyr narratives – cf. e.g. Prudentius *Peristephanon* 1.40–5. 5: echoes patristic condemnation of pagan deities – cf. e.g. Lactantius *Inst*. 5.10 <u>ritus inpios</u> *ac profanos deus uerus odio habet*, 2.3 *religiones et cultus deorum* <u>inane</u> *esse officium confitetur*. 6 **Quirini** may suggest the story that the statue of the infant Romulus (later the god Quirinus) was miraculously struck by lightning (Cicero *Div*.2.21); for Jupiter's traditional thunderbolt cf. e.g. *Aeneid* 10.567 *Iouis* ... *fulmina*. 7–8: cf. Seneca *Medea* 129–30 *ferro obuium / offerre pectus*, *Aeneid* 12.221 *iuuenali in corpore* (similarly sympathetically of the doomed youth

Turnus); the emphatic anaphora of the verb *obtulit* (vertically juxtaposed: an Horatian effect, cf. *Odes* 1.2.4-5 *terruit* ... / *terruit*) is neatly linked with the common pair of nouns *ferro / igni* (found e.g. at *Aeneid* 2.581, 7.692). 9: cf. Augustine *Civ.* 21.4 *flammis aestuant.* 10: cf. Horace *Odes* 2.13.32 *densum* ... *uulgus,* Ovid *Met.* 2.717 *densi circumstant sacra ministri,* Statius *Ach.* 1.484 *stabat anhela*; the grander *praetor* is loosely used here for a lower-ranking local official, as in Prudentius' account of the martyrdom of the provincial Eulalia (*Peristephanon* 3.97). 11: *i, lictor* is the traditional command of the Roman magistrate to his enforcing agent (Cicero *Rab.Perd.* 13, Livy 1.26.7); cf. also Ovid *Met.* 4.349 *calidis* ... *mersit in undis,* Seneca *HO* 1927-8 *sub undas / ... mergit.* 12-13: *merge* ... *mergitur:* for this kind of confirmatory repetition cf. Wills 1996: 238-40 (note the vertical juxtaposition of the two elements in polyptoton at line-start, cf. similarly Horace *Odes* 1.12.51-2 **Caesaris / Caesare*); cf. also *Aeneid* 7.811 *tingeret aequore plantas.* 14 *frigidus* ... *fons* is a Lucretian phrase (6.848- 9, 6.873, 6.879); for the poetic nominalization and partitive construction of *amoena florum* cf. Valerius Flaccus 1.842 *amoena piorum* (cf. also Horace *Odes* 2.3.14 *flores amoenae... rosae*). 15-16: cf. Apuleius *Apol.* 59 *secundo lauacro* (this rare noun is an Apuleian favourite, 20×), Silius 3.170 *mulcentem* ... *membra sopore,* Pliny *NH* 12.4 *recreans membra.* 17-18: cf. Seneca *Tro.* 1143 *stupet omne uulgus, Georgics* 4.452 *frendens* (of similar powerless frustration), Horace *Ep.2.1.47 elusus,* Ovid *Am.1.7.27 scelerumque ministrae.* 19-20: cf. Ovid *Met.1.583 imoque reconditus antro.* 21: cf. *Aeneid* 9.133 *nil me fatalia terrent*; for *fidei magister* of a Christian champion cf. Ambrose *Expl. Psalm.* xii.40 *fidei magistrum.* 22-3: cf. Horace *Epod.* 5.14 *mollire Thracum pectora* (another traditionally hard-hearted group). 23-4: *Stygius* suggests the false pagan view of the underworld involving the river Styx; cf. also Catullus 63.19 *mente cedat.* 25: cf. Propertius 3.16.17 *saeua canum rabies,* Statius *Silu.* 2.7.100 *rabidi* ... *tyranni.* 26: cf. Firmicus Maternus 3.5 *flagellis lacerare* (note how the line is neatly framed by the alliterating pair *flagrat* ... *flagellis*). 27-8 : cf. Phaedrus 2.7.8 *ferro* ... *sauciant,* Horace *Epod.* 4.4 *dura compede*; *planta* here means the whole foot not just its sole, a poetic metonymy (cf. e.g. *Aeneid* 8.458). 29: *sat datum* is a Vergilian phrase (*Aeneid* 2.291, 9.135), while *immanis furor* is from Augustine (*Ep.* 91.9, *Contra Don.*22). 30: cf. Horace *Epod.*5.89 *diris agam uos*; *hostia* is often used of Christian martyrs (*TLL* 6.3.3048.13ff). 30-1: cf. Ovid *Met.*8.739-40 *qui numina diuum / sperneret*; for the gerundive construction of *immolandam* here cf. Cicero *Rep.*2.36. 32: cf. *Culex* 112 *caede cruenta*.

33-48 The miraculous aftermath of the martyrdom. 33: cf. Ambrose *Exp. Psalm.*117.21 *corporis interempti* (and note the line-framing word order). 34-40: the role of the loyal disciple Levianus in saving the body of the martyr recalls that of Joseph of Arimathea for Jesus (Matthew 27.58-60), while the piecing together of the dismembered body recalls that of Hippolytus at Seneca *Phaedr.* 1105-8 and 1244-68. 34: cf. Ausonius *Ecl.* 10.11 *duplici celebrandus honore, Aeneid* 9.281 *fortibus ausis*. 35-6: cf. Juvencus 1.409 = 2.509 *carceris umbris*. 38-9: *truncum = truncatum* as at Lucan 8.436 (cf. also Lucan 8.677 *caput ense recidis*); for *rite componens* cf. Apuleius *Met.* 6.1.5 *rite componit*. 40: cf. Lucan 2.333 *condidit urna*. 41: cf. Horace *Odes* 1.22.13 **quale portentum*, Cicero *Diu.*2.59 *maximum ... portentum*, and Augustine *Serm.*254 *membra sacra* (of the crucifixion of Jesus). 42: cf. *Aeneid* 9.725 *latis umeris*, 7.573-4 *in urbem / ... reportant*. 43: cf. Seneca *NQ* 3.19 *lucis expertia* (for the miracle of the blind men given sight see introductory section above). 44: cf. Ovid *Ars* 3.655 *munere gaudet*. 45: note the line's elegant chiastic pattern of alliteration (*re-, pa-, pa-, re-*). 45-6: cf. Calp.Sic. 7.53 *auro ... refulgent, Aeneid* 5.366 *uelatum auro uittisque*, Ovid *Pont.*2.11.21 *palmae ... honores* (here *palma* indicates the traditional palm-branch of the Christian martyr, *TLL* 10.1.145.15ff). 47: cf. *Aeneid* 9.545 *saepta corona*, Augustine *Serm.*278 *aeternam coronam*, 315 *supernam coronam* (*superum* = genitive plural, cf. e.g. *Aeneid* 1.4). 48: cf. *Aeneid* 6.672 *reddidit heros* (for the Christian use of *heros* of martyrs see on I.9-10 above) – note the emphatic repetition of *redditur* at the start of both the first and the last line of the stanza.

49-64 The closing invocation of the saint and reference to the poet's own papacy (item 5 below also closes with a reference to Leo as author).

49: *Diue, quem* opens a Sapphic stanza similarly at Horace *Odes* 4.6.1 (there of Apollo) – cf. note on I.5 above; cf. also *Aeneid* 3.83 *templa* ... *uenerabar*. 50: for the quasi-polyptoton of adjective and cognate noun *Umbris, Umbriae* see Wills 1997: 240–1. 50–1: cf. Horace *Odes* 4.3.2 *placido lumine uideris*, *Aeneid* 6.330 *exoptata reuisunt*. 51–2: cf. Silius 16.683 *opima pace*, Flaminio *Carm.*1.8.17 *pacis gaudia candidae*. 53: *Diue* – cf. on 49 above, a prayer-like repetition of address; the same word-form similarly begins two Horatian Sapphic stanzas at *Odes* 2.16.1 and 5 (*otium* ... *otium*). *Pastorem*: see on 1.33–4 above. 54: for the priestly *infula* binding the head (here representing the episcopal mitre) cf. on item 3.19–20 below; cf. also Statius *Silv.* 5.2.35 *sociumque laborum* (the author shared the episcopate of Perugia with his addressee, see introductory section above). 55: cf. Horace *Odes* 3.16.7 *tutum iter* (again divinely influenced), *Aeneid* 6.733 *superna luce*; the idea of the guiding star here anticipates the coming nautical metaphor. 56: combines the original fishing-boat of St Peter with the idea of the 'ship of faith' (cf. Augustine *Ep.* 119.6 *fidei cumba*), perhaps recalling the classical 'ship of state' image (cf. e.g. Horace *Odes* 1.14); cf. also *Aeneid* 3.157 *tumidum* ... *aequor*. 58–9: cf. Horace *Odes* 4.4.76 *acuta belli*, CS 73 *spem bonam certamque*. 59–60: cf. *Psalms* 120.1 *leuaui oculos meos in montes, unde ueniet auxilium mihi*. 61–4: the ageing papal author seems to draw on the despairing words of the ageing king Latinus at *Aeneid* 7.594 and 598–9, but corrects his pagan pessimism and points to the haven of heaven rather than that of death: *'frangimur heu fatis' inquit 'ferimurque procella! / ... / nam mihi parta quies, omnisque in limine portus / funere felici spolior'*; *domitis procellis* and *uictor* point to the many trials the contemporary papacy needs to overcome (see volume Introduction). 62: cf. *Aeneid* 1.172 *optata* ... *harena*, Horace *Odes* 3.14.4 *uictor ab ora*. The self-naming of the poet at the end of a poem echoes Horace *Odes* 4.6.44 *uatis Horati* (also in a prayer), and is found again in item 5 (below). 63: cf. Horace *Odes* 1.14.2–3 *occupa / portum*; the repetition of *tandem* expresses feeling in this context of prayer, like that of *iam pridem* in the final prayer of *Georgics* 1 (1.501 and 503). For *uagus* of wandering on the sea cf. Tibullus 1.3.39–40 *uagus* … / … *nauita*. 64: the poem shares its last line with Horace's *Carmen Saeculare*, another divine hymn – cf. CS 44 **sospite cursu*.

2. Elegy on Mary, Helper of Christians

This elegiac poem[17] was composed in 1895 in honour of the Virgin Mary as 'Helper of Christians' (*Adiutrix Christianorum*), a version of her title *Auxilium Christianorum*, inserted in the Litany of Loreto by Pius V after the naval battle of Lepanto in 1571.[18] This title recognized the Virgin's supposed intervention in that key engagement on the side of the Christian Holy League, led by the Papal States and Pius' sponsorship, against the Ottomans; Pius also instituted the feast of the Holy Rosary (initially the feast of Our Lady of Victory) to celebrate the victory on 7 October, the date of the battle. The battle is the main subject of this poem (lines 19–54); Pecci may have been aware that he was here following in a rich poetic tradition, since there were many neo-Latin poems written soon after the battle celebrating the victory,[19] and of the rich reception in art of the victory which sometimes included Mary's supposed intervention.[20]

The key structural link in the poem is the element of the Rosary (a traditional set of linked prayers which involves the Virgin), which connects the Lepanto narrative with the poem's other narrative, that about the life of St Dominic (5–18). There we find a version of the story that in 1206 Dominic de Guzmán was in Provence trying to turn the heretical Albigensian sect back to Catholic doctrine, and was encouraged by a vision of the Virgin who gave him the Rosary as a weapon for orthodoxy, which led to the success of his mission.[21] St Dominic is mentioned in Pecci's series of epigrams on Mary and the Rosary, written in the same year (1895), which precede this poem in the 1902 edition of his poems; this juxtaposition may be referred to in the opening of this work (see on lines 1 and 3 below), which suggests a new start and a more ambitious poem. As pope, Leo XIII was a strong advocate of the Dominicans and St Thomas Aquinas.[22]

The poem had a practical intention in its original context. In a papal encyclical of the same year, 1895, Pope Leo set out plans for the building of a great basilica at Patras in Greece, the nearest major city to the site of the battle of Lepanto, in honour of Our Lady of Victory,[23] and this is clearly the prospective seaside shrine of the Virgin mentioned at the end of the poem. A commission was set up headed by a cardinal, but nothing had been built by 1902 and the enterprise seems not to have survived Leo's death in 1903.[24] This construction project may have been something of a contemporary propaganda move against the neighbouring Ottoman Empire in commemorating the most notable European victory against it several centuries previously; in 1895 the emperor Abdülhamid II was engaging in persecution of the Armenian Christians, some of whom were Catholic, including massacres which were widely reported in the West.[25] As in the ode on the 1400th anniversary of the conversion of Clovis (item 3 below), an apparently antiquarian topic can have a contemporary political aspect.

The framing of the poem as an aetiological narrative recounting the origin of or motivation for a sacred shrine, potential or actual, is one of several elements which make clear that this poem is modelled on Propertius 4.6, in the same elegiac metre. There the Roman poet presents a narrative of the similarly naval Battle of Actium (31 BCE) as the origin of the Palatine temple of Apollo, who (like the Virgin at Lepanto here) is said to have played a crucial role in Augustus' victory against Antony and Cleopatra. Both Actium and Lepanto were battles between Eastern and Western powers in which the West and its different religion triumphed; the battle-narratives in the two poems also have a similar structure, including a detailed account of the fighting and concluding with a final aetiological statement of the origin of a shrine or potential shrine (53–4 ~ 4.6.67–8).

Text and translation

AN. MDCCCXCV ADIUTRICI CHRISTIANORUM ELEGIA

At nunc, Virgo potens, uictrices te auspice palmas
  Maiori plectro concinuisse iuuat.
Per te namque almae uictoria nuntia pacis
  Plus semel ad ueteres risit amica patres.
Gallia, tu testis: metuendas arte maligna 5
  Vis inferna tibi struxerat insidias.
Tuque, olim uirtute, fide splendescere uisa,
  Heu priscum misere iam decus exueras!
Immunda late errorum uitiique scatebas
  Illuuie, gentes depopulante tuas. 10
Adfuit at Virgo: meritis, pietate uerendum
  Finibus Hispanis aduocat ipsa uirum;
Cui roseas blando cum traderet ore coronas
  Haec, ait, haec Gallis arma salutis erunt.
Hisce armis pugnae occurrit Gusmanius heros, 15
  Hac arte enisus clara tropaea tulit.
Occubuere hostes; rursumque effulsit auita
  Pulchrior in Gallis candidiorque fides.
Testor et Ioniis quas cernis Echinadas undis:
  Viuida adhuc facti fama per ora uolat. 20
Stant ex adverso instructae longo ordine puppes,
  In saeua ardescunt proelia iam ruere.
Utraque fert acies signum; haec caeleste Mariae,
  Lunae triste minax illa bicornis habet:
Ut raucae sonuere tubae, concurritur: ingens 25
  Continuo ad caeli tollitur astra fragor.
Aera tonant, reboat litus, micat ignibus aequor;
  Impauidi hac illac dant fera iussa duces.
Confracto latere et remis non una dehiscit

Vincenzo Pecci (1810–1903; Pope as Leo XIII 1878–1903)

ELEGY TO THE HELPER OF CHRISTIANS, 1895

But now, mighty Virgin, it is my pleasure to sing
With greater plectrum of triumphant victories under your auspices.
For it is through you that victory, harbinger of sweet peace,
Smiled more than once on our fathers of old.
France, you are a witness: an infernal force by evil arts   5
Had set up a fearsome ambush against you,
And you, once perceived to shine with virtue and faith,
Alas, had stripped off your glory of old!
You were unclean and teemed far and wide with the filth
Of error and vice, which was ravaging your peoples.   10
But the Virgin was there to help: she of her own accord
Summoned a man revered for piety from the shores of Spain.
To him, as she handed over the garlands of roses with kindly words,
She said 'These, these will be the weapons that bring safety to
   the French'.
With these weapons the hero Guzman confronted the fray,   15
By this means he strove and won famous victories.
The enemy fell to him, and once more their ancestral faith
Shone out finer and fairer amongst the French.
I call to witness the Echinades you can see in the Ionian waters:
Lively still is the report of the feat that flies through the lips
   of men.   20
The ships stand drawn up in opposition in a long line:
They are already on fire to rush into violent battle.
Both battle-lines bear a banner, the one the celestial standard
Of Mary, the other the grim flag of the twin-horned moon:
When the harsh trumpets blared, they came together: 25
A vast crash rose at once to the stars of heaven.
The air thunders, the shore resounds, the sea flashes with fire:
The commanders, unterrified, give their fierce orders here and
   there.
More than one ship gaped with shattered side and oars,

> Nauis, et immensi gurgitis ima petit. 30
> Iactata horrisono merguntur corpora ponto,
>   Humano spumans unda cruore rubet.
> Anceps stat fortuna: pari uirtute peracta,
>   Hinc inde euentu pugna iterata pari.
> Iamque iterum temptanda acies, cum percita fato 35
>   Nescio quo classis Turcica, sollicito
> Pulsa repente metu, refugit producere pugnam,
>   Et quamuis multo milite praeualida,
> Cedere uisa loco, et sese, mirabile dictu!
>   Ultro Christiadum dedere in arbitrium. 40
> Ingeminat tunc uictor io, nomenque Mariae
>   Conclamat resonis undique litoribus:
> Conclamant populi portentum, Virginis almae
>   Patratum dia bellipotentis ope;
> Romulidae imprimis, quis mirum ex hoste triumphum 45
>   Fatidico edixit praescius ore Pius.
> Inde quies et pax Europae asserta ruenti,
>   Inde stetit patriae religionis honos,
> Seraque posteritas (quid adhuc ignaua moratur?)
>   Heia! euentu dignum aggrediatur opus. 50
> Sublime attollat Pario de marmore templum
>   Ad litus, memori gesta ubi pugna loco.
> Hic Virgo templum teneat Regina, tumenti
>   Hic praecincta rosis imperet ipsa mari.

Vincenzo Pecci (1810–1903; Pope as Leo XIII 1878–1903)

And headed for the depths of the measureless main. 30
Bodies were tossed and sunk in the terrible-sounding sea,
The foaming wave was red with human blood.
The fortune of battle stood undecided: the fight was conducted
With equal courage, and repeated with equal outcome.
And battle was to be joined once again, when the Turkish fleet, 35
Sped by some kind of destiny, was suddenly driven back
By timorous fear, and shrank from extending the conflict.
And although it was mighty with many a fighter,
It was seen to leave the place of battle, and, marvellous to say,
To surrender itself into the power of the Christians. 40
Then the victor repeated the cry of triumph, and proclaimed
The name of Mary to the resounding shores on every side:
The peoples present proclaimed the miracle that was managed
By the holy help of the protective Virgin so mighty in war:
Above all the sons of Romulus, to whom the prescient Pius had
    foretold 45
From his prophetic mouth a wondrous triumph over the enemy.
Hence tranquillity and peace was defended for a Europe
Previously collapsing, hence the honour of its ancestral religion
    stood firm,
And may a later posterity, o, (why does it still delay in idleness?),
Attempt a work worthy of that feat: 50
May it raise a lofty shrine of Parian marble
By the shore, where the battle was waged, in the place that
    recalls it:
Here may the Virgin Queen occupy her shrine, here
May she, girded with roses, herself command the sea.

Commentary

1-4 An introduction announces a poem in praise of the Virgin Mary and her aid in key historical moments. The abrupt opening *At nunc* (1) recalls the first line of Propertius 2.10.1 *sed tempus lustrare aliis Helicona choreis* and may reflect a change of poetic gear from the previous sequence of shorter elegiac epigrams (see introductory section above), while *uirgo potens* Christianizes *uirgo potens nemorum* of Diana at Statius *Theb*.9.608, *uictrices . . . palmas* is a Propertian phrase (4.1.139-40) and *te auspice* adapts the pagan religious language of Roman military auspices to a Christian context. 2: *maiori plectro* as at Horace *Odes* 4.2.33 *maiore . . . plectro* refers to a grander and longer literary form (the alternative ablative *maiori* is found at Lucan 7.162 and Silius 13.409). 2 *concinuisse* is perfect for present infinitive as regularly in poetry – cf. Horace *Odes* 1.1.4 *collegisse iuvat*. 3: cf. Tibullus 1.10.67 *Pax alma*; for *nuntius pacis* cf. Cicero *In Vat.* 35, *Phil.* 12.11 4: cf. Catullus 61.212 *dulce rideat ad patrem*.

5-18 Mary's aid to St Dominic in his struggles with the heretical Albigensians is described (for the historical background see introductory section above). 5: for the trope of a (similarly French) location as a witness to great deeds cf. Tibullus 1.10.10 *testis et Oceani litora Santonici*, and for **arte maligna* see Silius 7.266. 6: *uis inferna* occurs at Cicero *Arat.* 34.271, *struxerat insidias* at Ovid *Met.* 1.198. 7: the asyndeton *uirtute, fide* is Ciceronian (*S.Rosc.* 27); France's earlier Christianity is celebrated in Pecci's ode celebrating the conversion of Clovis (item 3 below). 8: cf. *Aeneid* 6.878 *heu prisca fides*, Seneca *Ph.* 741 *decus omne priscum*. 9-10: note how the two elements of an alliterating noun-adjective pair (of separate Vergilian words: *Aeneid* 3.228, 3.593) are vertically juxtaposed at line-start. The forceful language here recalls patristic polemic against unorthodoxy (cf. e.g. Jerome *Prol.in Job* 75.6 *in stercore et uermibus scatebat errorum*, *Ep.* 48.4 *scatere uitiis*), while the metaphor of *depopulante* is that of a plague (cf. Gellius 2.1.5 *pestilentiae . . . quae Atheniensium ciuitatem . . . depopulata est*). 11 *adfuit* i.e. was present to help through her divine power (*OLD* s.v. *adsum* 13a); the description of St Dominic in 11-12 Christianizes the parallel pagan hero Aeneas (*Aeneid* 1.151 *pietate grauem ac meritis* ... *uirum*), while the phrasing of his Spanish origin is also Vergilian (*Aeneid* 10.719 *uenerat* ... *Corythi de finibus*). 13 *roseas* ... *coronas*: the garlands of roses seen in Dominic's vision of the Virgin when she presented him with the Rosary (Drane 1891: 120-37), Christianizing the rose-garland sometimes worn by pagan female deities (e.g. the Muse Thalia at Statius *Silv.* 2.1.116) by allusion to the traditional association of Mary with the rose (e.g. as the *rosa mystica* in the Rosary of Loreto;[26] for *blando* ... *ore* of persuasive speech cf. Ovid *Met.* 13.555. 14: for the Christian *arma salutis* cf. Paulinus of Nola *Carm.*22.64. 15: for the archaic *hisce* (= *his*) cf. *Lucr. 6.647, for *pugnae occurrit* cf. *Aeneid* 11.528 *occurrere pugnae*, and for the line-ending cf. *Aeneid* 6.651 *Troius *heros*, again pairing Dominic and Aeneas. 16: once more compares Dominic with great pagan heroes, echoing Horace *Odes* 3.3.9-10 *hac arte Pollux et uagus Hercules / enisus arcis attigit igneas* and Ovid *Her.* 9.104 *et tulit a capto nota tropaea uiro*. 17: *occubuere* echoes a line-opening found three times in Silius 5.540, 9.408, 16.542, while in lines 17 and 18 the noun/ adjective pair *auita* ... *fides* is vertically juxtaposed at line-end; for the metaphorical use of *effulsit* of virtues cf. Seneca *Ep.* 79.14 *innocentia ac uirtus* ... *effulsit* (this picks up the image of *splendescere* in line 7 above). 18: recalls the Christian poet Juvencus 2.339 *pulchra fides* as well as the pagan Tibullus 1.7.64 **candidiorque ueni*.

19-54 The Virgin Mary's intervention at the battle of Lepanto is recounted. As noted in the introductory section above, this section of the poem looks back to Propertius' narrative of the Battle of Actium in 4.6, specifically echoed a number of times in these lines. 19 *testor*: see on line 5 above for locations called to witness great deeds, and cf. *Aeneid* 5.803 *Xanthum Simoentaque testor*; *Ioniis* ... *undis* recalls Propertius 4.6.16 *Ioniae* ... *aquae*, while *Echinadas undis* repeats the line-ending of Lucan 6.364. 20: cf. *Georgics* 3.9 *uictorque uirum uolitare per ora* and *Aeneid* 9.194-5 *facti / fama*. 21: cf. *Aeneid* 6.901 *stant litore *puppes, Ilias Latina* 216 *instructae puppes,* and **longo ordine* 4× in the *Aeneid* (2.766,

6.482, 6.654, 8.722). 22: cf. *Aeneid* 2.347 *ardere in proelia*, 11.727–8 *in proelia saeua / suscitat*, Ovid *Met.* 5.166 *ruere ardet*, Lucan 4.151 *ruens in proelia*. 23: cf. Ovid *Fasti* 6.421 (= *Ex Pont.* 3.2.51) *signum caeleste* (in two different senses, astronomical and miraculous). 24: cf. Manilius 3.551 *signum* ... *triste* (astronomical), Horace *Carm.Saec.* 35–6 *bicornis*... / *Luna* (adapted here for the Muslim crescent emblem). 25–6: cf. Statius *Theb.* 3.708–9 *rauca* ... / *signa tubae*, *Aeneid* 7.637 *classica iamque sonant*, *Georgics* 4.78 *erumpunt portis, concurritur*, *Aeneid* 8.527 *fragor* ... *ingens*, Horace *Sat.* 2.7.29 *tollis ad astra*; *caeli* ... *astra* varies the common *sidera caeli* (*Aeneid* 1.259 etc.). 27: cf. *Aeneid* 9.541 and 12.757 *caelum tonat*, *Georgics* 3.223 *reboant siluaeque et longus Olympus*, *Aeneid* 1.90 **micat ignibus aether*. 28 *impauidi* recalls the Stoic hero of *Odes* 3.4.8 (*impauidum*); *hac illac* is a relatively colloquial expression from Terence (*Heaut.* 512), while for *fera iussa cf. Ovid *Rem.Am.* 496. 29 echoes the storm of *Aeneid* 1, picking up *latus* (of a storm-tossed ship) at 1.105 and *dehiscens* at 1.106. 30: cf. *Georgics* 1.29 *immensi* ... *maris*, *Ciris* 416 *magni* ... *gurgitis*, Lucan 4.127 *ima petit quidquid pendebat aquarum*. 31: cf. Ovid *Tr.* 1.2.39 *in immenso iactari corpora ponto*, Cicero *Tusc.* 2.10 (verse) *horrisono freto*. 32: cf. Lucan 3.572–3 *cruor altus in unda / spumat* (another naval battle), Ovid *Met.* 11.374–5 *sanguine litus / undaque prima rubet*. 33: cf. *Aeneid* 4.603 *anceps pugnae fuerat fortuna*; *pari uirtute* is a Ciceronian phrase (*Red.* 20, *Phil.* 7.6, 12.8, *Leg.* 1.34). 34: cf. Fronto *Princ.Hist.* 2.4 *bella* ... *pari euentu bellata*. 35: cf. *Aeneid* 4.413 *iterum temptare*; *percita is a Lucretian favourite (7×). 36–7: cf. Ovid *Her.*16.331 *Troica classis*, Ovid *Pont.*3.2.12 *sollicito* ... *metu*; for the sense and construction of *refugio* cf. Seneca *Ag.* 417 *refugit loqui mens aegra*, for the alliterative *producere pugnam* at line-end cf. Silius 9.135 *producere bellum. 38: cf. Horace *Odes* 1.15.6 *multo* ... *milite*. 39: *cedere* ... *loco* is a military phrase (Caesar *Civ.* 2.41.4, Sallust *Cat.* 9.4), while *mirabile dictu is a favourite Vergilian line-ending (7×). 40: *Christiades* is a standard neo-Latin expression for 'Christians'; for *ultro* ... *dedere* cf. *Georgics* 4.204, and for *in arbitrium cf. [Tib.] 3.6.14 *dominae misit in arbitrium*. 41–2: cf. Horace *Odes* 4.2.49–50 *io Triumphe, / non semel dicemus, io Triumphe*, Silius 11.488 *litora resonantia*, 6.285

resonae ... ripae (the same rare adjective). 43: *populi* stresses the international coalition of the Holy League (the Papal States, Spain, Venice, Genoa and several other Italian states), while *Virginis almae* Christianizes Statius *Theb*.11.132 **uirginis almae*, there of the pagan Astraea. 44: *dia* is an archaic poetic form (classical *diuina*), also found in Vergil (*Aeneid* 11.657); for its use with *ope* cf. Ovid *Fasti* 3.22 *diuina ... ope*, while *bellipotentis* claims for Mary the epithet of the pagan deities Mars (*Aeneid* 11.8) and Minerva (*Theb*. 8.716). 45 *Romulidae* (for the patronymic cf. Lucretius 4.683, *Aeneid* 8.638) focuses on the Italian Papal forces, naturally for this author; *quis* = *quibus*, while *ex* is the usual preposition indicating triumph over an enemy – cf. *Ilias Latina* 541 **ex hoste triumphos*. 46: echoes descriptions of pagan prophecy – cf. Lucretius 6.3 *ueridico ... ore profudit* (Epicurus), Silius 3.680 *fatidico ... murmure* (the oak of Dodona), *Aeneid* 6.66 (the Sibyl) *praescia uenturi*; *edixit* fits an authoritative papal statement (for the role of Pius V see the introductory section above). 47: cf. *Aetna* 357 *tanta quies illi est et pax*; for *assero* = 'defend' cf. *OLD* s.u.5; *Europae ruenti* is an exaggeration, but the Ottomans had captured Famagusta, the last Christian possession in Cyprus, a few months earlier. 48: the repeated *inde* points to a causal origin as often in Ovid's aetiological discourse (cf. e.g. *Fasti* 3.126-7), while *stetit* continues the metaphor of *ruina* as its polar opposite; for *patria religio* cf. Tacitus *Ann*. 15.55. 49: cf. Ovid *Pont*.1.4.24 *sera posteritate*. 50: *heia* is a colloquial exclamation brought into epic by Vergil (*Aeneid* 4.569, 9.38); cf. also Seneca *HF* 1281-2 *aggredi/ingens opus*. 51-4: for the proposed sanctuary see the introductory section above. 51: cf. Valerius Flaccus 5.187 *Pario de marmore*, Ovid *Her*. 21.105 *templum ... sublime*, *Aeneid* 6.69 *solido *de marmore templum*. 52: *ad* = 'beside', cf. *OLD* s.u.13; *memori* personifies the place as witness to events as in lines 5 and 19 above (for *memor* used of commemorative objects cf. *OLD* s.u.6). 53: cf. *Georgics* 3.19 *in medio mihi Caesar erit templumque tenebit*; *regina* recalls Mary's common title of *regina caeli* (on her queenship of heaven in the Catholic tradition see Carroll 1953). 53-4: note the final rhyme of noun and participle in agreement (for *tumere* with *mare* cf. e.g. Ovid *Ars* 3.259-60); *praecincta* *rosis* picks up Mary's links with the rose in the Rosary (see the introductory section above) and elsewhere, and may also allude to her common depiction in art surrounded by roses or wearing a garland or crown with roses (a future altarpiece might be imagined here).[27] 54: *imperet … mari* transfers to Mary the divine province of the pagan Neptune (*Aeneid* 1.138–9 <u>*imperium pelagi*</u> … / … *mihi sorte datum*).

3. Ode on the 1,400th anniversary of the conversion of Clovis

This ode in Sapphic stanzas[28] was written in 1896 to celebrate the 1,400th anniversary of the conversion in 496 of Clovis, king of the Franks, and the establishment of Christianity as the religion of France, presented here as the first Western nation outside Italy to become Christian; Pope Leo also proclaimed a jubilee in 1896 for the French church to celebrate the year.[29] The circumstances of Clovis' conversion are as follows: under pressure in the crucial battle of Tolbiac against the Alemanni, Clovis, already married to the Christian princess Clothilde, vowed to convert if the Christian God granted him victory, and when that victory was gained he was baptized along with his people on Christmas Day 496.

The episode is described in Gregory of Tours' *History of the Franks* written nearly a century later (2.30–1), an account which is clearly used by Pecci here, especially in his version of Clovis' vow (lines 9–24), which is an abbreviated paraphrase of *Hist.Franc.* 2.30:

> *Iesu Christi, quem Chrotchildis praedicat esse filium Dei uiui, qui dare auxilium laborantibus uictoriamque in te sperantibus tribuere diceris, tuae opis gloriam deuotus efflagito, ut, si mihi uictoriam super hos hostes indulseris et expertus fuero illam uirtutem, quam de te populus tuo nomine dicatus probasse se praedicat, credam tibi et in nomine tuo baptizer. Invocaui enim deos meos, sed, ut experior, elongati sunt ab auxilio meo; unde credo, eos nullius esse potestatis praeditos, qui sibi oboedientibus non occurrunt. Te nunc inuoco, tibi credere desidero, tantum ut eruar ab adversariis meis.*

(Jesus Christ, whom Clothilde proclaims to be the son of the living God, you who are said to give aid to those in trouble and to bestow victory on those who hope in you, I devote myself to you and ask for the glory of your aid, so that, if you grant me victory over these enemies and I come to know that power, which the people dedicated to your name declares that it has experienced, I shall believe in you and be baptised in your name. For I have called upon my gods, but, as I have found, they are far from my help; accordingly, I believe that they are of no power, since they do not come to help those who obey them. On you now I call, in you I long to believe, only let me be rescued from my enemies).

The poem falls into three sections: the story of Clovis, narrated at some length (5–24), a series of briefer highlights from the Christian history of France since 496 (25–52), and a closing wish for the continuing vigour of Christianity in contemporary France (53–76). In the central set of vignettes from French history, the first (33–40) is the Frankish king Pépin le Bref's double crossing of the Alps in 755–6 to aid Pope Stephen II in defeating Aistulf, King of the Lombards, followed by the so-called 'Donation of Pépin' (756), in which the pope's dominion over various Italian cities was formally recognized. This was often seen as the origin of the pope's temporal rule over the Papal States (see Noble 1984: 65–98) and thus was particularly important from the perspective of a papal poet. The second (41–4) is France's participation in the Crusades, especially the First Crusade, which captured Jerusalem with its Christian shrines in 1099 (41–2) and established its main leader the French nobleman Godfrey of Bouillon as its king, alongside further less successful Crusades (43–4) in which French kings were prominent (Louis VII in the Second of 1147–8, Philip II Augustus in the Third of 1189–92, and Louis IX (St Louis) in the Seventh and Eighth of 1248–54 and 1270). The third and fourth are Joan of Arc, who helped to save the French kingdom from an English takeover in 1429–31,[30] mentioned for her divine inspiration (45–8), and the suppression of the heretical followers of the French Jean Calvin in the religious civil wars of France of 1562–98 (49–52).

The poem is strongly Horatian in style and structure. As a celebratory ode invoking religious elements on a national anniversary occasion, it specifically recalls the *Carmen Saeculare* of 17 BCE, of the same length and in the same metre (nineteen Sapphic stanzas), written for Augustus' *ludi saeculares* which celebrated the passing of a period of 110 years in the history of Rome. As an ode which lists and commends great figures in the history of a nation, it also recalls Horace's view of Roman history in such poems as *Odes* 1.12, with a glance at Vergil's Show of Heroes in *Aeneid* 6 (see commentary on lines 33–4 below). The narrative framework of the Clovis episode (5–24) recalls that of the Regulus ode (*Odes* 3.5), in which the words of a past hero on a key historical occasion are presented as a dramatic speech (3.5.18–40).

Papal correspondence shows that the ode was sent to Cardinal Langénieux, Cardinal Archbishop of Reims, for use in an anniversary celebration in the same place where Clovis was baptized by St Remigius (Rémi), bishop of Reims and 'Apostle of the Franks', and the poem has clear resonances for a contemporary Catholic readership (both French and Italian) in 1896.[31] Its stress on the Donation of Pépin (39–40) points to the still raw loss of the Papal States in 1870, while the final exhortation to France to maintain its Catholic traditions (56–76) is addressed to a nation which had previously been an active defender of the papacy[32] but was then engaged in major secularization under the Third Republic. State lay education had already been established under the Jules Ferry laws of 1881–2, and in 1905 the radical government of Émile Combes would enact legislation which finally separated church and state in France.[33] The poem's close also glances at France's growing colonial empire of the 1890s and its links with Catholicism (see notes on lines 70–1 and 71–2 below). The poem was not without some wider impact in France: it was set as a cantata with chorus, bass and tenor by Théodore Dubois in 1899 and was performed in Paris as well as Reims.[34]

Text and translation

AN. MDCCCXCVI OB MEMORIAM AVSPICATISSIMI EVENTVS QVVM FRANCORVM NATIO PRAEEVNTE CLODOVEO REGE SE CHRISTO ADDIXIT. ODE.

Viuat Christus Qui diligit Francos.

GENTIUM custos Deus est: repente
Sternit insignes humilesque promit:
Exitus rerum tenet, atque nutu
Temperat aequo.
Teutonum pressus Clodoueus armis, 5
Ut suos uidit trepidos pericli,
Fertur has voces iterasse, ad astra
Lumina tendens:
'Diue, quem supplex mea saepe coniunx
Nuncupat Iesum, mihi dexter adsis: 10
Si iuues promptus ualidusque, totum
Me tibi dedam.'
Ilico excussus pavor: acriores
Excitat uirtus animos; resurgit
Francus in pugnam; ruit, et cruentos 15
Disiicit hostes.
Victor i, uoti Clodovee compos,
Sub iugo Christi caput obligatum
Pone; te Remis manet infulata
Fronte sacerdos. 20
Ludor ? en signis positis ad aram
Ipse rex sacris renovatur undis,
Et cohors omnis populusque dio
Tingitur amne.
Roma ter felix, caput o renatae 25
Stirpis humanae, tua pande regna:
Namque uictrices tibi sponte lauros
Francia defert.

1896: IN COMMEMORATION OF THE MOST AUSPICIOUS EVENT WHEN THE FRANKISH NATION, LED BY KING CLOVIS, BOUND ITSELF TO CHRIST. ODE.

'Life to Christ who loves the Franks'

God is the guardian of peoples: suddenly
He casts down the lofty and promotes the lowly:
He controls the outcomes of events, and controls them
With unbiased nod.
    Clovis, pressed by the arms of the Teutons,   5
When he saw his men anxious of danger,
Is said to have repeated these words, aiming
His eyes to the stars:
    'God, whom my wife often in prayer
Names as Jesus, be of favourable help to me: 10
If you aid me readily and resolutely, I will give
Myself wholly to you.'
    At once their fear was dispelled, and courage
Roused their spirits to greater boldness: the Frank
Rose again to battle, charged and scattered   15
His bloody enemies.
    Go on in victory, Clovis, after the fulfilment of your vow,
Place as you are bound your head under the yoke of Christ:
At Reims the priest awaits you with a headband
    On his forehead.   20
Am I deceived? Look, his standards laid aside
At the altar, the king is made new with holy waters,
And his whole host and people is dipped
    In the sacred stream.
Thrice happy Rome, you head of the reborn   25
Human race, open up your kingdom:
For France of her own accord offers you
    Laurels of victory.

Te colet matrem; tua maior esse
Gestiet natu: potiore uita 30
Crescet, ac summo benefida Petro
clara feretur.
Ut mihi longum libet intueri
Agmen heroum! Domitor ferocis
Fulget Astolfi, pius ille sacri 35
Iuris amator,
Remque romanam populantis ultor:
Bis per abruptas metuendus Alpes
Irruit, summoque Petro volentes
Asserit urbes. 40
Laetus admiror Solymis potitas
Vindices sancti tumuli phalanges:
Me Palaestinis renovata campis
Proelia tangunt.
O novum robur celebris puellae! castra 45
perrumpens inimica turpem
Galliae cladem repulit Ioanna
Numine freta.
O quot illustres animae nefanda
Monstra Calvini domuere, gentem 50
Labe tam dira prohibere fortes
Sceptraque regni!
Quo feror? tempus redit auspicatum
Prisca quo uirtus animis calescat:
Ecce, Remensis ciet atque adurget 55
Corda triumphus.
Gallicae gentes, iubaris uetusti
Ne quid obscuret radios, cauete;
Neue suffundat malesuadus error
Mentibus umbras. 60
Vos regat Christus, sibi quos reuinxit:
Obsequi sectis pudeat probrosis;

Vincenzo Pecci (1810–1903; Pope as Leo XIII 1878–1903)

She will cultivate you as her mother, she will long
To be your eldest child: she will grow with a better life, 30
And will be said to hold full faith
   In great Peter.
What a pleasure it is to me to gaze upon
The long column of heroes! There shines out
The tamer of fierce Aistulf, that holy lover 35
   Of sacred law
And avenger against him who laid waste the state of Rome:
Twice he rushed fearsomely through the sheer Alps,
And claimed for great Peter cities
   That welcomed him. 40
In joy I wonder at the ranks that gained control
Of Jerusalem, who claimed the holy tomb;
I am touched by the battles renewed again
   On the plains of Palestine.
O strange strength of the famous maid! Joan, 45
Bursting through the camp of the enemy
Drove back the shame of disaster from Gaul
   Relying on divine power,
O how many were the sterling spirits who tamed
The evil monsters of Calvin, with the strength 50
To protect the race and the throne of the kingdom
   From such dire taint!
Where I am off to? The auspicious time has come around
For old-fashioned virtue to grow warm in your minds:
Behold, the triumph of Reims rouses and 55
   Urges your hearts.
Tribes of Gaul, take care that nothing
Dim the rays of your radiance of old,
And that misleading error does not cast shadows
   Upon your minds: 60
Let your king be Christ, who has bound you to him:
Be ashamed to follow wicked sects:

Occidat liuor, sociasque in unum
Cogite uires.
Saecla bis septem calor actuosae 65
Perstitit uitae, renuens perire:
Currite ad Veslam; nouus aestuabit
Pectore feruor.
Dissitis floret magis usque terris
Gallicum nomen: populis vel ipsis 70
Adsit eois, Fideique sanctae
Vota secundet.
Nil Fide Christi prius: hac adempta
Nil diu felix. Stetit unde priscae
Summa laus genti, manet inde iugis 75
Gloria Gallos.

May ill-feeling perish, and gather your strength
  Allied in one place.
The heat of your energetic life has lasted   65
Twice seven centuries, refusing to die out:
Hurry to the river Vesle – a new passion
  Will seethe in your heart.
The race of Gaul flourishes ever
In lands far-scattered: may she aid even   70
The very peoples of the East, and prosper the prayers
  Of the holy faith.
Nothing is more important than faith in Christ: that removed,
Nothing is prosperous for long. From that same source
Of highest praise for its people of old, there continues 75
The ever-flowing fame of France.

Commentary

Epigraph: a quotation from the prologue to the Lex Salica, the ancient Frankish law code, the first version of which was compiled under the rule of Clovis after his conversion.[35]

1–4 A statement of God's power over mortals. 1–2 Christianizes and corrects Horace's address to Jupiter at *Odes* 1.12.49 *gentis humanae pater atque custos*, and adapts the same poet's account of the powers of the goddess Fortune at *Odes* 1.35.12–14 *ualet ima summis / mutare et <u>insignem</u> attenuat deus, /obscura <u>promens</u>*; *humiles* echoes the same theme in the Magnificat (Luke 1.52 *deposuit potentes de sede, et exaltauit humiles*). 3–4 *exitus rerum* is a favourite Ciceronian phrase in the singular (15×), while *nutu temperat aequo* recalls Horace on Jupiter again at *Odes* 3.4.45–8 *qui terram inertem, qui mare <u>temperat</u> / uentosum et urbes regnaque tristia / diuosque mortalisque turmas /imperio regit unus <u>aequo</u>* and the divine nod of Jupiter in Vergil (so *nutu* at *Aeneid* 9.106 and 10.115).

5–24 The conversion of Clovis. 5 *Teutonum . . . armis*: cf. *Aeneid* 4.228 *Graiumque . . . armis*. 6: cf. *Aeneid* 10.364–5 *Arcadas insuetos acies inferre pedestris / <u>ut uidit</u> Pallas Latio dare terga sequaci* (similarly introducing a speech in battle); *trepidos pericli* imitates the Vergilian genitive after the similar *metuens* – cf. *Aeneid* 5.716 *metuensque pericli*. 7 *fertur*: introduces a past speech from another source similarly at Horace *Odes* 1.7.23 (the source here of lines 9–12 is Gregory of Tours, see introductory section above for the longer parallel text briefly paraphrased here; Pecci shows no lexical matches); cf. also Horace *Ep.*1.18.12 *iterat uoces*. 7–8: cf. *Aeneid* 2.405 *ad caelum tendens ardentia lumina frustra*; *ad astra* suggests heaven as at *Aeneid* 9.641. 9: the speech-opening echoes the poem-opening of Horace *Odes* 4.6.1 *Diue, quem*, 'correcting' the Horatian address to Apollo. 9–10: cf. Ovid *Met.*14.607-8 (another divine naming) *<u>quem</u> turba Quirini / <u>nuncupat</u> Indigetem*, Statius *Ach.*1.716–17 (another prayer to Apollo) *adsis o memor hospitii, Iunoniaque arua / <u>dexter</u> ames*. 11–12: cf. Plautus *Mil.*

Vincenzo Pecci (1810–1903; Pope as Leo XIII 1878–1903) 221

567 *egomet me dedam tibi*, Cicero *Att*.9.4.1 *ne me totum aegritudini dedam* (both appropriately colloquial sources for a speech). 13 *ilico* – an archaic and relatively prosaic word not found in Augustan poetry; *excussus pauor* inverts the classical poetic use of *pauor* as subject not object of this verb (Seneca *Ag*.5 [Seneca] *Octauia* 123, Silius 6.556–7). 13–14: cf. *Aeneid* 11.800 *acris animos*, 3.342–3 *uirtutem animosque*.../ ... *excitat*. 15–16: cf. Horace *Odes* 1.2.39–40 *cruentum* / ... *hostem*, Seneca *Ag*.896 *dissicere*... *hostem*. 17: cf. Ovid *Am*.1.7.35 *I nunc*... *uictor*, Horace *Ars* 76 *uoti*... *compos*. 18: appropriately uses patristic language: cf. Ambrose *De Tobia* 9 *caput obligat*, while *iugum Christi* is a favourite expression of Ambrose (13×). 19–20: the woollen headband which marks a pagan priest is here Christianized as an episcopal mitre (so at item 1.II.54 above) – cf. *Aeneid* 10.537–8 *sacerdos*, / *infula cui sacra redimibat tempora uitta*; the priest is the future St Rémi, bishop of Reims, whose baptism there of Clovis (with his army as here) is narrated by Gregory of Tours (2.31). 22: cf. *Odes* 3.4.5–6 *An me ludit amabilis* / *insania?*, Catullus 95.5 *sacras*... *undas* (here Christianized as the waters of baptism); spiritual renewal through baptism is a common idea in patristic discourse – cf. e.g. Augustine *Ep*.190.16 *baptismate renouantur*. 23–4 *dio*... *amne* varies *sacris*... *undis*; for the archaic *dius* see on item 2 line 44 above, and for the phrase and *amnis* in the poetic sense of 'water' cf. Valerius Flaccus 4.338 *sacro*... *amne*; cf. also Ovid *Rem*.700 *tingere in amne*.

25–32 Celebration of the consequent ancient link between papal Rome and France. 25: cf. Ovid *Met*.8.51 *o ego ter felix*, Lucan 4.807 *felix Roma*. Rome as head (*caput*) of the world is a classical idea, especially in Ovid (*Am*.1.15.26, *Fasti* 1.209–10, 4.255–6, 5.93); *renatae* suggests the renewal of both Rome and humanity under Christianity. 26: cf. Lucretius 1.733 *humana*... *stirpe*, Petronius 121.1.116 *pande, age, terrarum sitientia regna tuarum*. 27: cf. *Eclogues* 8.13 *uictrices*... *lauros*. 28: cf. Horace *Odes* 2.16.16 *aufert. 29: cf. Seneca *HO* 580 *matrem colam*. 30: *potiore uita* = the 'better life' of Christianity. 31: *benefidus* is a poetic-style compound first found in sixteenth-century neo-Latin (Prospero Acrimato *pareneticum carmen* 2.68); Peter represents papal Rome as often.

33-40 Celebration of Pépin le Bref and his aid to the papacy (for the historical facts referred to here see introductory section above). 33-4: these lines recall Anchises surveying with similar pleasure the similarly long series of his Roman descendants in the Underworld of *Aeneid* 6; cf. 6.681 *lustrabat studio recolens*, 6.749 <u>agmine</u> *magno*. For *domitor* cf. Horace *Ep.* 1.2.19 *domitor Troiae*, and for *ferox* of 'barbarian' enemies of Rome cf. Horace *Odes* 3.2.3 (Parthians), 4.2.34 (Germans). 35: *fulget* recalls Anchises' description of his descendants again (cf. *Aeneid* 6.826 *illae autem paribus quas <u>fulgere</u> cernis in armis*); likewise Pépin's characterization as a lover of law echoes that of the Roman king Numa by Anchises at *Aeneid* 6.810-11 *primam qui legibus urbem / fundabit* (cf. also Seneca *Oed*. 876 *iuris ... sacri*); this and the claim of piety perhaps defend the reputation of Pépin, who brought about the deposition of the last Merovingian king Childeric III and his own election as monarch in 751. 37: again recalls the words of Anchises, this time on Marcellus the elder (*Aeneid* 6.857-8 *hic <u>rem Romanam</u> magno turbante tumultu / sistet*), as well as Horace's praise of Augustus as *Caesaris ultor* (*Odes* 1.2.44). 38: cf. Horace *Odes* 4.14.12 *Alpibus ... tremendis*, Seneca *HO* 1167 *montis abrupti*. 39-40: refers to the historically crucial Donation of Pépin (756) – see the introductory section above; *uolentes* fittingly echoes the willing submission of the peoples of the East to Augustus at *Georgics* 4.561-2 *uolentis / per populos*, while *asserit urbes* echoes the same phrase at Lucan 3.56.

41-52 Further Catholic highlights from French history: the Crusades, Joan of Arc and the sixteenth-century Wars of Religion (for the historical details see the introductory section above). 41: *admiror* continues the Anchises-like admiration of compatriots (see on 33-4 above), while *Solymis potitus* is the language of military prose (cf. Caesar *Civ*. 3.35.1 *omni Aetolia potitus est*). 42-4: *uindices ... phalanges* – cf. *Aeneid* 12.277 *animosa phalanx*, Seneca *HF* 255 *gnatos ... uindices*; *sancti tumuli* is the Holy Sepulchre, the traditional burial place of Jesus and the chief shrine of Jerusalem recaptured by the mostly French First Crusade in 1099, while 43-4 *renouata ... / proelia* (cf. Ovid *Met*. 5.155 *renouataque proelia*) looks to the series of crusades in which French

Vincenzo Pecci (1810–1903; Pope as Leo XIII 1878–1903) 223

leaders and forces participated; for *Palaestinis . . . campis* cf. Lucan 5.460 *Palaestinas . . . harenas*. 45: *nouum*: 'strange', i.e. not traditionally female; *celebris . . . puellae* = Joan of Arc, perhaps Christianising the pagan fame of the beloved (*puella*) of classical Latin elegy (Ovid *Am.* 1.10.59 *celebrare puellas*); the particular reference of *castra/ perrumpens inimica* (cf. *Aeneid* 5.671 *inimicaque castra*) is to her part in breaking through the English siege of Orléans and the city's relief in April–May 1429, a key moment of the Hundred Years' War. 47–8: cf. *Aeneid* 6.843 *cladem Libyae*, Valerius Flaccus 4.101 *numine freti*. 49–50: again recalls Anchises' admiration of his descendants (*Aeneid* 6.758 *illustris animas*); for *nefanda / monstra* cf. Seneca *Thy*. 632 *nefandi . . . monstri* (*domuere = domuerunt*, as at *Aeneid* 2.198). 51: *fortis* with infinitive is an Horatian construction (*Odes* 1.37.26, 3.3.50); note how the similarly shaped and rhyming verbs *domuere* and *prohibere* are here vertically juxtaposed in the same metrical position, also an Horatian feature (cf. e.g. *Odes* 1.31.1–2). *Labes* is standard in patristic Latin for the taint of heresy (*TLL* 7.2.772.45–61). 52: *sceptra* (poetic plural) = 'rule' (literally 'sceptres'), a common Vergilian metonymy (8× in *Aeneid*).

53–76 Closing exhortation to the French nation to preserve Christian values, evoking the high moralizing and nationalist tone of Horace's Roman Odes (*Odes* 3.1–6); the elaborate effects of word order in this section (see below) add to its hymnic force. 53–4: *quo feror?* suggests that the poet is in danger of distraction into history from his contemporary theme, echoing the self-redirection of Horace at *Odes* 3.3.70 *quo Musa tendis? Tempus redit* points to the return of the ancestral courage just described (cf. Grattius 323 *uirtutisque . . . priscae*), as in the classical pattern of the return of the golden age (cf. Horace *Carm.Saec.* 57–9 *iam Fides et Pax et Honos Pudorque / priscus et neglecta redire Virtus / audet*), while *auspicatum* Christianizes the Roman prophetic auspices as at item 2, line 5 above; for the metaphor of the heat of courage cf. e.g. *Aeneid* 6.130 *ardens . . . uirtus*. 55 *adurget*: a rare verb found in Horace (*Odes* 1.37.17). 57–8: the nicely alliterative *Gallicae gentes* has a historiograpical colour (cf. Sallust *Cat.* 40.1, Livy 27.39), while *iubaris . . . radios* indicates the sun as at Ovid *Met.*1.768

'*per iubar hoc*' *inquit* '*radiis insigne coruscis...*'. 59–60: cf. Lucretius 3.304 *suffundens... umbra*, Statius *Theb*.11.656 *malesuadus amor*. 62 *obsequi sectis* is a *figura etymologica*, with verb and object having the same derivation (*sequor*), while *probrosis... sectis* echoes patristic invective: cf. Tertullian *Apol*.3 *malam sectam*, Bachiarius *De Fide* 2 *probrosae heresis*. 62–3: these two lines begin with alliterative and metrically identical verbs in vertical juxtaposition (see on line 51 above). 63–4: military language, cf. Sallust *Jug*. 80.2 *in unum cogit*, *Ilias Latina* 133 *socias... uires*. 65–6 *actuosa uita* is a prosaic phrase (Valerius Maximus 2.1.10, Seneca *Dial*.9.4.8), as is *calor uitae* ([Quintilian *Decl.Mai*. 10.4.5); for the infinitive after *renuo* cf. Silius 17.24 *renuens procedere*; note how the alliterating and polar opposite verbs *perstitit* and *perire* enclose the line. 67–8: the Vesle is the river of Reims; *aestuo* (often used poetically of bodies of water, cf. *OLD s.u*.4) is thus an appropriate metaphor here; cf. similarly Ovid *Her*. 16.25 *pectoris ... aestum*, *Met*.2.175 *nouas feruoribus iras*. 69: note how participle and noun in agreement enclose the line; *dissitis... terris* looks to the worldwide French colonial empire of the 1890s (including parts of South America, Asia and Africa). 70–1: *nomen* = 'race' as in the common *Romanum nomen* (e.g. Ovid *Met*.1.201); *populis... adsit Eois* (cf. Lucan 7.56 *populique... Eoi*) is a euphemistic reference to contemporary expansion in Indo-China, e.g. in the acquisition of Laos in 1893 (see Aldrich 1996), while lines 71–2 suggest the role of Catholic proselytizing in the 'civilizing mission' of the French imperialism of the time (see e.g. Burrows 1986): for *sancta fides* see both *Aeneid* 7.365 (pagan) and Lactantius *Inst*.5.1.15 (Christian), while *uota secundet* echoes the same words at Seneca *HF* 645. 73–4: a pithy and sententious pair of phrases without verbs (*est* is twice omitted), in the manner of Horace (cf. e.g. *Odes* 3.4.65); for consecutive lines headed by *nil* cf. Horace *Odes* 3.25.17–18, and for 73 cf. Propertius 4.1.80 *nil prius esse fide* (here Christianized); for the idea of *nil diu felix* cf. Horace *Odes* 2.16.27–8 *nihil est ab omni / parte beatum*. 74–5: *priscae* picks up *prisca* (54) in similar reference to past glories; cf. Horace *Epod*.2.2 *prisca gens*. The correlatives *unde/inde* are vertically juxtaposed, each followed by a matching disyllabic adjective (for a smilar effect cf. Horace *Odes*

1.3.6–7). 75–6: *summa laus* is a frequent Ciceronian phrase, *iugis gloria* Christian, here fittingly echoing at the poem's close the close of a sequence (7) attributed to the twelfth-century French poet Adam of St Victor, celebrating the French St Genevieve: *Christo pro tot miraculis / laus frequens iugis gloria*.[36] 76: for the alliterative juxtaposition, a final flourish, cf. Hirtius *Gall.* 8.6.2 *gloria Gallos*.

4. Horatian hexameter poem on moderate diet

The translation of this poem in Latin hexameters[37] into English by the Scottish writer Andrew Lang soon after its publication in 1897[38] has been claimed as the moment when the then pope's Latin poetry was drawn to international attention.[39] The poem is written in the looser and more colloquial style of hexameter verse (*sermo* or 'talk') characteristic of Horace in his *Satires* and *Epistles*, and draws extensively on Horatian material from the *Satires*, with many close echoes of details from its classical originals.

Like the poems of Horace *Epistles* Book 1, this work is in epistolary form and directed to a friend. 'Fabricius Rufus' is likely to Latinize the name Fabrizio Ruffo, perhaps to be identified with Fabrizio Ruffo (1843–1917), Principe Di Sant' Animo, the son of Vincenzo Ruffo, Duc de Bagnara in Calabria, and a generation younger than Pecci.[40] This character might well have been connected with Pecci's friend Fulco Luigi Ruffo-Scilla, also from a noble family with Calabrian connections, who is addressed with the same Latinized surname as 'Ludouicus Rufus' by Pecci in a Latin poem celebrating his appointment as archbishop of Chieti in 1877.[41]

The poem's main topic of the virtues of a moderate diet frequently recalls in detail *Satires* 2.2, where Horace reports Ofellus' lecture on that subject;[42] that poem is also indicated as the chief model in the title of Pecci's poem which echoes it twice, and in the reuse of the name and didactic authority of the Horatian character Ofellus, who is treated by Pecci as by Horace as a figure of wisdom. This same technique of reporting someone else's opinions on diet is also found in *Satires* 2.4, where Catius reproduces the extensive lecture of an anonymous gourmand commending luxurious food, ironized by Horace; the material of this second lecture is effectively inverted here in Pecci's poem's lengthy condemnation of rich diet.[43] *Satires* 2.8, where Horace presents an ironic narrative by the comic poet Fundanius of the excessively elaborate dinner of Nasidienus, is also regularly echoed in this poem.[44]

After a brief introduction (1–5) the reported discourse of Ofellus falls into two parts, an exhortation to moderate diet (6–41) and a dramatic description of the evil effects of gluttony (42–85). The material for the first section corresponds to the similarly embedded speech of Ofellus in Horace *Satires* 2.2, which is largely dedicated to advocating a frugal diet, with only a brief final condemnation of luxurious eating (2.2.95–8). Pecci's second section, the major attack on gluttony (*ingluuies*), criticizes a vice commonly denounced in Horatian and other Roman satire,[45] but more importantly points to one of the seven deadly sins of Christian tradition,[46] neatly combining ancient and modern systems of ethical thought.

Text and translation

AN. MDCCCXCVII: TENVI VICTV CONTENTVS INGLVVIEM
FVGE.

AD FABRICIVM RVFVM EPISTOLA

Quo uictu immunem morbis et robore uitam
Ducere florentem possis, sermone diserto
Sedulus Hippocratis cultor rigidusque satelles
Haec nuper praecepta bonus tradebat Ofellus;
Multa et de tristi ingluuie grauis ore locutus.   5
'Munditiae imprimis studeas: sine diuite cultu
Mensa tibi, nitidae lances et candida mappa.
Apponi in mensa iubeas purissima uina;
Et uacuus curis grato praecordia potu
Demulce et recrea conuiuas inter amicos.   10
Sobrius at caueas, nimium ne crede Lyaeo,
Neu crebra pigeat calices perfundere lympha.
Candida lympha! datum uix quidquam hoc munere maius,
Vix quidquam uarios uitae magis utile in usus.
E munda Cerere atque excoctos delige panes,   15
Quas gallina dapes aut bos agnusue pararint
Sume libens; toto nam firmant corpore uires;
At mollire prius carnes, et fercula cures
Ne siser inficiat, ne faecula Coa vel allec.
Nunc age, prouideas tereti defusa catino   20
Ne desit mensae spumantis copia lactis.
Nil uitale magis, nil lacte salubrius: infans
Qui lac suxisti, senior bene lacte ualebis.
Degustanda simul profer dulcissima mella;
Attamen Hyblaeo parcus de nectare liba.   25
Tum laudata tibi sint oua recentia, sucum
Leni igne aut libeat modicis siccare patellis,

1897: BE CONTENT WITH A MODEST DIET AND AVOID GLUTTONY.

LETTER TO FABRIZIO RUFFO.

As to the diet by which you can lead a life immune to disease
And flourishing in strength, good Ofellus used lately to hand
   down
These precepts in eloquent speech, he, the careful cultivator
Of Hippocrates and his unrelenting servant;
He spoke too in serious tones of grim gluttony: 5
'Above all pay attention to cleanliness: let your table be
Free from rich luxury, your dishes shining, your napkins white:
Give orders that the purest wines are placed on the table,
And, free from cares, soothe and refresh your guts
With welcome drink amongst friends as your fellow-diners.   10
But make sure you are sober – do not put too much trust in wine,
And do not be reluctant to bathe your cups with frequent water.
Bright liquid! Hardly any other gift is greater than this,
Hardly anything is more useful for the various ends of life.
Choose well-baked bread from pure grain,   15
Consume freely the feast that the hen, the ox or the lamb provide,
For they reinforce the strength of the whole body:
But soften these meats first, and take care that rampion does not
Adulterate your courses, or dried Coan lees, or fish sauce.
Come now: make sure that, poured out in a round bowl,   20
The table is not short of abundance of foaming milk.
There is nothing more life giving, nothing healthier than milk:
You who have sucked milk as an infant will have good health
   from milk when older.
At the same time provide the sweetest honeys for tasting,
But be sparing in your consumption of the Hyblaean nectar.   25
Then let fresh eggs have your commendation, and feel free
To dry their yolks with slow heat or in small pans,

Sugere seu mollem pleno sit gratius ore;
Utcumque absumas erit utilis esca saluti.
Culta suburbano riguoque uirentia in horto   30
Adde olera et pubens decusso flore legumen.
Adde nouos quos laeta refert tibi uinea fructus,
Dulces pampinea decerptos uite racemos,
Pruna admixta piris, imprimis mitia poma,
Quae pulchre in cistis mensam rubicunda coronent.   35
Postremo e tostis succedat potio bacis,
Quas tibi Moka ferax e litore mittit Eoo:
Nigrantem laticem sensim summisque labellis
Sorbilla: dulcis stomachum bene molliet haustus.
De tenui uictu haec teneas, his utere tutus,   40
Ad seram ut ualeas sanus uegetusque senectam.
At contra' (haec sapiens argute addebat Ofellus)
'Nectere nata dolos, homines et perdere nata
Vitanda ingluuies, crudelis et improba Siren.
Principio haec illi sollers et sedula cura,   45
Instruere ornatu mensas cultuque decoras.
Explicat ipsa, uiden?, tonsis mantelia uillis;
Grandia disponit longo ordine pocula, lances,
Caelatas auro pateras, argentea uasa;
Mensa thymo atque apio redolet florumque corollis.   50
His laute instructis simulata uoce locuta
Conuiuas trahit incautos succedere tecto,
Et lectis blanda inuitat discumbere eburnis,
Continuoque reposta cadis lectissima uina
Caecuba depromit Coumque uetusque Falernum;   55
Quin exquisita stillatos arte liquores
E musto et pomis ultro potantibus offert.
Conuiuae umectant certatim guttura et una
Sucosas auido degustant ore placentas.
Ecce autem Lucanus aper, perfusus abunde   60

Or it might be more pleasant to suck them raw with full mouth:
However you eat it, this will be a food useful for health.
Add greens grown in a suburban estate in a well-watered garden, 30
And downy beans with their flowers removed,
Add the fresh fruits that the lush vineyard yields you,
Sweet clusters cut from the grape-vine,
Plums mixed with pears, above all ripe apples, which
In their ruddy colour are to encircle the table prettily in
    their boxes.   35
Afterwards let there follow the drink made from roast berries,
Which Mocha sends to you from its eastern shore:
Sip the dark liquid gradually and with the edges of your lips:
The sweet draught will nicely soften up the stomach.
On moderate diet hold to these ideas, use these and be safe,   40
So as to be well into late old age, healthy and vigorous.
But, on the other hand' (this wise Ofellus used to add, acutely)
'Gluttony, born to weave traps, born to destroy men,
Is to be avoided, that cruel and wicked Siren.
Her principal, cunning and constant concern is this,   45
To set out tables fair with ornament and luxury.
She lays out, do you see?, napkins with shorn nap,
Arranges vast glasses in a long row, platters,
Bowls chased with gold, vessels of silver: the table
Is fragrant with thyme and parsley and with garlands of flowers. 50
These rich preparations made, she speaks with deceiving voice
And draws in unsuspecting guests to come to the house,
And invites them charmingly to recline on ivory couches,
And at once brings out the choicest Caecuban wines,
Laid down in casks, Coan and old Falernian: 55
She even offers freely exquisite liquors skilfully distilled
From grape-must and fruit to them to drink.
The guests vie to wet their throats, and with them
They taste juicy cakes with greedy mouth.
Here the Lucanian boar, richly basted   60

Mordaci pipere atque oleo, profertur edendus,
Et leporum pingues armi et iecur anseris albi
Assique in uerubus turdi niueique columbi.
Carnibus admixti pisces: cum murice rhombi,
Ostrea et educti Miseno e gurgite echini. 65
Hos super, immanis patina porrecta nitenti,
Apparet squillas inter murena natantes.
Attonitis inhiant oculis; saturantur opime:
Cuncta uorant usque ad fastidia iamque Lyaeo
Inflati uenas nimio dapibusque grauati 70
Surgunt conuiuae, temere bacchantur in aula,
Insana et pugiles inter se iurgia miscent,
Defessi donec lymphata mente quiescunt.
Laeta dolum ingluuies ridet, iam facta suorum
Compos uotorum, et gaudet memor artis iniquae, 75
Ceu nautas tumida pereuntes aequoris unda,
Mergere conuiuas miseros sub gurgite tanto.
Nam subito exsudant praecordia et excita bilis
E iecore in stomachum larga affluit, ilia torquet,
Immanemque ciet commoto uentre tumultum; 80
Membra labant incerta, stupent pallentia et ora.
Corpore sic misere exhausto fractoque, quid ultra
Audeat ingluuies? Ipsum, pro dedecus!, ipsum
Figere humo ac (tantum si fas) exstinguere malit
Immortalem animum, diuinae particulam aurae.' 85

With tangy pepper and oil is brought out to be eaten:
And the rich shoulders of hares and the liver of a white goose,
And thrushes roasted on spits and snow-white doves.
Fish is mixed with meat: turbot with shellfish, oysters,
And sea-urchins taken from the sea at Misenum. 65
On top of these massive items, set out on a shining platter,
There appears a moray eel between swimming crayfish.
They gape with astonished gaze and are richly sated;
They devour everything to the point of disgust; and now,
Their veins swollen by excessive wine and weighed down 70
By their feasting, the guests arise and rage recklessly in the hall,
And they exchange deranged insults like boxers,
Until, exhausted by their maddened mind, they fall quiet.
Gluttony gladly laughs at her tricks, now in possession
Of all her wishes, and rejoices, mindful of her evil skill, 75
In drowning the miserable guests beneath such a great billow,
Like a swollen ocean wave drowns dying sailors.
For all of a sudden their insides ooze out, and bile is produced
From their liver and flows copiously into the stomach,
Tortures the guts and rouses a mighty motion in the stirred
 stomach: 80
Their limbs totter hesitantly, and their pale faces are stupefied.
Once the body is so exhausted and broken, what might gluttony
 dare further?
She might wish to fix, o shame, to the earth the immortal soul
Itself, itself, and (if so great an act is permissible)
To extinguish that particle of the divine breath. 85

Commentary

The title alludes to Horace *Satires* 2.2, the poem's main model (see introductory section above): cf. *Satires* 2.2.110 *contentus paruo*, 2.2.53 *tenui uictu*, 2.2.70 *uictus tenuis*.

1–5 Introduction to Ofellus' advice on simple diet and avoiding gluttony. These lines adapt the opening (lines 1–4) of Horace *Satires* 2.2, the poem's principal model (see introductory section above): *Quae uirtus et quanta, boni, sit uiuere parvo / – nec meus hic sermo est, sed quae praecepit Ofellus / rusticus ... / discite*. 1–2: *uictu ... uitam* – the supposed etymological connection between the two words (cf. Isidore *Orig.* 20.2.1) and their link in meaning (food and life: is stressed by their alliteration; for *immunem morbis* cf. Statius *Silv.*2.2.222 *immunis fatis*, for *uitam ducere* cf. *Aeneid* 2.461 and 4.340, for *uitam ... florentem* cf. Lucretius 3.1008 *aeuo florente*, and for *sermone diserto* cf. Ovid *Ars* 2.507 *sermone diserti. 3: cf. Horace *Ep.* 1.13.5 **sedulus ... minister*, *Ep.* 1.1.17 *uirtutis uerae custos* **rigidusque satelles*; for *cultor* of a devoted follower cf. Martial 5.5.1 *Sexte, Palatinae cultor facunde Mineruae*. The medical authority of Hippocrates of Cos (fifth century BCE) was well recognized in Rome (cf. e.g. Cicero *De Or.* 3.132). 4: *praecepta* echoes both *praecepit* of Ofellus' advice on diet at *Satires* 2.2.2 (above) and the use of *praecepta* of the gastronomic precepts reported by Catius in *Satires* 2.4 (2,11,95) – see the introductory section above, while *bonus ... Ofellus* varies Horace's commendation of Ofellus as *abnormis sapiens crassaque Minerva* (*Satires* 2.2.3). 5: cf. Seneca *Suas.*7.11 *multa fortiter de mortis contemptu locutus*, Ovid *Tr.*2.423 *cecinit grauis Ennius ore*; for *ingluuies* as a vice in satire cf. Horace *Satires* 1.2.8.

6–41 Ofellus' detailed guidance on a simple diet. 6 *imprimis* (or *in primis*) is a signposting term in didactic poetry (14× in Lucretius), here (as at Horace *Satires* 2.2.71 *in primis ualeas bene* and *Georgics* 1.338 *in primis uenerare deos*) marking a prime instruction; *studeas* is similarly didactic in tone, cf. Cicero *Phaen.*34.63 *caue ... studeas*. For the line-ending cf. Horace *AP* 409 *sine diuite uena, *Culex* 95 *non* *diuite cultu (*sit* should be understood here with *mensa*). 7: cf. Horace *Satires* 2.2.4 *inter lances mensasque nitentis*, Statius *Siluae* 1.6.31 *candidasque mappas*, and especially Horace *Epistles* 1.5.22-4 *ne sordida mappa / corruget naris, ne non et cantharus et lanx /ostendat tibi te*. 8 *apponi*: the standard term for serving food or drink at table (cf. Horace *Satires* 2.8.69 *ne male conditum ius apponatur*); for *purissima* cf. Ovid *Pont.* 3.1.162 *uinaque pura*. 9-10: cf. Silius 15.272-3 *uacui curis . . . mensas / instituunt*, *Priapea* 3.6 *pocula grata* (of wine), *Ciris* 346 *mulcens praecordia*, Horace *Epistles* 1.5.24 *fidos inter amicos*. 11: cf. *Eclogues* 2.17 **nimium ne crede colori*; *Lyaeus* = Bacchus 'the looser', 'wine' by 'god for thing' metonymy as often (e.g. Propertius 3.5.21 *mentem uincire Lyaeo*). 12: cf. Horace *Epodes* 16.27 *neu . . . pigeat*, Statius *Theb.* 8.766 *multa . . . lympha*, Calpurnius Siculus 4.123 *perfundere uino, Horace *Satires* 2.6.68 *siccat . . . calices* (inverted here). 13: cf. *Eclogues* 5.53 *An quicquam nobis tali sit* **munere maius?* 14: cf. Manilius 1.61 *uarios . . . usus*, Cicero *Tusc.* 1.48 (verse) *uitae uaria . . . mala*, Silius 12.649 *uitae . . . usus*, and for the *figura etymologica* (expressive conjunction of semantically related terms) *utile . . . usus* cf. Ovid *Met.*10.280 *utilis usu. 15: cf. *Copa* 20 *munda Ceres* (= bread, 'god for thing' as in *Lyaeo*, wine, in line 11 above; for the pairing of these two poetic metonyms cf. *Georgics* 2.229, *Aeneid* 4.58). For the healthy effect on the stomach of well-cooked bread (i.e. not harmfully undercooked) cf. e.g. Pliny *NH* 22.138. 16: cf. Virgil *Ecl.* 6.79 *quas Philomela dapes . . .* *pararit. 17 *libens* is adverbial ('gladly') as often in poetry (cf. e.g. Statius *Theb.*3.275 *perge libens*); *toto . . . corpore* is a Vergilian phrase (13×), *corpore uires* a Vergilian hexameter-ending (*Aeneid* 5.396). 18: cf. Lucretius 6.969 *carnem mollit*, Horace *Satires* 2.6.104 *fercula cena. 19: for this list of potentially harmful strong flavourings cf. Horace *Satires* 2.8.9 *siser, allec, faecula Coa* (for their details see Freudenburg 2021: 298). 20: *nunc age* is another didactic signpost term addressed to the reader (see on line 6 above), 14× in Lucretius, all similarly line-initial. 20: cf. Horace *Satires* 2.4.77 *angustoque . . . catino*, *Copa* 11 *cado . . .* *defusa. 21: cf. Horace *Satires* 2.3.123 *ne tibi desit?* 21: cf. *Aeneid* 3.66 **spumantia cymbia lacte*, *Georgics* 3.308 *largi copia lactis*. 22: the health-giving nature of milk is common to ancient and modern thought;[47] for the emphatic phrasing cf. Cato *Agr.* 157.5 *salubrius nihil est*, and especially Horace *Epistles* 1.1.18 *nil ait esse prius, melius nil caelibe vita*. 23 *lac sugere* is a favourite expression of Augustine (8×) and is found in the Vulgate (Deut. 33.19, Isaiah 60.16). 24: *degustare* implies an appropriately small sampling of this rich food (as at Ovid *Pont.* 4.10.18); cf. also *Georgics* 4.101 *dulcia mella*. 25: cf. Statius *Silu.* 3.2.118 *Hyblaeo . . . nectare* (similarly referrring to the Sicilian town of Hybla, famed for its honey); *liba* = 'merely taste' as at Horace *Satires* 2.6.67. 26–7: for eggs as Roman food cf. Horace *Epistles* 2.2.168, Juvenal 11.71, while for the construction of *laudata sint* (= *laudentur*) cf. Plautus *Poen.* 580 *fac modo ut condocta tibi sint dicta*. The reference is to frying or boiling/poaching eggs in the modern manner (for *patella* = 'pan' cf. Pliny *NH* 19.171). 28: sucking raw eggs seems to be more modern rather than Roman; cf. Ovid *Met.* 6.508 **pleno singultibus ore*. 29: for *utcumque* in this sense with subjunctive cf. e.g. Plautus *Bacch.* 662, and for *utilis saluti* cf. Augustine *Ep.* 60.1. 30: cf. Horace *Satires* 2.4.15–16 *cole suburbano qui siccis creuit in agris / dulcior: inriguo nihil est elutius horto* (*suburbanum* = suburban estate, OLD s.u. *suburbanus* 2), Columella 10.5.99 *uirentia lilia*. 31–2: for the colloquial anaphora of *adde* cf. Horace *Satires* 2.3.69–70 and 2.3.321; the *legumen* here seems to a species of flowering bean (broad or French); for *pubens* cf. *Aeneid* 4.514 *pubentes herbae*, while *florem decutere* is a patristic phrase (Ambrose *De Noe* 13, Jerome *Ad Gal*.2.4); cf. also [Ovid] *Nux* 132 *nouos fructus*, Lucretius 2.1157 (= 5.1372) *uinetaque laeta*. 33: cf. *Priapea* 2.8 *uirente dulcis uua pampino*, Ovid *Met*.10.100 *pampineae uites*; note how noun and epithet enclose the line. 34: cf. *Georgics* 4.145 *piris et . . . pruna*, *Eclogues* 4.20 *mixtaque . . . colocasia . . . acantho*, *Eclogues* 1.80 *mitia poma. 35: for *rubicundus* of fruit cf. Horace *Epistles* 1.16.8–9 *rubicunda . . . / corna*. 36: a periphrasis for coffee, unknown to the Romans, rounding off the meal (*postremo*); cf. *Georgics* 1.298 *tostas . . . fruges*. 37: for the personification of the exporting country cf. Horace *Epodes* 5.22–3 *herbas quas Iolcos atque Hiberia / mittit uenenorum ferax*, and for *litus Eoum* cf. Valerius Flaccus 5.245 *Eoo surgentes litore currus*. *Moka* is Mocha in Yemen, a key port in the nineteenth-century coffee trade to Europe. 38: cf. *Aeneid* 6.218 *calidos latices*, Apuleius *Met*.2.16.2 *sorbillat dulciter*. 39: cf. Pliny *NH* 2.227 *dulcis haustus*, Horace *Satires* 2.2.18 *stomachum bene leniet*. 40: cf. Horace *Satires* 2.2.53 *tenui uictu*, 2.2.70 *uictus tenuis* (evoking the poem's major model, see the introductory section above), Q.Cicero *Comm.Pet*. 4.1 *haec cura ut teneas*, Horace *Epistles* 1.6.68 **his utere mecum*. 41: cf. Seneca *HF* 364 *sera . . . senectus*, Horace *Satires* 2.2.81 *uegetus*, 2.2.71 *in primis ualeas bene*, *Epistles* 1.7.3 *sanum recteque ualentem*.

42-85 The dangers of gluttony according to Ofellus. Here that vice (a feminine noun (*ingluuies*) in Latin) is consistently personified from a stereotypical male perspective as an alluring and corrupting female figure. 42: cf. Horace *Satires* 2.2.2-3 *Ofellus / . . . abnormis sapiens*. 43: for the alliterative line-opening cf. Statius *Ach.* 1.320 **nectere, nate*; for *natus* + infinitive (note the emphatic anaphora of *nata* here) in the sense of 'destined to' cf. Horace *Epistles* 1.2.27 *fruges consumere nati*, and for *dolos nectere* Seneca *Phoen*. 119-20 *dolos / . . . Sphinx nectens* (another malevolent female). 44: cf. Horace *Satires* 2.3.14-15 *uitanda est inproba Siren / desidia*, 1.2.8 *ingrata . . . ingluuie*. 45: *principio* (37 times in Lucretius, always (fittingly) at line-start as here) is another didactic signpost term like *imprimis* (lines 6 and 34 above); cf. also Ovid *Pont*. 1.6.35 *sollers . . . cura*, Tibullus 1.5.33 **sedula curet*. 46: cf. *Aeneid* 3.231 *instruimus mensas*, Livy 34.7.9 *ornatus et cultus*, Statius *Silu.* 1.6.29 *decora cultu*. 47: for the inserted rhetorical question *uiden?* cf. Catullus 61.94, and cf. also *Georgics* 4.377 (= *Aeneid* 1.702) *tonsisque ferunt mantelia uillis*. 48: cf. Juvenal 13.147-8 *grandia . . . / pocula*, Ovid *Fasti* 3.301 *disponit pocula* and the Vergilian *longo ordine* (*Aeneid* 2.766, 6.482, 6.654, 8.722). 49: cf. *Aeneid* 1.640 *caelataque in auro*, Statius *Theb*. 1.540-1 *auroque nitentem / . . . pateram*, Horace *Satires* 2.7.72-3 *uasa / . . . argentea*. 50: cf. *Georgics* 4.169 *redolentque thymo*, *Eclogues* 6.69 *floribus atque apio*, *Copa* 13 *flore *corollae*. 51: *laute* = 'richly, luxuriously', as at Horace *Satires* 2.8.67; cf. *Aeneid* 4.105 **simulata mente locutam*, 3.320 **uoce locuta est*. 52: cf. Ovid *Met*. 7.19 *trahit inuitam*, *Aeneid* 11.146 **succedere tectis*. 53: cf. Horace *Satires* 2.6.103 *lectos . . . eburnos*,

Aeneid 1.708 *toris . . . discumbere*. 54-5: cf. Horace *Epodes* 9.1 *repostum Caecubum*, Martial 1.18.2 *condita . . . cadis*, *Georgics* 1.341 **mollissima uina*, Horace *Satires* 2.8.15 **Caecuba uina*, *Satires* 2.3.115 *Chii ueterisque *Falerni*. 56-7: a periphrasis for modern post-prandial spirits or liqueurs such as *grappa* (from grape residue) and *limoncello* (from lemon zest); cf. Valerius Maximus 4.3.7 *exquisita arte*, Ovid *Met*. 10.501 **stillataque cortice murra*, Columella 10.1.43-4 *pomis . . . / et musto*, *Culex* 85 **ultro . . . offert*, *Georgics* 4.146 *ministrantem . . . *potantibus*. 58: cf. *Epicedion Drusi* 422 *guttura tinxit aqua*, *Aeneid* 4.704 = 9.230 **et una*. 59: cf. Martial 11.86.3 *dulcesque placentas*, Ovid *Rem.* 209 *auido . . . deuoret ore*; for *degustare* see on line 24 above. Note the elegant, interlaced word order here (ABCBA, the so-called Golden Line).[48] 60: cf. Horace *Satires* 2.8.7 *in primis *Lucanus aper*, 1.7.32 **perfusus aceto*; **ecce autem* is a Vergilian formula introducing a new narrative development (9× in *Aeneid*, all *line-initial), while **abunde* ends Horatian hexameters at *Satires* 1.2.89 and *Epistles* 1.4.10. 61: cf. Ovid *Ars* 2.417 *piper urticae mordacis semine miscent*, Petronius 138.1 *oleo et minuto pipere*, Horace *Epistles* 1.16.7 **edendi*. 62-3: (over)elaborate dishes from Roman satire – cf. Horace *Satires* 2.4.44 *leporis . . . armos*, 2.8.88 *ficis pastum iecur anseris albae*, Juvenal 5.114 *anseris . . . magni iecur*, Horace *Satires* 2.7.73-4 *assis / . . . turdis*; for *niueique columbi* cf. Catullus 68.125 *niueo . . . columbo* (and for a cock-pigeon as a delicacy cf. Apicius 6.4.4), 64-5: cf. the fish and seafood of Horace *Satires* 2.4.32-3 *murice Baiano melior Lucrina peloris, / ostrea Circeis, Miseno oriuntur echini*; for the *rhombus* as a luxury dish in satire cf. Horace *Satires* 2.2.42-9, Juvenal 4.39. 66-7: cf. Horace *Satires* 2.8.42-3 *adfertur squillas inter murena natantis / in patina porrecta*. 68: cf. *Ciris* 132 *cupidis Minoa inhiasset ocellis*; *opime* (adverb) occurs in classical Latin only at Plautus *Bacch.* 373. 69-71: cf. Horace *Epodes* 4.11 *ad fastidium* (for the poetic plural *fastidia* of satiety with food cf. Horace *Satires* *2.2.14, *2.4.78), *Eclogues* 6.15 *inflatum . . . uenas . . . Iaccho* (for *Lyaeo* cf. on line 11 above), *Aeneid* 1.210 **dapibusque*, Livy 1.7.5 *cibo uinoque grauatum*, Plautus *Pseud.* 296 *a mensa surgunt satis poti*, *Mil.* 856 *bacchabantur* *aula*, Georgics 4.90 =*Aeneid* 1.142 *in aula. 72: cf. Ovid *Fasti* 1.73–4 *insanaque* . . . / *iurgia*, Statius *Silu*. 4.4.39 *miscent iurgia*, *Aeneid* 12.720 *illi inter sese multa ui uulnera miscent* (of duelling animals); *pugiles* = *[ut] pugiles* (simile) as often in poetry (e.g. Horace *Ep*. 2.2.98). 73: cf. Lucan 5.211 *fessa* *quiescunt, Catullus 64.254 *lymphata mente. 74: gluttony (for the term *ingluuies* see on line 5 above) is strongly personified here, deceptive and laughing like Venus at Horace *Odes* 3.27.67 *perfidum ridens Venus*; cf. also Tibullus 1.2.89 *laetus rides*, *Eclogues* 6.23 *dolum ridens*. 75: cf. Silius 17.540 *iam compos uoti*, *Aeneid* 4.618 *pacis* *iniquae. 76: cf. Ovid *Fasti* 3.595 *tumidas . . . *undas, *Ars* 1.171 *aequoris unda. 77: cf. Juvenal 6.424 *conuiuae miseri*, *Aeneid* 6.741 **sub gurgite uasto*, 10.557 *gurgite mersum*. 78–9: cf. *Georgics* 1.88 *exsudat inutilis umor* (similarly intransitive), Horace *Satires* 1.9.66 *meum iecur urere bilis*, 2.2.75–6 *dulcia se in bilem uertent stomachoque tumultum / lenta feret pituita*, Celsus 2.7.6 *intestina torquentur*. 80: cf. Livy 42.16 *ingentes tumultus ciere*; note the elegant line-enclosing noun-adjective pair *immanem* . . . *tumultum*. 81: cf. Statius *Theb*. 6.871 *membra labant, 9.531 *incertique labant* . . . *gressus*, *Aeneid* 10.822 *ora* . . . *pallentia*; note how the nouns *membra* and *ora*, balanced in sense as body-parts, frame the line. 82–3: cf. Silius 12.318 *corpore sic toto, Seneca *Ep*. 60.7 *corpus exhaurit*, 101.12 *corpore fracto*, *Aeneid* 3.480 **quid ultra / prouehor* . . .?; for *ingluuies* see on line 5 above, for the forceful anaphora cf. Statius *Silu*. 4.2.38 *ipsum, ipsum*, and for the emphatic exclamatory *pro* cf. Horace *Odes* 3.5.7 *pro curia inuersique mores!*, Florus *Epit*.1.36 *pro dedecus!* 84–5 recall Horace *Satires* 2.2.77–9 *quin corpus onustum / hesternis uitiis animum quoque praegrauat una /atque adfigit humo diuinae particulam aurae* in a final close echo of the poem's chief model (see introductory section above); cf. also Lucan 10.63 *si fas* (sc. *est*), *Epic.Drus.* 129 *si talia dicere fas est*, Cicero *Sen*.66 *exstinguit animum* and 82 *animi immortales*, Lucretius 3.754 **immortalem animam*.

5. Ode on the coming of the new century

This ode, in Alcaic stanzas,[49] was written to mark the coming of the new century on 1 January 1900. Understandably, given its papal author, it was rapidly translated into a variety of vernacular languages in Europe, and English versions appeared in both the UK and the United States.[50] Its connection with a *saeculum* (confirmed in the title) naturally suggests links with Horace's lyric *Carmen Saeculare*, similarly celebrating the inauguration of a significant new calendrical age (the Roman *saeculum* of 110 years), though Horace's poem is in a different lyric metre (Sapphics) and wholly positive about the coming age in contrast with the pessimism of Pecci's poem; in its chronological commemoration it also resembles Pecci's ode on the anniversary of the conversion of Clovis (item 3 above).

Its Alcaic metre provides a clue to another and more significant Horatian source, the cycle of six Alcaic Roman Odes which opens the third book (*Odes* 3.1-6). There too we have condemnations of the immorality of the current age alongside recognition of its material advances, and firm hopes that a saviour figure will bring about a good outcome for the future (Augustus in Horace, Jesus in Pecci). Other Horatian odes on Augustus such as 1.12 are also drawn on, alongside further odes which evoke the darker sides of recent Roman history (such as 2.1 on civil war). The poet's self-presentation also echoes aspects of that of the ageing Horace in *Odes* Book 4, not least in the last line in which he signs off with his own name, echoing the closure of *Odes* 4.6.

The poem can be divided into three parts. The opening section (1–16) begins with the contrast between the last century's scientific advances and its moral decadence, exemplified for the poet in the sufferings and oppression of the Papacy at the hands of the secular state of Italy. The middle section (17–32) expands on the moral decline of the nineteenth century, lamenting the rise of secularism and its concomitant human pride. The final section (33–56) addresses a prayer to Christ to steer the world in a better direction, and concludes with a personal reference to the poet himself.

The pessimistic tone of Pecci's poem reflects contemporary problems for the Catholic Church from the perspective of its head. Chief amongst these was the antagonistic relationship between the Italian state and the Vatican, which at this time still refused to recognize Italy formally and forbade Catholics to vote in its elections. Lines 11–15 point to the loss of the Papal States a generation earlier, characterized by the poem as involving war, deceit and oppression. This refers to the military occupation of Rome by the Italian state in 1870 after Pius IX was abandoned by his French garrison, and to the subsequent uncertain status of the pope isolated, prisoner-like, in the Vatican, not resolved until the creation of the Vatican State by the Lateran Treaty of 1929.[51]

There is an interesting contemporary parallel to this ode in the 1900 poem 'The Passing of the Century' by the then English Poet Laureate Alfred Austin (1835–1913), another public ode written to mark the inauguration of the twentieth century.[52] Austin was a conservative Catholic who had visited Rome and had taken an interest in church affairs there,[53] and might well have known Pecci's poem. Austin's poem in six twelve-line stanzas also points to the nineteenth century as an age of war, beginning at the time of the Napoleonic conflict, and similarly looks to the guidance of God for the new age.[54]

Text and translation

AN. CHRISTI MDCCCC PRIDIE KALENDAS IANUARIAS A lESV CHRISTO INEVNTIS SAECVLI AVSPICIA

Cultrix bonarum nobilis artium
Decedit aetas: publica commoda
   Viresque naturae retectas
     Quisquis auet memoret canendo.
Saecli occidentis me uehementius   5
Admissa tangunt: haec doleo et fremo.
   Pro! Quot retrorsum conspicatus
     Dedecorum monumenta cerno!
Querarne caedes sceptraque diruta,
An peruagantis monstra licentiae,   10
   An dirum in arcem Vaticanam
     Mille dolis initum duellum?
Quo cessit urbis, principis urbium,
Nullo impeditum seruitio decus,
   Quam saecla, quam gentes auitae   15
     Pontificum coluere sedem?
Vae segregatis numine legibus!
Quae lex honesti, quae superest fides?
   Nutant semel submota ab aris
     Atque ruunt labefacta iura.   20
Auditis? Effert impia conscius
Insanientis grex sapientiae
   Brutaeque naturae supremum
     Nititur asseruisse numen.
Nostrae supernam gentis originem   25
Fastidit excors: dissociabilem,
   Umbras inanes mente captans,
     Stirpem hominum pecudumque miscet.
Heu quam probroso gurgite uoluitur
Vis impotentis caeca superbiae: 30
   Seruate, mortales, in omne

31 DECEMBER 1895: PROPHECY FOR THE NEW CENTURY WHICH BEGINS FROM JESUS CHRIST

A noble age which has nourished good character
Departs: let he who wishes record in song
The general gains and the revealing
Of the forces of nature:
    I am more strongly affected by the crimes   5
Of the waning age – these I lament and murmur against.
Alas! As I turn and look backwards,
How many reminders of disgrace I see!
    Should I lament the slaughters and the ruined royal realms,
Or the monstrosities of rampant licence,   10
Or the accursed war against the Vatican citadel
Begun by a thousand deceptions?
    Where now is the glory of the city, the queen of cities,
Once hindered by no form of slavery,
The city which the ages and ancestral peoples   15
Have revered as the seat of the popes?
    Alas for laws sundered from divine power!
What law of virtue or what fidelity remains?
Ordinances shake once separated from altars,
They totter and collapse.   20
    Can you hear? The guilty band
Of unwise wisdom produces impieties,
And strains to assert
The supreme godhead of brute nature.
    It senselessly despises the heavenly origin   25
Of our human race: catching at empty shadows
With its mind, it blends the unmixable
Stocks of men and beasts.
    Alas, with how vile a torrent rolls on
The blind force of uncontrolled pride: 30
Keep, you mortals, for all time

> *Iussa Dei metuenda tempus.*
> *Qui uita solus certaque Veritas,*
> *Qui recta et una est ad superos uia,*
> *Is reddere ad uotum fluentes* 35
>   *Terrigenis ualet unus annos.*
> *Nuper sacratos ad cineres Petri*
> *Turbas piorum sancta petentium*
>   *Is ipse duxit, non inane*
>   *Auspicium pietas renascens.* 40
> *Iesu, futuri temporis arbiter,*
> *Surgentis aeui cursibus annue:*
>   *Virtute diuina rebelles*
>   *Coge sequi meliora gentes.*
> *Tu pacis almae semina prouehe;* 45
> *Irae, tumultus, bellaqua tristia*
>   *Tandem residant: improborum*
>   *In tenebrosa age regna fraudes.*
> *Mens una reges te duce temperet,*
> *Tuis ut instent legibus obsequi:* 50
>   *Sitque unum Ovile et Pastor unus,*
>   *Una Fides moderetur orbem.*
> *Cursum peregi lustraque bis novem,*
> *Te dante uixi. Tu cumulum adiice:*
>   *Fac, quaeso, ne incassum precantis* 55
>   *Vota tui recidant Leonis.*

The formidable commands of God.
   He who alone is life and the sure Truth,
Who is the direct and only way to heaven,
He alone has the power to give abundant years   35
To the children of earth in answer to their prayer.
   Recently he himself led to the consecrated ashes
Of Peter crowds of the pious
Seeking holy things: such reviving piety
Is no empty indication.   40
   Jesus, who controls future time,
Assent to the advance of the age now arising:
With your divine might compel rebel peoples
To follow a better course.
   Promote the seeds of gentle peace;   45
Let passions, disorders and grim wars
At last subside; drive the deceptions
Of the wicked into the realms of darkness.
   Let one mind under your command direct the rulers
So that they are eager to obey your laws: 50
Let there be one Fold and one Shepherd,
Let one Faith control the world.
   I have run my course, and I have lived
Ninety years, your gift. Add the culmination:
Bring it about, I beg, that the wishes of your Leo   55
May not fall to earth in vain.

Commentary

1-16 The poet points to the passing of an age rich in material progress but also afflicted by moral decline. 1: cf. Ovid *Ex Ponto* 2.5.65 *artis... ingenuae cultor*; *bonae artes* is a common Ciceronian phrase (7×). 2: cf. Horace *Epistles* 2.1.3 *publica commoda*. 3: cf. Lucretius 1.29-30 *quod sic natura tua ui /... ex omni parte retecta est*. 5: for *saecli occidentis* cf. *occasus saeculi*, used by patristic writers of the end of the material world (*TLL* 9.2.341.50ff); the paired verbs of rejection *doleo et fremo* recall Horace *Odes* 3.1.1. *odi... et arceo*. 6: *admissa* = 'crimes' (as at Ovid *Met*.14.92). 7: *fremo* = 'murmur against, object to' (cf. Valerius Flaccus 5.523-4 *ausa... /... fremit*). 7: for the Horatian exclamation *pro* cf. *Odes* 3.5.7 and note on item 4 lines 82-3 above; *retrorsum* is also Horatian (four of its six occurrences in classical Latin poetry are in Horace – cf. esp. *Epistles* 1.1.75 *spectantia... retrorsum*) while *conspicor* belongs to the colloquial language of Plautus (30×). 8: cf. *Aeneid* 12.944-5 *oculis... saeui monimenta doloris /... hausit*. 9: cf. Statius *Theb*. 12.552 *querimur caesos*, Propertius 2.28.54 *diruta regna*. 10: cf. Horace *Odes* 4.15.9-11 *ordinem / rectum euaganti frena licentiae / iniecit* (of the moral disorder conquered by Augustus); *monstra* parallels the dangerous beasts subdued by Hercules (cf. similarly *monstrum* at Horace *Odes* 4.4.63). 11-12: cf. *Aeneid* 11.217 *dirum exsecrantur bellum*, Horace *Odes* 1.20.7-8 *Vaticani / montis*, Ovid *Met*.7.726 *per mille dolos*; for the grand archaic *duellum* (= *bellum*) cf. Horace *Odes* 3.5.38, 3.14.18, 4.15.8. The reference is to the capture of papal Rome by the Italian army on 20 September 1870, including an incursion into St Peter's Square, which was preceded by complex attempts at a diplomatic settlement; *dirum* ('accursed') perhaps alludes to Pius IX's excommunication of the invading army on 1 November of the same year.[55] 13-16: for the forceful rhetorical question cf. Horace *Odes* 4.13.17 *Quo fugit Venus...?* 13-14: cf. Horace *Odes* 4.3.13 *Romae, principis urbium*, *Culex* 360 *Roma decus magni... orbis*; *impeditum seruitio* refers from a rhetorical papal perspective to the Vatican's 'enslaved' position after 1870. 15: for the insistent anaphora of the relative pronoun cf. Horace *Odes* 4.13.19-20 *quae spirabat amores, / quae me surpuerat mihi*, and for *gentes auitae* cf.

Vincenzo Pecci (1810-1903; Pope as Leo XIII 1878-1903) 247

Statius *Theb*.4.383 *gentis auitae* (though here *auitus* seems to mean simply 'long-established' rather than the classical 'ancestral'). 16: *pontificum sedes* is a papal phrase for Rome since Gregory the Great (*Reg.Epist.* 9.148); for the shape of the line here cf. Horace *Odes* 2.14.28 **pontificum potiore cenis*.

17-32 The poet laments the moral decline of the nineteenth century, the rise of secularism and associated human pride. 17-18: cf. Horace *Odes* 3.24.35-6 *quid leges sine moribus / uanae proficiunt*? The line attacks the newly secular laws of European Catholic countries such as Italy and France. For *numen* = 'divine power' generally cf. Horace *Odes* 4.4.74, and for the indignant repeated rhetorical interrogative in the same line cf. Horace *Odes* 4.13.17-18 *Quo fugit Venus, heu, quoue color, decens / quo motus?*, for *superest* in a similar context cf. Ovid *Ars* 2.637 *quid tuti superest . . . ?*, and for substantival *honestum* ('virtue') cf. Horace *Satires* 1.6.63, *Odes* 4.9.41. 19-20: cf. Ovid *Met*.10.375 *sic animus labefactus uulnere nutat*; *submota ab aris* elegantly varies 17 *segregatis numine* (altars, shared by Roman and Christian cultic practice, here stand metonymically for religion). 21-2: cf. Horace *Odes* 3.4.5-6 **auditis?*; for *impia* used substantivally (= 'impieties') cf. e.g. Seneca *Ep.* 95.58, for *conscius . . . grex* cf. Ovid *Fasti* 2.100 *conscia turba*, and for *insanientis grex sapientiae* cf. Horace *Odes* 1.34.2 **insanientis dum sapientiae*. 23: for *brutae . . . naturae* cf. Horace *Odes* 1.34.1 *bruta tellus*, 24: for the three-word final line of the Alcaic stanza with enclosing alliteration cf. Horace *Odes* 2.1.12 *Cecropio repetes coturno*. 25-6: cf. Ovid *Met.* 5.190 *nostrae primordia gentis*; *supernus* means 'heavenly, divine', here with Christian colour but also perhaps inverting Servius on *Aeneid* 4.654 *anima, quae superna est et originem suam petit*; for *fastidit* = 'rejects' cf. Horace *Epistles* 2.1.22, for *excors* = 'senseless' cf. Horace *Satires* 2.3.67, *Epistles* 1.2.25, and for the rare adjective *dissociabilis* cf. Horace *Odes* 1.3.22.27: for the metaphor cf. Lucan 2.303 *inanem persequar umbram*, and cf. also (in the different sense of 'enjoy') *Eclogues* 2.8 *umbras . . . captant*. 28: cf. *Aeneid* 6.728 *hominum pecudumque genus*, Augustine *Contra Iulianum* 6.7 *hominum stirpe*; for *miscere* used similarly of the undesirable combination of opposing elements cf. Horace *Epistles* 1.16.54 *miscebis sacra profanis*. 29–30: cf. Ovid *Tristia* 3.4b.52 *heu quam uicina, Ilias Latina* 915–16 *uasto gurgite praeceps/uoluitur*, Prudentius *Cath.* 11.33 *caeca uis mortalium*, Livy 42.46 *impotentem superbiam*. 31–2: for *seruare* of keeping to ordinances cf. Horace *Epistles* 1.16.41 *qui leges iuraque seruat*, and for the solemn apostrophe *mortales* cf. Propertius 2.27.1. *In omne tempus* is a Ciceronian phrase (4×); cf. also Ovid *Met.* 15.641 *iussa dei*, Statius *Theb.* 3.702 *iussa uerenda*.

33–56 The poet calls on Christ to turn the world in a better direction, and ends with a reference to himself. 33–4: these lines combine Horace's list of the powers of Jupiter with Jesus' self-characterization as the route to God: cf. Horace *Odes* 3.4.45–8 (Jupiter) <u>qui</u> *terram inertem,* <u>qui</u> *mare temperat / uentosum et urbes regnaque tristia / diuosque mortalisque turmas / imperio regit *unus aequo*, John 14.6 *Ego sum uia, et ueritas, et uita. Nemo uenit ad Patrem, nisi per me*; for *ad superos* of ascent to (pagan) heaven cf. *Aeneid* 12.224. 35–6: for *ad uotum* = 'according to (his) wish' cf. Seneca *Ep.* 15.3, for *annos reddere* cf. Ovid *Met.* 7.295–6 and for *terrigenae* = 'mortals' cf. Lucretius 5.1427. 37–40: the reference here is to Christmas 1899, the opening of the jubilee year 1900; in this context faithful Catholics were able to earn a plenary indulgence by a pilgrimage to Rome which involved visits to St Peter's (*cineres Petri*) and the three other major basilicas of the city (*sancta*);[56] God is here represented as leading the pilgrims via inspiration to go. 37–8: cf. Silius 16.579 *sacratos cineres*, 13.552 *turba piorum*. 39–40: understand *est* with *pietas* as subject and *auspicium* as complement (*auspicium* is adapted from the language of Roman religion – cf. similarly notes on items 2.1 and 3.53–4 above). 41–52: this prayer to Christ echoes prayers to and descriptions of pagan gods (Venus at Lucretius 1.2–31 and in Ovid *Amores* 3.2, Jupiter in Horace *Odes* 1.12 and 3.1) as well as the familiar Christian image of the good shepherd. 41: for divine control of future time cf. Horace *Odes* 3.29.29–30 *prudens futuri emporis *exitum / caliginosa nocte premit deus*; the divine cosmic controller (*arbiter*) is an idea shared by pagan and Christian thought (cf. Seneca *Ep.* 16.5, Ambrose *De Apol.Dau.* 10.52). 42: cf. Lucan 7.390 *aeui uenientis,*

Ausonius 4.10 Green *aeui cursum*, Ovid *Am*. 3.2.56 *inceptis adnue, diua, meis*. 43: *uirtus diuina* is a Ciceronian phrase (12×), *gens rebellis* a biblical term (Esth. 13.5). 44: cf. Seneca *Phaedr*. 174–5 *furor cogit sequi /peiora*, *Aeneid* 3.188 *meliora sequamur*; *gentes* echoes a standard term in early Christinianity for non-Christian 'heathen' peoples (*TLL* 6.2.1862.42ff), suggesting again contemporary secularization in Catholic countries. 45: cf. the poet's appeal to Venus for peace at Lucretius 1.31–2 *nam tu sola potes tranquilla pace iuuare / mortalis*; for *pax alma* cf. Tibullus 1.10.67, while *semen pacis* is a biblical image (Zach. 8.12). 46–7: for *tristia bella* cf. *Aeneid* 7.323, Horace AP 73, and for the general idea cf. *Aeneid* 9.642–3 *iure omnia bella / . . . uentura resident*. 47–8: cf. Phaedrus 17.4 *pectoris fraudem improbi*, Prudentius *Apotheosis* 747 *regna tenebrarum*, Proverbs 4.19 *uia impiorum tenebrosa*; for *improbus* of the wicked in early Christian discourse cf. *TLL* 7.1.689.71–2, 692.58–60. 49: for *mens una* of the Christian god cf. Arnobius 1.34, for *temperare* of the universally controlling role of the supreme deity cf. Horace *Odes* 1.12.16, 3.4.45, and for the supreme deity's command of kings cf. Horace *Odes* 3.1.6 *reges in ipsos imperium est Iouis*. 50: the laws of God are a frequent biblical idea (e.g. Leuiticus 18.5); cf. also Cicero *Tusc*. 1.101 (verse) *legibus obsequimur*. 51: for the Christian image of the good shepherd cf. note on item 1.I.33–4 above and especially Paulinus of Nola 3.15.164–5 *seruabat pastor ouile / exemplo Domini*. 52: cf. Tertullian *Exh.Cast*. 7 *Vnus deus, una fides*, Ovid *Pont*. 2.5.75 *orbis moderator* (of the prince Germanicus). 53–6: the poem ends with a prayer of the poet for his personal wishes, like Horace *Odes* 1.31.17–20, and with the poet's own name, similarly found in the last line of Horace *Odes* 4.6 (see on 56 below) as well as in the last stanza of item 1.II (above). 53–4: cf. *Aeneid* 4.653 *uixi et quem dederat cursum Fortuna peregi*, and Horace's characterization of his age in *lustra* (five-year periods) at *Odes* 4.1.6 *circa lustra decem* and 2.4.23–4 *cuius octavum trepidauit aetas / claudere lustrum*; *cumulum adiice* varies the classical *cumulum addere* (Cicero *Fam*. 13.15.3, Ovid *Met*. 1.205–6), as at Cassiodorus *Psalm*. 70 *adieci cumulum*. 55–6: cf. Ovid *Tristia* 3.14.7 *fac, quaeso*; *incassum* is Vergilian (4×), while for the idea of prayers falling back from heaven in vain cf. Propertius 1.17.4 *uota cadunt*. The final self-naming *tui* ... *Leonis* (as noted above) recalls the similar 'signature' of Horace in the last line of *Odes* 4.6 (44), *uatis Horati* and the concluding use of *Leo* at item 1.II.62 above.

Appendix: Table of Latin Metres

[| = end of metrical foot, / = most regular caesura (= central division of line after a word); - = long syllable, v = short syllable, x = *anceps*, which may be either long or short]

Latin hexameter (six feet)

- v v | - v v | - / v v | - / v v | - v v | - x [v v can always be substituted by -]

Latin elegiac couplet (= hexameter plus pentameter, five feet)

- v v | - v v | - / v v | - / v v | - v v | - x [v v can always be substituted by -]
- v v | - v v | - / - v v | - v v | - v v | - [v v can always be substituted by – in feet 1 and 2]

Hendecasyllable (eleven syllables)

- - - v v - v - v - - [the first two syllables can also be – v or v -]

Horatian lyric metres

(i) Alcaic stanza

This is a four-line stanza composed of two Alcaic hendecasyllables (eleven-syllable lines) followed by a nine-syllable line and a ten-syllable line:

```
x - v - - / - v v - v x
x - v - - / - v v - v x
   x - v - - - v - x
     - v v - v v - v – x
```

The caesura in lines 1–2 occasionally occurs after an earlier syllable of the hendecasyllable.

(ii) Sapphic stanza

This is a four-line stanza composed of three Sapphic hendecasyllables rounded off by a five-syllable adonean:

```
- v - - - / v v - v - x
- v - - - / v v - v - x
- v - - - / v v - v - x
    - v v – x
```

The caesura in lines 1–3 occasionally occurs after the sixth syllable of the hendecasyllable.

(iii) Third Asclepiad stanza

This is a four-line stanza of two asclepiads followed by a pherecratean and concluded by a glyconic:

```
- - - v v - / - v v - v x
- - - v v - / - v v - v x
- - - v v - x
- - - v v - v x
```

(iv) Fourth Asclepiad stanza

This is a two-line stanza consisting of a pherecratean followed by an asclepiad:

```
- - - v v - x
- - - v v - / - v v - v x
```

Iambic dimeter (Ambrosian hymn stanza)

This is a four-line stanza consisting of identical iambic dimeters.

x - x – x – x x
x - x – x – x x
x - x – x – x x
x - x – x – x x

Notes

Introduction

1. Collected in Trout 2015.
2. For Ambrose's hymns see Walsh and Husch 2012: 1–46, for the poems of Paulinus see https://www.thelatinlibrary.com/paulinus.poemata.html with Dressler 2023, for those of Venantius Roberts 2017.
3. See Van Heck 1995.
4. See e.g. IJsewijn 1988 and 1995, Laureys 2022.
5. For an English translation of his poems to 1978 see Woytila 1994.
6. For good recent summary of biographies of Barberini with literature see Wiendlocha 2005: 279–95 and Lutz 2020.
7. For further analysis of his poems for the Farnese see Harrison 2023.
8. See IJsewijn 1983.
9. See *Lyrica* 1.1, 1.3, 1.5, 1.10 and 1.20; 1.21 praises Urban's poetry in particular. IJsewijn 1988: 236–37 suggests that Urban felt some jealousy of the younger, very talented poet.
10. See Wiendlocha 2005: 288–9 on breviary reforms.
11. Printed later as *Lucus* 25–8 (for a text and translation see Drury and Moul 2014: 272–5, and for an analysis Doelman 2008–9).
12. See especially Köchli 2017.
13. For a recent, well-documented, concise biography cf. Rosa and Montanari 2000: 3.336–48, and for a substantial study see Angelini et al. 2000.
14. For Christina's life and relations with Alexander see Buckley 2004.
15. See Krautheimer 1985.
16. See Laureys 2001.
17. See Claren et al. 2003; the two had met some years earlier during Chigi's German service (ib. xii–xiv), and Balde had addressed a long epodic poem to Chigi in 1643 (*Silvae* 9.17).
18. For a brief summary biography see Malgeri 2000, for a chapter-length account Chadwick 1998: 273–331, and for a volume-length account see Ernesti 2019.
19. For an excellent contextualization see Laureys 2022: 586–96.

20 For its rich classical teaching see Fois 1991. The Jesuit curriculum laid down in the *Ratio Studiorum* of 1599 (still in force for Pecci in the 1820s; for a modern edition see Pavur 2005) prescribed a range of reading in Vergil, Horace and some other Latin poets, and its delivery involved extensive memorization of ancient authors and regular composition in Latin prose and verse.
21 Chigi does this for special effect too – cf. Chigi item 7's opening, which echoes the opening of Horace *Odes* 1.3 very closely (see commentary), and Chigi item 8 lines 23–6 which more or less repeat Lucan 3.55-8.
22 Some of Barberini and Chigi's poems have been freely paraphrased in rhyming English verse by Nixon 2020; for Pecci there are the loose and dated English translations in Pecci 1886 and Pecci 1902.

Chapter 1

1 For his life and career see the Introduction to this volume.
2 For the reception and editions of his Latin poetry see the literature collected by IJsewijn 1988: 237 n.19, the list in Wiendlocha 2005: 326–8, and the discussion in Rietbergen 2006: 95–142.
3 See Harrison 2023 for more on these early poems for the Farnese family.
4 See Rietbergen 2006: 101–5.
5 Usually after an elegiac lipogrammatic poem showing how poetry can be harnessed to pious and ethical purposes (*Poesis probis et piis ornata documentis primaeuo decori restituenda*).
6 Note also the controversial reworkings of canonical Latin hymns inserted in his 1631 papal revision of the Breviary; for these see Springhetti 1968: 183–90, Rietbergen 2006: 132–3.
7 There is no conventional numeration of the poems, but all editions contain a full list of contents at the beginning for navigation purposes.
8 Edited by the emerging Oxford scholar Joseph Brown(e), later Provost of Queen's College and Vice-Chancellor of the University (see Hunt and Skedd 2008), who admired Barberini for the quality and high moral tone of his poetry and presented his work as a salutary contrast to the immorality of contemporary English verse (Barberini 1726: v–vi, xi).
9 For a helpful sketch of this dichotomy see Comiati 2022.

10 For an analysis of the Alcaic stanza see Appendix: Table of Latin Metres.
11 For this event and its major significance see Israel 1995: 219.
12 *Miscellanea* 1 and 8 – for texts, translations and commentaries see Ford and Watt 1982, McGinnis and Williamson 1995. Note also Jean Dorat's cycle of Horatian *Odae Triumphales* (1558) on the successful Calais campaign.
13 The large collection of poems on the battle in Gherardi 1572 contains a number of Alcaic odes (380–408), including one by Aurelio Orsi addressed to Antonio Colonna, the victorious Papal admiral (395–7), a likely model for Barberini.
14 See Wright et al. 2014: xvi–xvii and the notes on *Alexander* below.
15 See e.g. McLaughlin 1995: 143–4, 272–3.
16 For an analysis of the Latin hexameter see Appendix: Table of Metres.
17 The mention of English opponents in line 61 can only refer to this; Leicester's expedition arrived in the Netherlands at the end of 1585 (see e.g. Adams 2008), so the eclogue dates from 1586 at the earliest.
18 See Houghton 2019.
19 See Grant 1965: 331–42 and especially 342–4 on victory poems, including other pastorals involving celebrations of Lepanto. A nice example is Fracastoro's eclogue of 1534–5 in praise of Gian Matteo Giberti, bishop of Verona, *Carmina* 51 (for a modern edition see Gardner 2013: 317–41, 496–9).
20 It matches the *Eclogues* (average ~82 lines) in length; Claudian's panegyrics are much longer, and the *Panegyricus Messallae* is 211 lines.
21 See Ware 2012, esp. 30–1.
22 These earlier eclogues were unpublished before Wiendlocha's edition (2005), which thus enabled a full understanding of this opening.
23 *Umbra* occurs 15 times in the *Eclogues, pecudes* at *Eclogues* 2.8 and 6.49, *ilex* at *Eclogues* 6.54, 7.1 and 9.15, *calamus* = reed-pipe 8 times in the *Eclogues*, *avena* = straw-pipe at *Eclogues* 1.2 and 10.51.
24 For recent accounts of the issue see Mondin 2007 and Kayachev 2011.
25 Compare the similar rhetorical questions in similar contexts in Ennius (*Ann.*164 Sk), Lucretius (5-1-6) and Horace (*Odes* 1.6.13–16).
26 Already encountered in Ode II – see item 1 above.
27 See Wright et al. 2014: xvii–xviii, Jordan 2004.
28 See Kurat 1961.

29 The specific reference is unclear, but the allusion may be to post-Lepanto Ottoman raids on Venetian colonies in Dalmatia (modern Croatia).
30 The briefer version of the perfect *uidere* is picked up in Barberini's *sensere*, which itself echoes the same form in the same ode of Horace, this time used of Drusus' own army realizing his qualities (4.4.25–7 <u>sensere,</u> *quid mens . . . / . . . / posset*). For the use of this ode in Barberini's own Alcaics on the Duke see item 1 above. See also Seneca *Oedipus* 471–2, again using *sensere* of feeling the power of a victorious opponent (Bacchus): *regna securigeri Bacchum* <u>sensere</u> *Lycurgi/* <u>sensere</u> *terrae Zalacum feroces*.
31 Noted by Wiendlocha 2005: 219.
32 For the details (and the Dutch fireships mentioned here) see Israel 1995: 216–19.
33 Referring to the unsuccessful expeditions on the Dutch side of the Duke of Anjou (1582–3) and the Earl of Leicester (1585–6, see above).
34 The latter parallel is noted by Wiendlocha 2005: 219.
35 The parallel is noted by Wiendlocha 2005: 219.
36 Israel 1995: 185.
37 See e.g. Spencer 2002.
38 See e.g. Djurslev 2019.
39 Harrison 2023 presents a more discursive analysis of this poem.
40 For an analysis of the Latin hexameter see Appendix: Table of Latin Metres.
41 At this time the Signatura was divided into two sections, the *Signatura gratiae* for examining petitions for favours, and the *Signatura iustitiae* for contentious cases. It is clear from the poem's title that Magalotti was an official of both. For the history of the Signatura in this period see Weber 2005.
42 For recent reassessments of Magalotti's career see Köchli 2004 and Paliotto 2009: 46–62.
43 The actual location and even the historicity of Alba Longa are in fact disputed issues – see Grandazzi 2008: 445–514.
44 See e.g. Petrillo 1995.
45 For the extensive Renaissance tradition of neo-Latin *Silvae* see Galand and Laigneau 2013.
46 For his career see Coleman 1988: 146.
47 Traces of this major complex remain in the papal gardens at Castel Gandolfo and other nearby locations: for a recent account see Liverani 2008.

48 *Carmen* 8; for a recent text, translation and notes see Gardner 2013: 228–30, 464–7.
49 For detailed documentation on Paul and the achievements of his papacy see Reinhard 2009.
50 See http://www.vatican.va/various/basiliche/sm_maggiore/en/storia/cappella_borghese.htm. *Celsa testudine culmen* (89) refers to the fourteenth-century *campanile* with its vaulted pyramidical roof, the highest in Rome (for *testudinatus* = 'vaulted' see Vitruvius 2.1.4).
51 See https://palazzo.quirinale.it/Storia/storia.html.
52 See http://stpetersbasilica.info/index.htm.
53 See Coleman 2006: xx and Lipsius 1604: 21.
54 *Dulce* here may allude to the Epicurean idea that proper pleasure was the highest good.
55 For his biography see https://www.treccani.it/enciclopedia/virginio-cesarini_(Dizionario-Biografico).
56 For an image see https://commons.wikimedia.org/wiki/File:Van_Dyck_Virginio_Cesarini.jpg.
57 For an analysis of the hendecasyllable see Appendix: Table of Latin Metres.
58 He is addressed by Barberini in a Sapphic ode of much the same period commending his zeal for study (Barberini 1634: 264–7).
59 For his career and works see https://www.treccani.it/enciclopedia/giovanni-battista-ciampoli_(Dizionario-Biografico)/
60 That on Laurence can be dated to 1619, that to Mary Magdalen to 1611–18, that to St Louis to 1619: see Rietbergen 2006: 109–10. These first three were the centrepiece of the first edition of Barberini's Latin poems, published in Paris, where he had been papal nuncio in 1604–7 (Barberini 1620).
61 See e.g. Quintilian 10.1.61 *Nouem uero lyricorum longe Pindarus princeps spiritu, magnificentia, sententiis, figuris, beatissima rerum uerborumque copia et velut quodam eloquentiae flumine.*
62 See conveniently Mazzoli 2014.
63 For a convenient account of neo-Latin 'Pindaric' odes see Revard 2014, and for the Dorat poem and its context see Demerson 1979.
64 The first strophe and antistrophe have the same number of lines (12, cf. Barberini), but neither of the following pairs do (strophe 2 = 23 lines, antistrophe 2 = 10 lines, strophe 3 = 14 lines, antistrophe 3 = 12 lines). For the poem see Lewalski and Haan 2012: 276–83.

65 Barberini also wrote an epigram commending Regulus' self-sacrificial courage (Barberini 1634: 219–20).
66 See Ryan 2012: 449–59.
67 Barberini 1634: 62–9.
68 Philip II of Spain had become king of Portugal too in 1581 and the two countries were united under Habsburg rule until the establishment of the house of Braganza in 1641.
69 See Rietbergen 2006: 112.
70 As noted by the scholar-printer Antonius Stephanus (Antoine Estienne) in his preface to the 1620 edition (Barberini 1620: 4; Estienne also points out that Barberini avoids the Catullan hendecasyllable in these strophic odes as potentially appearing irreligious).
71 See https://www.iranicaonline.org/articles/spain-relations-persia-16-17-century.
72 For the silver mines of Peru under Philip II see Kroeber 1958.
73 See several essays in Campbell 2014, especially Newmyer 2014.
74 Included in the Book of Daniel in the Septuagint and Vulgate but found in the apocryphal books in non-Catholic texts. For a convenient discussion see Davies 2001: 363–5.

Chapter 2

1 For his life see the Introduction to this volume.
2 Additions were made to later editions (see below), but none seem to date from after 1650 (and neither Chigi 1656 nor Chigi 1660 contains any indication that the poet is now pope). For a useful brief account of the collection see Barthold 2003: 6–16.
3 Confirmed by the printer's note to the reader in Chigi 1645. For the history and character of this academy see Quiviger 1991.
4 Reprinted in all later editions. It is very likely the work of Fabio Chigi himself – cf. Laureys 2022: 589.
5 For his career as cardinal and artistic patron see Stumpo 1980.
6 The fourth edition of 1660 (Chigi 1660) contains one fewer poem, leaving out number 61 in Chigi 1656 (a two-line epigram on a flower sent to a girl) and I have chosen to use the text and numeration of Chigi 1656. This

edition is also used (and photographically reproduced) in Hugenrot 1999, a helpful modern edition of all the poetry with German translation and brief annotations, on which I have regularly drawn in what follows.
7   See commentary on item 5 below.
8   For a full account of poem 90 see Barthold 2006.
9   See Nisbet 2014: 379–86.
10 For a full modern edition see Barthold 2003.
11 See Barthold 2003: 18–19.
12 For a modern edition see Muret 2012.
13 For a modern edition see Bloemendal 2020.
14 See Barthold 2003: 5.
15 See Barthold 2003: 12 and Comiati 2022: 550–3.
16 Hugenrot 1999: 2.254–7; see also similarly Barthold 2003: 3 n.25 and 11.
17 For an analysis of the Alcaic stanza see Appendix: Table of Latin Metres.
18 See e.g. Tarrant 1995.
19 For an analysis of the Third Asclepiad stanza see Appendix: Table of Latin Metres.
20 See e.g. Griffin 1997.
21 See e.g. Avagianou 1991.
22 Hugenrot 1999: 2.52 suggests that *uellus* is retained accusative with a proleptic *niueam* ('so as to make it white as to its fleece'), but this seems an unnatural interpretation, and it is not at all clear what the 'fleece' of the earth might be (certainly not fleecy snow in this context of warm spring sunshine).
23 Which indeed ensued after Chigi's arrival in Rome in 1626 – see the Introduction to this volume.
24 Published in his *Lyricorum Libri Tres* (Cologne, 1625).
25 For an analysis of the Alcaic stanza see Appendix: Table of Latin Metres.
26 For an analysis of the Latin hexameter see Appendix: Table of Latin Metres.
27 The subtitle reminds us that the graphite pencil was already known in the sixteenth century – it was famously depicted by the Swiss scientist Conrad Gessner in his *De Omni Rerum Fossilium Genere* (1565), fol.104v.
28 See e.g. Gowers 2012: 183.
29 See https://it.wikipedia.org/wiki/Palazzo_Comunale_di_Narni.
30 See Gowers 2012: 208–9.

31 For useful information and bibliography see http://www.perfettaletizia.it/archivio/servizi/loreto/scheda_english.html.
32 For the Salone see Uguccioni 2007.
33 Cf. Gowers 2012: 214.
34 For an analysis of the Alcaic stanza see Appendix: Table of Latin Metres.
35 On his career see Merola 1964.
36 For his career see Stumpo 1986 and Solinas 1989.
37 See Buchanan *Miscellanea* 1 (in Ford and Watt 1982 or McGinnis and Williamson 1995); Dorat's cycle of Horatian *Odae Triumphales*, 1558 (in Demerson 1979); for the Lepanto poems see Wright et al. 2014.
38 As illustrated by his portrait by Philippe de Champaigne – see https://commons.wikimedia.org/wiki/File:Champaigne_portrait_richelieu_eb.jpg.
39 For an analysis of the Alcaic stanza see Appendix: Table of Latin Metres.
40 For his biography see Pellegrini 2015.
41 See e.g. Reichel 1896: 237–8.
42 Scala 1619.
43 For an analysis of the Fourth Asclepiad stanza see Appendix: Table of Latin Metres.
44 In what follows, '*Golden Legend*' refers to the text of the life of Mary (no. 96) in the modern annotated translation in Ryan 2012: 374–82.
45 See e.g. Heinzmann and Köhler 1994.
46 Hugenrot 1999: 2.99, an improbably tenuous link in my view.
47 See e.g. Glei and Seidel 2006.
48 Cf. Suetonius *Nero* 34 *solutilem* . . . *nauem* (and the discussion in the commentary on line 36 below).
49 A literal quotation of the Vulgate text of the creation narrative of Genesis 1.2.
50 For an analysis of the Latin hexameter see Appendix: Table of Latin Metres.
51 For his libretti see Ziosi 1999.
52 See Berce 2007.

Chapter 3

1 For a convenient detailed list of editions see that at http://onlinebooks.library.upenn.edu/webbin/book/lookupname?key=Leo%20XIII%2C%20

Pope%2C%201810%2D1903; Pecci 1902 shows the interest in the United States, Pecci 1903 that in Germany, and Pecci 1901 provides translations of the Secular Ode into twelve different European languages.
2. For these poems and their background in Pecci's theological interests see Dinan 2022.
3. For its character and history from its 1692 foundation see Dixon 2006.
4. For his connection see Pecci 1902: 296–7.
5. See e.g. Waquet 2001.
6. Pecci 1886 and 1902 (both by Catholic priests in the United States).
7. See Pecci 1902: xiii.
8. *Ars Photographica* in Ambrose's iambic dimeter: *Expressa solis spicula / Nitens imago, quam bene/ Frontis decus, uim luminum / Refers, et oris gratiam. / O mira uirtus ingeni, / Nouumque monstrum! Imaginem / Naturae Apelles aemulus / Non pulchriorem pingeret* (see Pecci 1902: 44–5).
9. E.g. Ludovico Graziani's 1900 *Bicyclula* and Pietro Rosati's 1904 *De telegrapho acrocodilo*; for a list of prize-winning submissions in the period cf. https://it.wikipedia.org/wiki/Certamen_poeticum_Hoeufftianum.
10. For Pecci's ecclesiastical career see Introduction above.
11. It is clearly based on the several medieval Latin narratives of this martyrdom, none later than the eleventh century – on these see further BHLms (*Bibliotheca Hagiographica Latina manuscripta*) at https://www.bollandistes.org/research-center/electronic-publications s.u. 'Constantius'.
12. Pope in either 167–74 or 170–7 – see *Annuario Pontificio* 2012.
13. Translation by H. T. Henry from Pecci 1902: 83.
14. For these two metres see Appendix: Table of Latin Metres.
15. For the church and its associated rituals see Zappelli 2008; the saint's day is still celebrated in similar mode – see https://www.umbriaeventi.com/festa-di-san-costanzo-perugia-9889.htm.
16. For the literary features of Prudentius' martyr narratives see Palmer 1989.
17. For an analysis of the elegiac couplet see Appendix: Table of Latin Metres.
18. For the text of the Litany see e.g. https://www.preces-latinae.org/thesaurus/BVM/Laurentanae.html.
19. For a modern edition of a selection see Wright et al. 2014.
20. E.g. by Paolo Veronese https://www.wga.hu/html_m/v/veronese/11/2lepanto.html.

21 For the traditions about St Dominic and the Rosary see Pecci 1902: 289–90, Drane 1891: 120–37.
22 See Chadwick 1998.
23 See the annotations in Pecci 1902.
24 See the annotations in Pecci 1902.
25 See Rodogno 2011: 185–211.
26 https://www.preces-latinae.org/thesaurus/BVM/Laurentanae.html
27 *Praecincta rosis* might indicate either garland or a surrounding setting of roses. Mary is depicted with a crown set with roses in the celebrated Ghent Altarpiece of the van Eyck brothers from the fifteenth century – see https://en.wikipedia.org/wiki/Ghent_Altarpiece- and in a rose bower by Stephan Lochner of the same period – see https://en.wikipedia.org/wiki/Madonna_of_the_Rose_Bower. For the link of Mary and flowers in art see Salvador-Gonzalez 2014.
28 For an analysis of the Sapphic stanza see Appendix: Table of Latin Metres.
29 See Pecci 1902: 301.
30 For Joan's military role see De Vries 1999. In 1894 Leo had authorized a commission in Rome to look into the case for Joan's canonization (see Kelly 1996: 220–3); she was eventually canonized in 1920.
31 For the correspondence see Pecci 1902: 299.
32 E.g. in helping to overthrow the Roman Republic in 1849, and in providing a garrison for Rome in the 1860s which was only withdrawn at the start of the Franco-Prussian war in early 1870 – see further Kertzer 2004.
33 For the growing secularism of the Third Republic see Akan 2017: 30–134.
34 See Walker 2021: 210–24.
35 For a text see https://la.wikisource.org/wiki/Lex_Salica/Prologus_et_Epilogus, and for more detail see http://www.leges.uni-koeln.de/en/lex/lex-salica/
36 For a modern text and translation see Mousseau 2013: 48–50.
37 For an analysis of the Latin hexameter see Appendix: Table of Latin Metres.
38 The 1902 edition used here represents the author's final version; for its differences of detail from the original 1897 version see Pecci 1902: 306–8.
39 Pecci 1902: xiii; but Pecci 1886 had already made some of his shorter poems known in the United States.

40 For a brief biography see https://www.geni.com/people/Fabrizio-Ruffo-Principe-Di-Sant-Animo/6000000033247019000.
41 Pecci 1902: 56-7. Pecci appointed him a cardinal in 1891: for a brief biography cf. https://www.findagrave.com/memorial/26632960/fulco-luigi-ruffo-scilla.
42 See notes on the title and on lines 3, 6, 7, 39, 40, 42, 64–5, 69–71, 78–9 and 84–5 below.
43 This poem is recalled in specific detail at lines 4, 7, 20, 30, 52–3, 64–5 and 69–71 (see notes there).
44 At lines 8, 19, 41, 51, 54–5, 60, 62–3, 66–7 (see notes there).
45 For the regular topic of over-consumption of food in Roman satire generally see e.g. Gowers 1993.
46 See e.g. Prose 2003.
47 cf. e.g. Constantinou and Skouroumouni-Stavrinou 2022.
48 For discussion of this feature see Wilkinson 1963: 215–17.
49 For an analysis of the Alcaic stanza see Appendix: Table of Latin Metres.
50 Pecci 1902 xiii, 314–17. For an anthology of versions in twelve European vernacular languages cf. Pecci 1901.
51 See e.g. Kertzer 2004.
52 It appeared in *The Times* on New Year's Eve 1900, thus marking the year of 1901 not Pecci's 1900 as the start of the new century (for the contemporary debate on this issue see e.g. https://www.historylink.org/File/2012).
53 Austin 1911 1.90–250.
54 For a text see Austin 1902: 104–9 and Austin 2012: 536–7.
55 For the whole episode see Kertzer 2004.
56 For the details cf. *The Catholic Telegraph* 68: 20 (18 May 1899) p. 6 'Jubilee Year', available online at https://thecatholicnewsarchive.org/?a=d&d=TCT18990518-01.2.38&e=-------en-20--1--txt-txIN--------

Bibliography

Adams, S. (2008), 'Dudley, Robert, earl of Leicester (1532/3–1588), courtier and magnate', *Oxford Dictionary of National Biography* https://www.oxforddnb.com/

Akan, M. (2017), *The Politics of Secularism: Religion, Diversity, and Institutional Change in France and Turkey*, New York.

Aldrich, R. (1996), *Greater France: A History of French Overseas Expansion*, New York.

Amore, A. and Bonfiglio, A. (2013), *I martiri di Roma*, Todi.

Angelini, A., Butzek, M. and Sani, B. (eds) (2000), *Alessandro VII Chigi (1599–1667): il papa senese di Roma moderna*, Siena.

Annuario Pontificio 2012 (2012), Vatican City.

Austin, A. (1902), *A Tale of True Love and Other Poems*, London.

Austin, A. (1911), *The Autobiography of Alfred Austin, Poet Laureate, 1835–1910*, London.

Austin, A. (2012), *Alfred Austin: Poems*, poemhunter.com [available online at https://www.poemhunter.com/alfred-austin/ebooks/?ebook=0&filename=alfred_austin_2012_3.pdf]

Avagianou, A. (1991), *Sacred Marriage in the Rituals of Greek Religion*, Bern.

Barberini, M. (1620), *Illustrissimi et Reverendissimi S. R. E. Card. Barberini Iustitiae Praefecti Signaturae Poemata*, Paris.

Barberini, M. (1634), *Maphaei S. R. E. Card. Barberini nunc Urbani Papae VIII Poemata*, Antwerp.

Barberini, M. (1642), *Maphaei S. R. E. Card. Barberini nunc Urbani Papae VIII Poemata*, Paris.

Barberini, M. (1726), *Maphaei S. R. E. Card. Barberini postea Urbani PP VIII Poemata*, Oxford.

Barthold, C. (2003), *Fabio Chigis Tragödie Pompeius: Einleitung, Ausgabe und Kommentar*, Paderborn.

Barthold, C. (2006), '*Grani digressus Aquis, venturus ad Urbem Mosellae dominam*: Fabio Chigis Reise nach Trier im Jahre 1650', *Neulateinisches Jahrbuch* 8: 13–105.

Berce, Y-M. (2007), *La sommossa di Fermo del 1648*, Fermo.

Bloemendal, J. (2020), *Daniel Heinsius: Auriacus, sive Libertas saucia (Orange, or Liberty Wounded), 1602*, Leiden/Boston.

Buckley, V. (2004), *Christina, Queen of Sweden*, London.
Burrows, M. (1986), '"Mission civilisatrice": French cultural policy in the Middle East, 1860–1914', *Historical Journal* 29: 109–35.
Campbell, G. L. (ed.) (2014), *The Oxford Handbook of Animals in Classical Thought and Life*, Oxford.
Canning J. (1987), *The Political Thought of Baldus de Ubaldis*, Cambridge.
Carroll, E. R. (1953), 'Our Lady's queenship in the magisterium of the church', *Marian Studies* 4: 29–81.
Chadwick, H. (1998), *A History of the Popes 1830–1914*, Oxford.
Chigi, F. (1645), *Philomathi Musae Iuveniles*, Cologne.
Chigi, F. (1656), *Philomathi Musae Iuveniles*, Paris.
Chigi, F. (1660), *Philomathi Musae Iuveniles*, Amsterdam.
Claren, L., Kühlmann, W., Schibel, W., Seidel, R. and Wiegand, H. (eds) (2003), *Jacob Balde SJ: Urania Victrix – Die Siegreiche Urania. Liber I–II – Erstes und zweites Buch / Urania Victrix. Liber I–II – Urania Victorious. Books One and Two*, Tübingen.
Coleman, K. M. (1988), *Statius: Silvae IV*, Oxford.
Coleman, K. M. (2006), *M. Valerii Martialis Liber spectaculorum*, Oxford.
Comiati, G. (2022), 'Horace across seventeenth-century Italian literature: Carlo de' Dottori and his odes', in Enekel and Laureys 2022: 547–79.
Constantinou, S. and Skouroumouni-Stavrinou, A. (2022), 'Premodern "Galaktology": Reading Milk in Ancient and Early Byzantine Medical Treatises', *Journal of Late Antique, Islamic and Byzantine Studies*, 1: 1–40.
Davies, P. R. (2001), '26. Daniel' in J. Barton and J. Muddiman (eds), *The Oxford Bible Commentary*, Oxford, 565–71.
Demerson, G. (1979), *Jean Dorat: Les Odes latines*, Clermont-Ferrand.
De Vries, K. (1999), *Joan of Arc: A Military Leader*, Stroud.
Dinan, A. (2022), 'Pope Leo XIII's hymns for the feast of the holy family', *Antiphon: A Journal for Liturgical Renewal* 26: 134–55.
Dixon, S. M. (2006), *Between the Real and the Ideal: The Accademia degli Arcadi and Its Garden in Eighteenth-century Rome*, Newark, Del.
Djurslev, C. T. (2019), *Alexander the Great in the Early Christian Tradition: Classical Reception and Patristic Literature*, London.
Doelman, J. (2008–9), 'Herbert's *Lucus* and Pope Urban VIII', *George Herbert Journal* 32: 43–53.
Drane, A. T. (1891), *The History of St. Dominic*, London/New York.
Dressler, A. (2023), *Selections from the Poems of Paulinus of Nola, Including the Correspondence with Ausonius: Introduction, Translation, and Commentary*, London.

Drury, J. and Moul, V. (2015), *George Herbert: The Complete Poetry*, London.
Enekel, K. A. E. and Laureys, M. (eds) (2022), *Horace across the Media: Textual, Visual and Musical Receptions of Horace from the 15th to the 18th Century*, Leiden/Boston.
Ernesti, J. (2019), *Leo XIII – Papst und Staatsmann*, Freiburg.
Fabbri, P. (ed.) (1999), *Musica in torneo nell'Italia del Seicento*, Lucca.
Fois, M. (1991), 'L'insegnamento delle lettere al Collegio Romano', *Archivum Historiae Pontificiae* 29: 42–60.
Ford, P. and Green, R. P. H. (eds) (2009), *George Buchanan: Poet and Dramatist*, Swansea.
Ford, P. J. and Watt, W. S. (1982), *George Buchanan: Prince of Poets*, Aberdeen.
Freudenburg, K. (2021), *Horace Satires Book II*, Cambridge.
Galand P. and Laigneau S. (eds) (2013), *La silve: histoire d'une écriture libérée en Europe, de l'Antiquité au XVIIIe siècle*, Turnhout.
Gardner, J. (2013), *Girolamo Fracastoro: Latin Poetry*, Cambridge, MA.
Gherardi, P. (1572), *In foedus et uictpriam contra Turcas iuxta sinum Corinthiacum Non. Octob. MDLXXI. partam poemata uaria*, Venice.
Glei, R. F. and Seidel, R. (eds) (2006), *'Parodia' und Parodie: Aspekte intertextuellen Schreibens in der lateinischen Literatur der Frühen Neuzeit*, Berlin/Boston.
Glomski, J., Manuwald, G. and Taylor, A. (eds) (2023), *Baroque Latinity: Studies in the Neo-Latin Literature of the European Baroque*, London.
Gowers, E. (1993), *The Loaded Table*, Oxford.
Gowers, E. (2012), *Horace: Satires Book 1*, Cambridge.
Grandazzi, A. (2008), *Alba Longa, histoire d'une légende: recherches sur l'archéologie, la religion, les traditions de l'ancien Latium*, Paris.
Grant, W. L. (1965), *Neo-Latin Literature and the Pastoral*, Chapel Hill.
Griffin, J. (1997), 'Cult and personality in Horace', *Journal of Roman Studies* 87 (1997) 54–69.
Harrison, S. J. (ed.) (1995), *Homage to Horace: A Bimillenary Celebration*, Oxford.
Harrison, S. J. (2023), 'Maffeo Barberini's poems for the Farnese family in 1580s Rome' in Glomski et al. 2023: 121–36.
Heinzmann, F. and Köhler, M. (1994), *Der Magdalenenaltar des Lucas Moser in der gotischen Basilika Tiefenbronn*, Regensburg.
Houghton, L. B. T. (2019), *Virgil's Fourth Eclogue in the Italian Renaissance*, Cambridge.
Hugenrot, H. (1999), *Fabio Chigi: Philomathi Musae Iuveniles / Des Philomathus Jugendgedichte* [2 vols], Cologne.

Hunt, W. and Skedd, S. J. (2008), 'Browne, Joseph, (1700–1767)', *Oxford Dictionary of National Biography*. https://www.oxforddnb.com/.

IJsewijn, J. (1988), 'Scrittori latini a Roma dal Barocco al Neoclassicismo', *Studi Romani* 36: 229–49.

IJsewijn, J. (1995), 'Latin literature in 17th-century Rome', *Eranos* 93: 78–99.

Israel, J. (1995), *The Dutch Republic: Its Rise, Greatness and Fall*, Oxford.

Jordan, J. (2004), 'Galley warfare in Renaissance intellectual layering: Lepanto through Actium', *Viator* 35: 563–80.

Kayachev, B. (2011), '*Ille ego qui quondam*: Genre, Date, and Authorship', *Vergilius* 57: 75–82.

Kelly, H. A. (1996), 'Joan of Arc's last trial: The attack of the devil's advocates', in Wheeler and Wood 1996: 205–36.

Kertzer, D. (2004), *Prisoner of the Vatican: The Popes, the Kings, and Garibaldi's Rebels in the Struggle to Rule Modern Italy*, Boston.

Köchli, U. (2004), 'Verflossener Ruhm – verwechselte Gebeine: Der vergessene Kardinalstaatssekretär Lorenzo Magalotti', in A. Karsten (ed.), *Jagd nach dem roten Hut: Kardinalskarrieren im barocken Rom*, Göttingen, 140–55.

Köchli, U. (2017), *Urban VIII. und die Barberini: Nepotismus als Strukturmerkmal päpstlicher Herrschaftsorganisation in der Vormoderne*, Stuttgart.

Körkel, B., Licht, T. and Wiendlocha, J. (eds) (2001), *Mentis amore ligati: Lateinische Freundschaftsdichtung und Dichterfreundschaft in Mittelalter und Neuzeit. Festgabe für Reinhard Düchting zum 65. Geburtstag*, Heidelberg.

Krautheimer, R. (1985), *The Rome of Alexander VII 1655–67*, Princeton.

Kroeber, C. B. (1958), 'The mobilization of Philip II's revenue in Peru, 1590–1596', *The Economic History Review* 10: 439–49.

Kurat, A. N. (1961), 'The Turkish expedition to Astrakhan in 1569 and the problem of the Don-Volga Canal', *The Slavonic and East European Review* 40: 7–23.

Lampridio, B. (1550), *Benedicti Lampridii Necnonio Bap. Almathei Carmina*, Venice.

Laureys, M. (2001), 'Ein Freundeskreis im barocken Rom: Einige Bemerkungen zu den *Septem illustrium virorum poemata*', in Körkel et al. 2001: 217–32.

Laureys, M. (2022), '"As closely as possible after the model of Horace"? Degrees of Horatianism in James Alban Gibbes' Lyric Poetry', in Enekel and Laureys 2022: 580–623.

Lewalski, B. K. and Haan, E. (eds) (2012), *The Complete Works of John Milton III: The Shorter Poems*, Oxford.

Lipsius J. (1604), *Iusti Lipsi Dissertatiuncula apud principes: item C. Plini Panegyricus liber Traiano dictus, cum eiusdem Lipsii perpetuo commentario*, Antwerp.

Liverani, P. (2008), 'La villa di Domiziano a Castel Gandolfo', in M. Valenti M. (ed.), *Residenze imperiali nel Lazio*, Monte Porzio Catone, 53–60.

Lutz, G. (2020), 'URBANO VIII, papa', *Dizionario Biografico degli Italiani* 97. https://www.treccani.it/enciclopedia/papa-urbano-viii_%28Dizionario-Biografico%29/

Malgeri, F. (2000), 'Leone XIII', *Enciclopedia dei Papi* 3.575–93. https://www.treccani.it/enciclopedia/leone-xiii_(Enciclopedia-dei-Papi)

Mazzoli, G. (2014), 'The Chorus: Seneca as Lyric Poet' in A. Heil and G. Damschen (eds), *Brill's Companion to Seneca: Philosopher and Dramatist*, Leiden/Boston, 561–74.

McGinnis, P. J. and Williamson, A. H. (eds) (1995), *George Buchanan: The Political Poetry*, Edinburgh.

McLaughlin, M. L. (1995), *Literary Imitation in the Italian Renaissance*, Oxford.

Merola, A. (1964), 'Barberini, Francesco', *Dizionario Biografico degli Italiani* 6. https://www.treccani.it/enciclopedia/francesco-barberini_%28Dizionario-Biografico%29/

Mondin, L. (2007), 'Ipotesi sopra il falso proemio dell'*Eneide*', *CentoPagine* 1: 64–78.

Mousseau, J. (2013), *Adam of Saint-Victor: Sequences*, Leuven.

Muret, M-A. (2012), *Marc-Antoine Muret: Jules César/Iulius Caesar* [introduction, édition et notes de Giacomo Cardinali, traduction de Pierre Laurens], Paris.

Newmyer, S. (2014), 'Being the one and becoming the other: Animals in ancient philosophical schools', in Campbell 2014: 507–32.

Nisbet, G. (2014), 'Epigrams – the Classical tradition', in P. Ford, J. Bloemendal and C. Fantazzi (eds), *Brill's Encyclopaedia of the Neo-Latin World*, Leiden/Boston, 379–86.

Nixon, R. (2020), *Pope Urban VII and Pope Alexander VII: Selected Poetry*, Eugene.

Noble, T. F. X. (1984), *The Birth of the Papal State, 680–825*, Philadelphia.

Paliotto, L. (2009), *Ferrara nel Seicento: quotidianità tra potere legatizio e governo pastorale*, Ferrara.

Palmer, A.-M. (1989), *Prudentius on the Martyrs*, Oxford.

Pavur, C. (2005), *The Ratio Studiorum: The Official Plan for Jesuit Education*, St Louis.

Pecci, V. (1886), *The Latin Poems of Leo XIII Done into English Verse*, Baltimore. https://archive.org/details/latinpoemsofleox00leoxuoft/mode/2up

Pecci, V. (1901), *Carme secolare del sommo pontefice Leone XIII tradotto in varie lingue*, Rome.

Pecci, V. (1902), *Poems, Charades, Inscriptions of Pope Leo XIII, With English Translations and Notes by W. T. Henry*, New York/Philadelphia. https://archive.org/details/adesins00leox/page/n7/mode/2up

Pecci, V. (1903), *Leonis XIII P. M. carmina, inscriptiones, numismata*, Cologne.

Pellegrini, M. (2015), 'Petroni, Pietro', *Dizionario Biografico degli Italiani* 82. https://www.treccani.it/enciclopedia/pietro-petroni_(Dizionario-Biografico)/

Petrillo, S. (1995), *I papi a Castel Gandolfo*, Velletri.

Prose, F. (2003), *Gluttony*, New York.

Quiviger, F. (1991), 'A Spartan academic banquet in Siena', *Journal of the Warburg and Courtauld Institutes* 54: 206–25.

Reichel, O. J. (1896), *A Complete Manual of Canon Law: Volume I*, London.

Reinhard, W. (2009), *Paul V. Borghese (1605–1621): mikropolitische Papstgeschichte*, Stuttgart.

Revard, S. (2014), 'Neo-Latin lyric poetry in the Renaissance' in P. Ford, J. Bloemendal and C. Fantazzi (eds), *Brill's Encyclopaedia of the Neo-Latin World*, Leiden/Boston, 399–411.

Rietbergen, P. J. A. N. (2006), *Power and Religion in Baroque Rome: Barberini Cultural Policies*, Leiden/Boston.

Roberts, D. H., Dunn, F. M. and Fowler, D. (eds) (1997), *Classical Closure*, Princeton.

Roberts, M. (2017), *Venantius Fortunatus: Poems*, Cambridge, MA/London.

Rodogno, D. (2011), *Against Massacre: Humanitarian Interventions in the Ottoman Empire, 1815–1914*, Princeton.

Rosa, M, and Montanari, T. (2000), 'Alessandro VII' in *Enciclopedia dei Papi* 3: 336–48.

Ryan, W. G. (2012), *Jacobus de Voragine. The Golden Legend: Readings on the Saints*, Princeton.

Sacré, D. (2007), 'An unknown edition of two Latin poems of Maffeo Barberini (Urban VIII)', *Humanistica Lovaniensia* 56: 337–42.

Salvador-Gonzalez, J. M. (2014), 'Sicut lilium inter spinas: Floral metaphors in late medieval Marian iconography from patristic and theological sources', *Eikon Imago* 6: 1–32.

Scala, B. (1619), *Vita beati Petri Petroni Senensis Cartusiani*, Siena.

Solinas, F. (ed.) (1989), *Cassiano dal Pozzo: Atti del Seminario Internazionale di Studi*, Rome.

Spencer, D. (2002), *The Roman Alexander: Reading a Cultural Myth*, Exeter.

Springhetti, A. (1968), 'Urbanus VIII P.M. Poeta Latinus et Hymnorum Breviarii Emendator', *Archivum Historiae Pontificiae* 6: 163–90.

Stumpo, E. (1980), 'Chigi, Flavio', *Dizionario Biografico degli Italiani* 24. http://www.treccani.it/enciclopedia/flavio-chigi_%28Dizionario-Biografico%29/

Stumpo, E. (1986), 'Dal Pozzo, Cassiano iunior', *Dizionario Biografico degli Italiani* 32. https://www.treccani.it/enciclopedia/dal-pozzo-cassiano-iunior_%28Dizionario-Biografico%29/

Tarrant, R. J. (1995), '*Da capo* Structure in Some Odes of Horace', in Harrison 1995: 32–49.

Trout, D. (2015), *Damasus of Rome: The Epigraphic Poetry*, Oxford.

Uguccioni, A. (2007), *Il Palazzo Ducale di Pesaro*, Pesaro. http://www.prefettura.it/pesarourbino/allegati/Download:Il_palazzo_ducale_di_pesaro_guida_illustrata_di_anna_uguccioni-5722098.htm

Van Heck, A. (1995), *Enee Silvii Piccolominei postea PII PP II Carmina*, Vatican City.

Walker, J. (2021), *Sacred Sounds, Secular Spaces: Transforming Catholicism Through the Music of Third-Republic Paris*, Oxford.

Walsh, P. G. and Husch, C. (2012), *One Hundred Latin Hymns*, Cambridge, MA.

Waquet, F. (2001), *Latin, or, The empire of a Sign: From the Sixteenth to the Twentieth Centuries*, London.

Ware, C. (2012), *Claudian and the Roman Epic Tradition*, Cambridge.

Weber, C. (2005), 'Il referendariato di ambedue le Segnature: una forma speciale del "servizio pubblico" della Corte di Roma e dello Stato pontificio' in A. Jamme and O. Poncet (eds), *Offices et papauté (XIVe–XVIIe siècle): charges, hommes, destins*, Rome, 565–86.

Wheeler, B. and Wood, C. T. (eds) (1996), *Fresh Verdicts on Joan of Arc*, New York.

Wiendlocha, J. (2005), *Die Jugendgedichte Papst Urbans VIII*, Heidelberg.

Wilkinson, L. P. (1963), *Golden Latin Artistry*, Cambridge.

Wills, J. (1996), *Repetition in Latin Poetry*, Oxford.

Woytila, K. (1994), *The Place Within: The Poetry of Pope John Paul II*, New York.
Wright, E. R., Spence, S. and Lemons, A. (2014), *The Battle of Lepanto*, Cambridge.
Zappelli, M. R. (2008), *Perugia, Borgo San Pietro: da Sant'Ercolano a San Costanzo*, Todi.
Ziosi, R. (1999), 'I libretti di Ascanio Pio di Savoia: un esempio di teatro musicale a Ferrara nella prima metà del Seicento', in Fabbri 1999: 135–65.

Index of Names and Places

Alba Longa 34
Ambrose of Milan 1
Antium/Anzio 66
Antwerp 11
Aquinas, Thomas 5
Augustus, Emperor 110, 185, 194, 241
Austin, Alfred 241

Barberini family 1–3
Barberini, Francesco, Cardinal 135
Barberino Val d'Elsa 1
Balde, Jakob 117–18, 5
Bernini, Gianlorenzo 3, 5
Borromini, Francesco 3
Buchanan, George 12

Calvin, Jean 211
Carpineto Romano 5
Caravaggio, Michelangelo Merisi da 3
Castel Gandolfo 34
Catullus 59
Castro, War of 3
Certamen Poeticum Hoeufftianum 182
Cesarini, Virginio 58
Chigi family 4–5, 93
Christina of Sweden, Queen 4
Ciampolli, Giovanni Baptista 67
Clement VIII, Pope 2
Clovis 210
Collegio Romano 5, 7
Collegium Urbanum 3
Constantius, St 182–4
Crusades 211

Damasus, Pope 1
Del Ponzo, Cassiano 135
Dominic, St 200
Domitian, Emperor 35
Don John of Austria 18

Daniel, Book of 69
Dorat, Jean 67
Dubois, Théodore 212

epistle, poetic form 34, 36

Farnese, Alessandro (Cardinal) 2
Farnese, Alessandro (Duke of Parma) 2, 11–12, 20–1
Ferrara 164
Fracastoro, Girolamo 36
François de Sales, St 96

Galilei, Galileo 4, 67
Gregory of Tours 210
Gregory XIII, Pope 54
Gregory XVI, Pope 5

Herbert, George 3
hieros gamos 105
Horace 7, 11–12, 35, 59, 67, 71, 94, 96, 104, 110, 120, 135, 146, 152–3, 164, 181, 184–5, 192, 212, 225–6, 240
Huguenots 135

Indo-China 224
Innocent X, Pope 163

Jansen, Cornelis 4
Joan of Arc 211
John Paul II, Pope 1

Kepler, Johannes 111

Lampridio, Benedetto 67
La Rochelle 135
Lang, Andrew 225
Lateran Treaty 241
Laurence, St 68
Lepanto, Battle of 12, 200,

Loreto 154
Louis XIII of Framce 135
Louis XIV of France 4–5
Lucan 164
Lucretius 97

Magalotti, Lorenzo 34
Marche 121
Marino, Giambattista 11, 96
Marseille 152
Martial 36, 60
Mary Magdalen 152
metres, Latin 251–3
Milton, John 67
Mons Albanus 53
Monte Cimino 53
Monte Soratte 53

Nemi 55
Nero, Emperor 161
Netherlands, The 11–12
Newman, John Henry 5

Orsi, Aurelio 2
Ottoman Empire 201
Ovid 94, 164

Palazzo Quirinale 54
Papal States 211, 241
pastoral poetry 20–1
Paul V, Pope 2, 4, 37
Paulinus of Nola 1
Pépin le Bref 211
Persia 82
Peru 82
Perugia 5–6, 182–4
Petroni, Pietro 146
Philip II of Spain 11

Philip III of Spain 82
Piccolomini, Enea Silvio (Pope Pius II) 1
'Pindaric' ode 10, 67–8
Pio di Savoia, Ascanio 164
Pius IX, Pope 6
Pompey the Great 94, 146
Porzio, Flaminio 54
Propertius 201
Prudentius 68–9

Reims 212
Richelieu, Cardinal 135
Rosary, Holy 200
Ruffo, Fabrizio 225

Salic Law 220
S. Maria Maggiore, Basilica 53
Sarbiewski, Maciej Kazimierz 3, 110
Scaevola, Mucius 146
Siena 4, 93, 146
Statius, *Silvae* 35

Thirty Years' War 2
Tiefenbronn 153

Urban VIII, Pope 95, 110
Urbino, Duchy of 3, 121

Valerian, Emperor 83
Vatican State 241
Venantius Fortunatus 1
Vergil 21, 36, 55, 153, 164, 212
Vida, Girolamo
Virgin Mary 104–5, 181, 200–1
Voragine, Jacobus de 69, 83, 152

Westphalia, Treaty of 163

www.ingramcontent.com/pod-product-compliance
Lightning Source LLC
Chambersburg PA
CBHW071810300426
44116CB00009B/1269